Sanitation
in
Developing
Countries

Sanitation in Developing Countries

Edited by
Arnold Pacey

for
Oxfam
and the
Ross Institute of Tropical Hygiene

JOHN WILEY & SONS
Chichester · New York · Brisbane · Toronto

Library of Congress Cataloging in Publication Data :

Main entry under title:

Sanitation in developing countries.

    Papers presented at a conference held at Pembroke College, Oxford, July 5-9, 1977.
    Includes indexes.
    1. Underdeveloped areas — Sanitation — Congresses.
2. Underdeveloped areas — Sewage disposal — Congresses.
I. Pacey, Arnold. II. Oxfam. III. London School of Hygiene and Tropical Medicine. Ross Institute of Tropical Hygiene.
RA567.S26   628'.4'091724   78-4215
ISBN 0 471 99655 6

Printed in Great Britain by Unwin Brothers Limited, The Gresham Press, Old Woking, Surrey.

Acknowledgements

The contents of this volume were brought together as a result of a conference held at Pembroke College, Oxford, between 5-9 July 1977. The conference was made possible by financial support from the U.K. Ministry of Overseas Development, the Leverhulme Trust, and Marston Excelsior Ltd., to whom the organizers are very grateful. Much hard work was also put in by many people associated with Oxfam and the Ross Institute.

All this support has contributed to the production of the present volume, but in addition the editor is personally very much indebted to Andrew Jenkins, the conference organizer, and to Catherine Goyder. He is also especially grateful to Oxfam staff members who have drawn diagrams, typed drafts, and checked the text. In relation to Chapter 7, a particular debt is owed to the London Embassy of the Socialist Republic of Vietnam for help with information and a translation; the Embassy also gave permission for Figures 7.1 and 7.2 to be used.

For permission to reproduce other copyright material the editor is grateful to the following:

International Development Research Centre, Ottawa, Canada, for Figures 3.1 to 3.6; and for Figure 5.3
Witold Rybczynski for Figures 7.3 and 7.4
Spokesman Books, for quotations in Section 7.2
The World Bank, for much of Section 3.3
UNICEF, for Table 1.1

Contributors Grouped by Location of Current Work Affiliation

(Details of contributors' postal addresses can be found via the name index.)

AFRICA

Mr. Michael D. Blackmore
Mr. Robert A. Boydell
Dr. V. de V. Clarke
Professor B.Z. Diamant
Mr. V. Handa
Ms. Nomtuse Mbere
Dr. P.R. Morgan
Dr. Krisno Nimpuno
Dr. P.A. Oluwande
Mr. S.E. Owusu
Professor A.M. Wright

ASIA

Dr. John Briscoe
Mr. Michael Chia
Ms. A.S. Gadkari
Mr. V.S. Govindan
Mr. B.K. Handa
Dr. Vijay Kochar
Mr. S.W. Kulkarni
Mr. M.S. Maitra
Mr. J. Bertrand Mendis
Mr. S. Muthuswamy
Mr. P.V.R.C. Panicker
Mr. V. Raman
Professor Hillel I. Shuval
Dr. John D. Skoda
Mr. S.K. Subramanian
Dr. B.B. Sundaresan

CARIBBEAN & SOUTH AMERICA

Dr. Duncan Mara
Professor Salomao A. Silva
Mr. G.O. Unrau

EUROPE

Professor D.J. Bradley
Dr. Donald Curtis
Mr. R.R. Daniel
Dr. Richard Feachem
Mr. James McL. Fraser
Ms. Catherine Goyder
Mr. Peter Hawkins
Mr. James Howard
Dr. B.J. Lloyd
Dr. Joan K. McMichael
Professor M.B. Pescod
Mr. John Pickford
Dr. Pieter H. Streefland

NORTH AMERICA

Mr. D.C. Gunnerson
Dr. DéAnne S. Julius
Dr. J.M. Kalbermatten
Mr. H.H. Leich
Dr. Michael G. McGarry
Professor Witold Rybczynski
Professor Gerhard Schad
Professor Abel Wolman

Contents

ix

Foreword

Expectation of life in many poor countries is barely half of what most of us enjoy in the rich industrial world. That half of life that people lose, they lose for many reasons, but a significant number are a direct result of poor sanitary conditions.

In reviewing that problem and what might be done about it, this book discusses four main themes: the relationship between sanitation and health (Chapter 2); latrine technology (Chapters 3 to 8); the implementation of improvements in excreta disposal (Chapters 9 and 10); and finally, the treatment·and recycling of wastes (Chapters 11 and 12). Although the book originated as a series of papers presented at a conference, the material has been organized to provide a coherent perspective on each of these themes, and to cover most, if not all the key issues.

The conference was remarkable for being one of the first international meetings on non-sewered waste disposal. It came early in the present revival of interest in low-cost sanitation, and presentation of work in progress was encouraged. Consequently, many of the papers show developing thoughts and concepts and incomplete data. Inevitably, therefore, this book loses in roundedness and balance what it gains in immediacy. The reader should take it as an interim statement and not as the definitive account of a stable subject; therein lies its interest.

The book, like the conference from which it grew, is sponsored by Oxfam and the Ross Institute of Tropical Hygiene and it may be worth indicating how these two bodies came to work together on such a project.

Oxfam was founded in 1942 to send help to children in Nazi-occupied Greece; since then its work for the relief of hunger and poverty has grown in many directions. Now concerned entirely with the Third World, this work includes programmes in agriculture, nutrition, water supply, primary health care, and community development. This is work that attacks the causes of poverty, and for it to be successful, the people whose needs are met must themselves be fully involved through their own individual efforts, and in helping to decide ultimate goals. Thus the ideal Oxfam seeks to attain is to be 'a partnership of people', working together 'for the basic human rights of food, shelter and reasonable conditions of life'. This ideal also governs the way Oxfam, as a registered charity, raises its funds from the British public, mainly through voluntary work by several thousand unpaid helpers.

As Oxfam's involvement in long-term development has grown, so too has its interest in all aspects of public health. Small projects supported by Oxfam in Zaire, India and Brazil are discussed in Chapter 10 of this book. But the biggest involvement in sanitation grew out of experience in refugee camps in West Bengal in 1971. Conditions were so appalling, with a massive outbreak of cholera, that Oxfam decided to develop some system for simple excreta control which could be applied in any future emergency of this type. From this decision came the sanitation unit described in Section 9.4, and from it also came the conference from which this book originates.

The Ross Institute of Tropical Hygiene, in contrast, is a university department but has responsibilities going beyond the usual academic bounds, providing training and advice on the prevention of tropical diseases. The Ross Institute forms part of the London School of Hygiene and Tropical Medicine within London University. It began as an organization promoting particularly malaria control, and training those working in the tropics in the necessary techniques.

When Ronald Ross discovered the life cycle of the malaria parasite, rather than pursuing academic research on the subject, he tried to apply his discovery to practical problems, and he tried to work out how best to control malaria by attacking the mosquito. His tradition was carried on by Malcolm Watson, working in Malaysia, who showed that if one knew enough about a particular kind of mosquito one could control it relatively simply. If one knew enough, it seemed, one could do things more cheaply, and therefore make the limited funds go further than before.

Funds for sanitation in developing countries are strictly limited, and so perhaps it is Watson's philosophy that we need to adopt — by better understanding of the problem, to make limited funds more effective in solving it. This not only means seeking out low-cost techniques (which are well represented in this book). It also means trying to achieve a clearer understanding of the relationship between sanitation and health — which is attempted here in Chapter 2. Additionally it means understanding how human behaviour can affect the transmission of disease in many detailed and subtle ways. This latter subject is dealt with particularly in Section 10.4, and Chapters 8, 10, and 11 all contain material dealing with important social and behavioural aspects of sanitation. It is in developing these necessary kinds of understanding, rather than with low-cost technology, that the Ross Institute is most active in its work for better sanitation in developing countries.

Both Oxfam and the Ross Institute, involved in quite different ways in the field, earnestly hope that the contents of this book will provide some practical help towards the solution of increasingly urgent health problems, and so will be for the benefit of many millions of our fellows in the world community.

Guy Stringer,
Deputy Director,
Oxfam.

David Bradley,
Director,
Ross Institute of Tropical Hygiene.

1
Defining the Problem

1.1 DATA ON EXCRETA DISPOSAL[1]

Reports from the field

Two reports from Bangladesh pose the problem to which this book seeks answers. One describes a town of such size that its sanitation services should be disposing of 50 tons of human excreta daily. In fact, only one-tenth of this amount is adequately dealt with, leaving a balance of more than 40 tons to accumulate in ditches and gutters, on roads and in houses. 'The ground lies thick with human faeces, much of them containing intestinal worms which are pecked out by the birds. Drainage channels which pass through the town and were intended to convey sullage or storm-water are now almost choked with solids undergoing anaerobic fermentation. . . Flies are everywhere and are numerous on the meat and fish that are exposed for sale.'[2]

The other report describes a survey carried out in rural areas throughout Bangladesh[3] which showed that less than 5 per cent of adults and even fewer children had access to an adequate latrine (Table 1.1). Of the majority without

Table 1.1 Latrines used in rural Bangladesh; answers to the question, 'what type of latrine do the members of your household use?'

	Adults (per cent)	Children (per cent)
Water-seal latrine	1.7	1.1
Pit or bore-hole latrine	3.0	0.3
Open latrine	46.2	11.4
No fixed place	49.0	86.0

adequate sanitation, about half the adults had no fixed place for defecating, and half used open latrines which offer some privacy, but rely on sloping ground or a shallow trench for drainage (Figure 1.1).

In defining the problems of sanitation in developing countries, it is necessary to ask, how widespread are such problems in the developing world? What do they

1

Figure 1.1 Open latrine in Bangladesh (photo: Nick Fogden, Oxfam)

mean in terms of living conditions and human dignity? What is their significance for people's health? What disease hazards are posed in crowded cities, and how do health risks compare in the countryside? To what extent are the problems alleviated by the provision of safe water supplies, better housing, or hygienic excreta disposal?

The two reports from Bangladesh, both of them presented at the conference from which this book originated, throw light on many specific aspects of these questions. In particular, both mention the large amount of illness which may be attributed to poor environmental conditions. The report on the rural areas described an attempt to measure the incidence of diarrhoeal disease.[4] And in Saidpur, the town with almost no excreta disposal, 'fifty per cent of the hospital cases. . . are people with gastrointestinal diseases, which are also the major cause of death in children. Parasitic infection of the town's population is more or less total.'

It would be wrong to assume that the whole of this immense burden of illness is due solely to inadequate excreta disposal. The survey covered water supplies and housing as well, and it is clear that there is a complex relationship between diarrhoeal diseases and a wide range of environmental factors—a relationship which is strongly influenced by people's habitats, especially with regard to hygiene. Thus although instances have been reported (Section 1.2) where an improvement in excreta disposal has been followed by a clear-cut fall in the incidence of certain illnesses, this does not always happen, and a recurring theme in this chapter is the need for more precise evaluation to demonstrate the connection between sanitation and health. One author argues that sanitation services have often been neglected because the health benefits arising from effective sanitation are not sufficiently evident (Section 1.4). With regard to parasitic worms (helminths), the study of their life cycles can help elucidate the relative importance of water supply, excreta disposal and personal hygiene in preventing disease (Chapter 2).

World statistics on sanitation

To what extent are the conditions revealed by these Bangladesh surveys typical? The World Health Organization (WHO) includes Bangladesh and India in its South East Asia region. The population of rural areas in that region totals some 760 million people, of whom only 6 per cent were estimated by WHO[5] to have 'adequate' excreta disposal facilities in 1975. This compares with a proportion of 4.7 per cent of adults in rural Bangladesh with proper latrines, according to the UNICEF survey (Table 1.1). The WHO figures for rural Bangladesh appear to be incomplete, but judging by the UNICEF data, conditions in country areas are not untypical of the region as a whole.

However, the WHO data also indicates that sanitary conditions in the South East Asia region are significantly worse than elsewhere. Taking the developing countries as a whole, 15 per cent of rural people were estimated to have adequate excreta disposal facilities in 1975 (Table 1.2). In particular, rural Africa and Latin America are estimated to be much better provided for than South East Asia.

Table 1.2 WHO statistics on excreta disposal in developing countries (excluding China); from *World Health Statistics Report,* 29 (10), (1976), p. 570.

	People served adequately by public sewers or household systems in 1975	People lacking adequate sanitation in 1975
Rural sector	209 millions (15 per cent)	1190 millions (85 per cent)
Urban sector	437 millions (75 per cent)	145 millions (25 per cent)

It would be wrong, however, to assume any great accuracy in the WHO data. The figures available from different countries vary greatly in reliability, detail, and in the criteria used. Sometimes, as with the Bangladesh survey, one can discover how many people have access to particular types of latrine. Sometimes, in contrast, one is told how many latrines exist per unit of population—in North Vietnam, for example, there was one latrine for every 1.4 households in 1972 (Section 7.2). It is sometimes difficult to know how such figures can be compared with the WHO percentage of people with adequate sanitation.

At first sight, data for the urban sector collected by WHO look more encouraging, with three-quarters of urban populations benefiting from adequate excreta disposal. But whatever the significance of this statistic, it can say little about the slum areas and squatter settlements in which sanitation is not only lacking, but where congestion and poverty defeat most plans for improvement. In these areas, and in other places where excreta disposal arrangements have broken down, people are living in conditions of the most extreme kind, surrounded by accumulations of excreta, and with health hazards compounded by overcrowding (Figure 1.2).

Figure 1.2 Living conditions for the urban poor in Bangladesh (photo: Oxfam)

It is in circumstances such as these that the problem of sanitation in developing countries is seen at its most urgent and disturbing, and where the greatest ingenuity is demanded of engineers and public health workers in trying to devise solutions. One of the most important chapters in this book (Chapter 9) describes some of the novel and unorthodox techniques which have recently been devised to alleviate situations of this kind.

1.2 AVAILABILITY OF LATRINES IN A DEVELOPING COUNTRY

A.M. Wright, S.E. Owusu and V.K. Handa[6]

Sanitation and health in rural areas

The significance of generalized data on the availability of adequate excreta disposal becomes much more evident when it can be compared with the detailed results of surveys from specific localities. Information of this kind is available from a research programme being carried out in Ghana by members of the Civil Engineering Department at the University of Science and Technology, Kumasi.[7]

The background to the programme is that even though a number of water supply and electrification projects are under way in rural areas of Ghana, there has not yet been any comparable work for the improvement of rural excreta disposal. Yet rural latrines are an important means of breaking the cycles of such communicable diseases as cholera, typhoid, schistosomiasis, hookworm infection and amoebiasis. Debility and mortality from these diseases is partly accountable for the slow pace of development in rural areas.

Although the relationship between sanitation and the spread of disease is a complex one, the effectiveness of sanitation in the control of communicable diseases has been demonstrated in several instances. Schliessman[8] has reported that the construction of privies in Costa Rica helped to reduce by 50 per cent the death rate from diarrhoea and enteritis between 1942 and 1954. Studies in several other . developing countries have shown what a reduction in diarrhoeal disease can be brought about by better water supply and sanitation facilities[9]; and a recent study by Azurin and Alvero[10] shows that over a period of five years, the provision of sanitary facilities for human waste disposal can reduce the incidence of cholera by as much as 76 per cent. In view of these demonstrated links between excreta disposal and health, it is imperative that extensive rural latrine programmes be initiated in Ghana and in other developing countries to buttress and sustain other rural development programmes.

Survey objectives

The survey of rural latrines which forms part of this research programme was conducted on both a national and a regional level.

The principal objective of the national survey was to find out the type and number of communal and private latrines in the rural areas of the country. Accordingly, questionnaires were prepared to elicit this information. In addition, questions were asked on the following: main occupation; source, reliability, quality, and adequacy of water supply; common diseases in the areas; and major causes of death. This section, however, deals only with the information obtained on latrines.

About 20 villages were selected from each of the 9 regions of Ghana for the survey. In most cases the village population was less than 2000. But there were cases where the population exceeded 6000. The actual survey was conducted by the regional staff of the Environmental Health Division of the Ministry of Health.

Based on the results of the national survey, five settlements were selected from each region for the more detailed regional survey. For large communities, a 10 per cent random sample of households was studied in detail, but in small settlements, a 50 per cent sample was adopted. In each house, one female and one male person was interviewed. In addition, in one out of every four houses, children (between 7 and 15 years) were interviewed. As in the case of the national survey, the interviews were conducted by field staff of the Environmental Health Division of the Ministry of Health following briefing and initial supervision by research staff from the University.

These surveys were carried out to obtain data on the following:

(i)   Pattern of use of private and communal latrines in the settlements.
(ii)   Ablution materials.
(iii) Accessibility of respondents to available communal latrines.
(iv)   Attitudes to available communal latrines.
(v)   Desired improvements in existing systems and
(vi)   Education and income of respondents.

Results of the national survey

The distribution of private and communal latrines in eight regions which participated in the survey is presented in Table 1.3. The table shows that four types of latrines are used in the rural areas of Ghana: the pit latrine, the bucket latrine, the aqua-privy, and the conventional water closet. Of these, the pit latrine and the bucket latrine are used both as private and as communal latrines. The water closet is used only in private houses whereas the aqua-privy is constructed only for public use.

In private houses, the most popular latrine is the bucket latrine, followed by the water closet and the pit latrine, in that order. In contrast, the most popular type of communal latrine used in Ghana is the pit latrine followed by the aqua-privy, and, to a much smaller extent, by the bucket latrine.

On average, there is one communal latrine for every 389 rural persons. This average is exceeded in four out of the eight reporting regions. The Volta Region has the least number of both private and communal latrines. Whereas 1713 persons in the Volta Region are served by one communal latrine, the results show that only 184 persons are served by one communal latrine in the Upper Region.

Latrine-use patterns in the Upper and Volta Regions

Table 1.4 shows the use made of private and communal latrines in the sample villages as revealed by two of the regional surveys. The table shows that in both regions, some people have been using the bush for defecation all their lives. In the Upper Region, as many as 68.8 per cent of the respondents claim to have used the open bush for defecation since birth; however, only 1.2 per cent of the respondents in Volta Region make this claim. It may also be seen from the table that whereas bucket latrines are used only in private houses in the Upper Region, they are used both as private latrines and as communal latrines in the Volta Region. Furthermore, whereas the most popular facility for defecation in the Volta Region is the pit latrine, the open bush is still the most popular system in the Upper Region.

Anal cleaning materials

The most popular anal cleaning materials used in the rural areas are stones and

Table 1.3 National Distribution of Private and Communal Latrines in Ghana*

Region	Upper	Northern	Bron-Ahafo	Ashanti	Central	Western	Volta	Greater Accra	TOTALS
No. of Villages sampled:	14	20	20	20	20	17	20	20	151
Estimated population:	24 200	26 582	31 280	16 817	30 846	28 719	32 600	10 977	202 310
Main occupations:	Farming Fishing Hunting	Farming Fishing	Farming Fishing	Farming Pottery Charcoal	Farming Fishing	Farming Fishing Mines	Farming	Farming	Farming Fishing Hunting Pottery Mines
Private rural latrines :									
Pit	20	42	53	7	37	35	23	45	262
Bucket	368	112	29	218	18	93	5	–	843
Water closet	303	1	–	2	1	15	–	–	322
Total:	691	155	82	227	56	143	28	45	1 427
Population served by one latrine :	35	165	381	74	550	200	1 166	244	141
Communal rural latrines :									
Pit	58	79	72	51	37	7	18	65	387
Bucket	2	–	1	–	1	12	1	–	17
Aqua-privy	73	22	–	9	7	5	–	–	116
Total	133	101	73	60	45	24	19	65	520
Approx. number per village :	10	5	4	3	2	1	1	3	3
Population served by one latrine :	184	262	428	280	686	1 195	1 713	169	389

(* There were no returns from the Eastern Region)

Table 1.4 Latrine use patterns in two regions of Ghana

	Respondents using specified latrine			
Type of latrine	UPPER REGION		VOLTA REGION	
	Number	Per cent	Number	Per cent
Latrine at own house:				
Bucket	9	5.3	11	4.4
Pit	11	6.5	7	2.8
Water closet	4	2.3	–	–
Latrine at nearby house:				
Bucket	–	–	2	0.8
Pit	–	–	7	2.8
Communal facility:				
Bucket	–	–	43	17.1
Institutional pit latrine	1	0.6	1	0.4
Other pits	19	11.2	177	70.5
Aqua-privy	9	5.3	–	–
Used open bush since birth:	117	68.8	3	1.2
TOTALS	170	100.0	215	100.0

leaves, old newspapers, and corn cobs. Taking the Volta Region, for example, the number of respondents using the various materials was as follows:

Toilet rolls	12	(4.8 per cent)
Newspapers and other paper	58	(23.1 .. ..)
Rags	10	(4.0 .. ..)
Corn cobs	54	(21.5 .. ..)
Stones and leaves	25	(10.0 .. ..)
Combination of the above	86	(34.2 .. ..)
Water	6	(2.4 .. ..)

Even in the Upper Region, where most of the population is presumed to be Muslim, only 1.2 per cent used water for ablution. This seemed surprising, but it seems that the choice of ablution material depends very much on availability. Thus the general scarcity of water in the Upper Region may account for its limited use.

Communal latrines

The survey showed that in both regions, the majority of respondents must walk over 50m to the available communal latrines. However, whereas only 1.2 per cent of respondents in the Upper Region indicated that their communal latrines were within 50m of their homes, 31 per cent of respondents in the Volta Region indicated that they lived within 50m of a communal latrine. Communal latrines appear to be very fully used in the Volta Region, whereas in the Upper Region, fewer people use these latrines, and almost 69 per cent use the open bush instead.

In both regions, large numbers of people expressed dissatisfaction with the available communal latrines specifying smells, fly and rodent nuisance, lack of privacy, untidiness of the squatting area, and distance of the latrines from home. Only a small proportion of people liked the squatting type of latrines; almost 79 per cent complained that the squatting type was not comfortable to the user, especially to old people and pregnant women.

Desired improvements

During the survey, information was sought on the type of improvement respondents would like to have in the existing private and communal latrines.

With private latrines, there was a desire for more regular collection of night soil where bucket systems are used. People also wanted squatting holes to be covered when not in use to minimize fly and odour nuisance. They wanted windows in toilets and would like conventional water closets.

It was felt that more communal latrines were needed, with superstructures of improved physical appearance and offering more privacy. People also wanted better control of odours and flies, and the provision of seats instead of squat holes.

In view of the general dissatisfaction with communal latrines, however, a more appropriate strategy might be to persuade people to accept private latrines that do not have the shortcomings of the communal system. Possible types of latrine which may prove acceptable are the hand-flushed, off-set pit latrine (with water seal), and the off-set dry pit latrine known as the Reed Odourless Earth Closet (ROEC). The former could be used where water is always available, and the latter where water is scarce.

National distribution of rural latrines

The survey showed that private and communal latrines are used in all regions of Ghana, but that there is considerable variation in the number available. In the sample villages of the Upper Region, there appear to be 10 communal latrines per village, which is so surprising that a second survey has been planned to verify the returns. In Volta Region, where there seem to be fewer latrines of all types than elsewhere, 8 out of the 20 villages had no communal latrine, and there was one private latrine for 1166 persons. In contrast, in Ashanti, the survey found one private latrine for every 74 people.

In the country as a whole, there are 141 persons to every private latrine, and 389 for every communal latrine. The low figures for ownership of private latrines suggest that a private latrine is not considered a necessary part of a house. In this connection, it would also be interesting to find the relative occurrence in rural houses of kitchens and bathrooms.

From Table 1.4 it can be seen that 6.5 per cent of people in Ghana's Upper Region have access to a private pit latrine, and 5.6 per cent in the Volta Region. These figures can be compared with similar data from the Bangladesh survey[11], which found that 3.0 per cent of adults had access to pit latrines (Table 1.1). A significantly better provision of sanitation in Ghana seems to be indicated, and the same conclusion is evident at every point where comparison between these two quite different surveys can be made. The same contrast is reflected in the WHO statistics for the two countries, or for the two regions in which they are set. Surveys like the one in Ghana tend to show that the WHO figures are over-optimistic, but it appears that the contrasts between different countries and regions recorded by WHO are realistic.

1.3 THE SEARCH FOR SOLUTIONS

Abel Wolman[12]

Human and technical factors

Research on statistical data about the availability of sanitation facilities in less economically favoured countries goes on forever. How many people cannot conveniently and safely drink water, wash themselves, and avoid contact with their own bodily discharges? Their number is high. According to WHO, more than two-thirds of people in developing countries have less than reasonably adequate facilities. Yet the WHO figures are probably more optimistic than real. Few urban excreta disposal systems are sufficiently well maintained and operated to provide consistently effective sewage disposal. Of equal importance is the fact that no figures disclose whether sanitary facilities are actually used to assure modest levels of personal hygiene. Even in the most 'developed' industrial countries, 'Wash your hands' is not yet a universally accepted or acceptable precept!

What is to be done about these tremendous problems? Sanitation and hygiene clearly have much to do with human behaviour. Moreover, the operation of water supplies and excreta disposal systems depends on human organisation—on regularity of servicing, training of manpower, adequate management, and so on. These matters keep cropping up throughout the book, especially in Chapter 10.

With human factors playing so central a part, can it be right to look only for technological solutions to sanitation problems? Search for the perfect well pump or perfect privy may well characterize sanitary history. We are left with the uncomfortable conclusion, long predictable, that no such devices really exist or can be devised. The success of any particular unit depends upon its individual and communal acceptance, understanding, and use, rather than upon the simplicity or complexity of its design.

But of course, choices do have to be made about technology, and there are advantages implicit in the low-cost, labour intensive solutions now being so eagerly sought. Choice of technology, which is discussed more fully in Chapter 3, does not rest only on broad criteria of cost and labour, but also on each local situation. There are times and places where sophisticated technology is appropriate, but in most rural areas it is certainly contra-indicated.

A profitable area for inquiry is to search out the technology used in developed countries 50 to 75 years ago. It was simple and low cost. The old septic privy was useful and effective (Section 4.3). The hypochlorite tank feeder may still cost less than 10 dollars. The hardy slow sand filter may nicely be revived. The new and fancy device, which has all the virtues we can summon up, may yet be invented. Whether it will be successful depends much upon who uses it, cherishes it, and prefers it—and that raises the question of the acceptance of new technology, which will be returned to frequently in this book.

A warning note must be sounded, however. Most calculations for *urban* facilities make clear that so-called simplified designs rarely lead to significant reductions in capital or operating costs. And only time will tell whether the growing list of small, simple, labour-intensive technologies will find its way into world-wide application.

Resources and money

Shortage of resources forces us to reconsider the use of waste materials, particularly human excreta. History is replete with examples of the use of excreta in the enrichment of agricultural soils. It is equally replete with records of the resulting disease incidence. The question naturally arises as to whether this means of disposal may be made safe and profitable; and this question is taken up at length in Chapters 11 and 12.

Why were these uses gradually abandoned? The health hazard was only one reason. Transport costs, in urban areas, were another. The advent of chemical fertilizer offered a preferable alternative, both in cost and convenience.

In rural areas, one might well revive re-use practices, if the disabilities which led to their abandonment can be resolved. Undoubtedly, fish and agricultural crops profit by organic enrichment. Can such uses of excreta be carried out with safety, economy, and ecological equilibrium? And with what kinds and densities of population? The conservation ethic certainly drives us toward such an assessment. Recent cholera epidemics arising from affected vegetables, fish, and molluscs, require that the decisions must be founded upon more than a compound of nostalgia and utopia.

In the simpler past, it was assumed that clean water supplies and efficient excreta disposal were good things in themselves. It was taken for granted that such facilities would be used, and would result in increased health, safety and comfort. In the present climate, the emergence of the economist brings on the stage a new series of questions, challenging the cherished assumptions of the past. He demands proof that these practices actually reduce disease or enhance productivity. Both of these things are difficult to establish. Efforts are being pursued with full awareness of the methodological complexities of isolating cause and effect and benefit-cost ratios. Such enquiries should not interrupt activity toward providing amenities for the survival and well-being of people.

The programmes which concern us cost money. WHO estimates that, with modest expansions, water supply and excreta disposal facilities in both urban and rural areas should require some 35 to 40 billion U.S. dollars by 1980. For the people thus benefited, the annual per capita investment would be in the neighbourhood of $3.00. The total capital required often intimidates people, until it is demonstrated that with the vast numbers of persons to be served, the per capita cost is surprisingly low. Money, indeed, is perhaps not the dominant constraint in moving forward with sanitation programmes. The amount to be spent is more than modest when compared with world expenditure for military arms and defence of 300 billion dollars, or $100 per annum for every man, woman and child in the developing world.

Motivation, management, and manpower

The key to successful achievement in the arena here discussed depends not only upon the clear intent of governments, but on motivation by people themselves. Simple acceptance of the latter point, however, does little to define or to accelerate the logistics by which to accomplish our aims. It is one thing to assert that we must have 'a sustained effort to bring about active community participation in planning, implementation, maintenance and operation of the system.' A totally different and more difficult problem remains as to how to accomplish this. How can one reach, persuade, and motivate, in less than a millenium, the people in hundreds of thousands of villages spread over the globe? By what machinery, and by whom? The 'barefoot' somebody, the nurse, the educator, the western agricultural county agent?

These questions must be answered, while we accept the dictum that understanding and acceptance are essential guarantees to water supply and excreta disposal programmes.

Historically, the reverse assumption was frequently dominant. If the facilities were provided, people, in the course of time, would use them. In the western world this assumption was amply verified by the clear demonstration that all people of all origins like to wash! Is this assumption to be so easily discarded, while we engage in the slow process of education and persuasion of more than a billion people? In any event, the different approaches should not be lightly or arbitrarily abandoned.

No enterprise is successful without an institutional, managerial structure, and a body of informed personnel at various levels of operation. The skilled professional at the top cannot function, no matter how highly motivated, without the cadres down to the village workers, locally accepted and earthily trained for the simple, but highly important tasks.

In those regions of the world where programmes have been most successful, such forces have been deliberately created over the last few decades. Can this be accomplished everywhere? Can we devise procedures to serve more people, more rapidly than in the past?

1.4 EXCRETA DISPOSAL IN RELATION TO WATER SUPPLY

M.B. Pescod[13]

The current situation

In most countries, programmes for water supply and sanitation have usually been developed separately. Different organizations often administer these programmes, and no co-ordination is attempted. This leads to poor environmental conditions where water supply has been provided without drainage, and sometimes, the health of the population affected is put at risk. Even where this does not happen, the full advantage of a complete sanitation service is not gained if the water supply component of the package is separated from the waste disposal component.

It is obvious that the authorities in many developing countries have essentially disregarded the problem of excreta disposal. Few urban areas are sewered, and domestic wastes are handled in a variety of ways, depending on local conditions, and on the way unofficial practices have developed to suit social and cultural preferences. In some few locations, night soil collection systems are operated, either by the authorities or privately, but more generally, on-site disposal is adopted. Septic tanks and cess pits or seepage pits are widely used, even where ground conditions are unsuitable and, inevitably, pollution of groundwater and surface water results. Sometimes these systems are connected into surface drainage, creating foul conditions in streets subject to flooding and generally contributing to surface water pollution. Increasing urbanization has overloaded the natural assimilative capacity of the environment in most large cities in developing countries, and the presence of black-coloured, odorous surface water is but one offensive manifestation of the absence of effective sanitation. Squatter or shanty settlements in major cities create particular problems because water supply and sanitation facilities are non-existent and health hazards are high.

In rural areas, population densities are lower and natural assimilation of human wastes has been less damaging in physical terms, but lack of sanitation may have a greater impact on health than in the urban context because people still largely depend on surface water for their potable supply.

Understanding the benefits of sanitation

An increased awareness of the importance of sanitation by the authorities is necessary if sanitation programmes are to be more effective in the future. The difficulty here is that it is hard to define precisely what the benefits of a sanitation system amount to, even though some general benefit may be obvious. Past attempts to justify sanitation in terms of health-benefit-to-cost ratios have not been successful, and there have been few serious studies of the effects of sanitation on the health of the population served. It is, of course, difficult to separate the effects of sanitation from benefits occurring for other reasons, and one basic problem is the lack of reliable health data in many developing countries, particularly for rural areas.

Some pilot studies are being carried out at present, for example in India (one is described in Chapter 2, Section 2.6). In this work, health information is collected from a population both before and after a sanitation programme is implemented. One of the working groups at the conference on which this book is based[14] suggested that evaluation studies of this kind should consider the following major questions.

(a) Who uses the sanitation facilities, who does not use them, and why?
(b) How are excreta-related diseases actually being transmitted in the community?
(c) What are the effects of the sanitation programme on the community's health status?
(d) How has the programme affected people's perceptions, particularly as regards hygiene and health?
(e) Who cleans and maintains the latrines, who neglects these jobs, and why?
(f) Could the programme be extended? How much does it cost? Should alternative methods be considered?

This kind of evaluation should be included in the planning stage of any sanitation programme, as base-line data will normally be required, and should continue as the programme progresses, leading to successive modifications in the technology or organization involved to deal with any snags that are revealed. One problem, however, is that the planning period allowed in many projects is too short to allow for this kind of intensive evaluation. There is also a great need for information on the methodology of evaluation; methods which have proved successful in actual surveys have rarely been described in published accounts.

Urban conditions and administration

Urban sanitation has not developed in many of even the largest cities in developing countries, although water supplies are constantly being upgraded. Many cities have no sewerage at all, and one of the major problems is the very large investment required to provide it. Although many 'master plans for sewerage' exist, very few major schemes have been attempted in recent years. Programmes for improving the water supply to over-populated cities have gone ahead while the communities continue to depend on the traditional means of wastes disposal.

This policy of continuing to provide for an ever-increasing demand for water without making an improvement in the sanitation system will increase the risk of major epidemics and decrease the general quality of urban life.

There is no question that establishing a national policy on water supply and sanitation will be the most effective measure to ensure that this sector is given the priority it deserves in receiving allocations from the national budget. Priorities and approaches in urban and rural water supply and sanitation must be established at the central level so that all agencies involved can work within a national framework. A balance between water supply provision and sanitation services can only be achieved in practice if the national policy includes this intention. Minimizing the numb   involved in the planning and implementation of water supply

and s   ture of programmes will
lead   l or regional (perhaps
metr   l or regional programme,
but   upport system. In many
cou   npracticable for political
reas   ed should be charged with
co-   gency should be provided
wit   he demands made upon it
and

sir   ve approach would be for a
ra   waste disposal, but this is
do   y is responsible only for
di   ustry deals with industrial
a   single, comprehensive water
i   e and incorporate sanitation
r   ome master plan. It is more
                  rban sanitation on a regional

basis rather than   otal master plan of sewerage
and drainage. A combined water authority with income from water rates or charges would be in a better financial position to implement sanitation services in a developing country than a sewerage authority without a conventional revenue source.

Integrated rural development

Increasing attention is now being given to integrated rural development, and this provides an opportunity for water supply and waste disposal to become a co-ordinated activity along with other rural development projects. If this can be achieved, there are likely to be financial benefits to water supply and sanitation projects through the increased economic level of communities receiving development assistance.

The financial implications of rural water supply and sanitation programmes in developing countries really go beyond the boundaries of the rural areas and impinge on urban residents, because if significant progress is to be made, the more affluent urban communities must accept the burden of subsidizing rural schemes. But it is also essential that rural dwellers be induced to pay the maximum amount possible for a water supply service and sanitation facilities. Their cash earnings are often low, so contributions will often need to be in the form of labour or materials. Plans for construction, operation and maintenance need to allow for this. The administrative structure of the responsible agency should allow for the regular collection of contributions, which should at least cover the cost of operation and maintenance, and it should provide an adequate maintenance service. In the past, many projects which were handed over to the residents on completion subsequently failed because there was no organized system of operation and maintenance.

Acceptability of technology

The most important aspect of water supply and sanitation system is their acceptability by the communities concerned, and this can only be satisfactorily achieved by involving the users at all stages of programme planning and implementation. A scheme will only be successful if it is accepted by the community and if it continues to operate; if communities are expected to support and, in rural areas, operate projects, then they must not only be kept informed of developments but must also be involved in the planning and decision-making processes. Only if planners and designers gain a thorough understanding of local attitudes and opinions will they be able to provide systems which are socially successful. Selling the desirability of sanitation along with water supply should be an important aspect of this early dialogue in a programme. It has been found that rural development agencies, or health-care staff have much better rapport with local people than the more distant personnel from the water supply authority. These workers have generally built up a respect for their impartiality and, since trust is an essential factor in collaboration, they should be used to provide the vertical links between the planners and designers on the one hand and the community on the other. Inevitably, they will also have a crucial role to play in making people aware of the health benefits which should arise from improvements in water supply and sanitation.

In technological design terms, an appropriate system of water supply and sanitation for a community in a developing country must be low in cost and acceptable to the recipients. Here, the form of the water supply has a profound influence on the sanitation system possible. A house connection will provide different opportunities for sanitation than will a public standpipe, and an intermittent water supply will produce its own constraints on system design. Nevertheless, social acceptability is essential and attempts to change habits must be carefully tested before a large-scale programme is implemented. *Appropriate* standards and criteria for design must be adopted if the level of service is to match the needs of the community and the realities of the duty.

In low-income urban areas, the technology of rural sanitation is often more appropriate than an extension of urban sewerage technology. At the same time, urban techniques and urban thinking are almost never appropriate in the rural sector.

Manpower training is not often attuned to the needs of simple water supply and sanitation systems. Professional engineers are educated to a high theoretical level and are unwilling to apply their minds to mundane systems, while technicians are in short supply in many developing countries. The managerial ability of professionals employed by water supply and sanitation authorities in some countries is extremely limited, and this is partly due to the low salaries paid to government employees and the poorly-qualified graduates attracted to government service. Manpower needs for water supply and sanitation projects must be assessed for the different levels of attainment, and training programmes should form part of the national policy.

Towards the year 2000

While it may be possible to think in terms of the total urban population of developing countries being adequately served with safe water and even modest sanitation services by the year 2000, it is inconceivable that rural communities can be provided with similar levels of service. Only with a significant degree of self-help could total coverage of rural areas with safe water supply be achieved by the same date and, if a similar approach is adopted, rural sanitation might be extended to not more than half the population. Changes of attitude on the part of the people and institutional changes in government will be necessary to achieve the needed balance between water supply provision and sanitation services. To reach the targets indicated, international, national and local finance must be allocated to water supply and sanitation programmes at unprecedented levels, and the administrative and technological systems must be geared to handling them efficiently.

NOTES AND REFERENCES

1. Section 1.1 is compiled from data presented by B.Z. Diamant, James McL. Fraser, James Howard, J. Bertrand Mendis, M.B. Pescod, and Abel Wolman.
2. Report by James McL.Fraser and James Howard; a fuller version appears in Chapter 9 (Section 9.1).
3. Report by John D. Skoda, J. Bertrand Mendis and Michael Chia; a fuller version appears in Chapter 2 (Section 2.5).
4. For further discussion of the diarrhoeal attack rate as revealed by this survey, see Section 2.5
5. World Health Organization, *World Health Statistics Report,* 29 (10), (1976), pp. 544-632.
6. Affiliation of all three authors: University of Science and Technology, Kumasi, Ghana; A.M. Wright is Professor of Civil Engineering.
7. The survey is undertaken by the Environmental Quality Division of the Civil Engineering Department at Kumasi. The work is supported by the International Development Research Centre of Canada. The field assistance of the Environmental Health Division of the Ministry of Health is gratefully acknowledged.
8. D.J. Schliessman, 'Diarrhoeal diseases and the environment', *Bulletin of WHO,* 21 (3), (1959), pp. 381-6.

18

9. W.J. van Zijl, 'Studies on diarrhoeal diseases in seven countries,' *Bulletin of WHO*, 35 (1966), pp. 249-61.
10. J.C. Azurin and M. Alvero, 'Field evaluation of environmental sanitation measures against cholera', *Bulletin of WHO*, 51 (1974) pp. 19-26.
11. Paragraph added by the editor.
12. Abel Wolman is from The Johns Hopkins University, Baltimore, Maryland 21218, U.S.A.
13. M.B. Pescod is Tyne and Wear Professor of Environmental Control Engineering, University of Newcastle upon Tyne, England.
14. See Chapter 6 (Section 6.2) for the report of the working group on pit latrines.

2

Towards an Engineering View of Health

2.1 FACTORS AFFECTING THE IMPACT OF SANITATION ON HEALTH

D.J. Bradley[1]

Varieties of excreta-related disease

There are very many infections which depend for their persistence on passing from the excreta of one person to the mouth of another. All of these are likely to be affected by excreta disposal methods. All of them are likely to decrease, often greatly, with the installation of a conventional sewerage system and an adequate water supply. However, it is now clear that the costs of providing conventional sewerage greatly exceed the resources available in many developing countries. And as with water supply, when resources allow only partial improvements, it is necessary to look critically at the health benefits likely to be attained.

If the engineering design of sanitation systems can be based on a *precise* understanding of the ways in which people's health may benefit, there is a better chance of achieving significant benefits with low-cost solutions, thereby helping more people with the same resources. There is a need, therefore, for a view of health which has regard to the sanitary engineer's capacity for making interventions. The aim of this chapter is to present four or five different ways of approaching this much-needed engineering view of health.

The hazards to health associated with inadequate excreta disposal are effectively due to infective disease. Even if the different numbered types of viruses and serotypes of enterobacteria are ignored, there are still more than fifty infections relevant to this discussion. They are usually classified according to the causative agent, or pathogen, of which there are four main kinds mentioned in this book: viruses, bacteria, helminths and protozoa. This classification is of some value, but a rather different approach may be more useful to the engineer, based on knowledge of the processes by which these infections spread. This new approach should also be based, I suggest, on a consideration of four variables, two relating to the pathogen—its persistence and latency—and two to the human body and its responses—age and immunity.

19

Latency and persistence

The two key variables that determine the nature of excretal transmission of infection may be regarded as *latency* and *persistence*. The first term I use to cover the interval between passage of the excreta and their becoming infective to others. In the case of most viral and bacterial infections, there is no latency, and the microbes are immediately infectious—Figure 2.1 (a). The requirements for safe disposal of excreta containing these agents are far more stringent than for those infections where there is a prolonged period before the excreta present a health hazard—Figure 2.1 (c). This is the case in most helminth infections where the excreted eggs have to mature before becoming infective. This latent period will require certain temperature and often humidity conditions, and possibly a specific soil environment, as in the case of hookworms. It may also require an intermediate host, in which case a further series of constraints on transmission follow, discussed below. It is this latency which, for example, separates diseases where night soil cartage is largely risk free from those where the fresh night soil is a major health hazard.

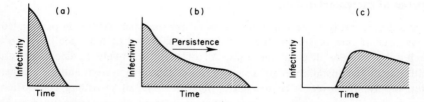

Figure 2.1 The *latency* and *persistence* of infections: (a) no latency, little persistence; (b) no latency, long persistence; (c) significant latency, long persistence.

The second key variable is persistence. How rapidly do the disease agents die under various conditions? The infection in Figure 2.1 (b) is clearly more persistent than the one in Figure 2.1(a). Often the agents with a latent period of development before infectivity are then very persistent in the environment—Figure 2.1(c). Persistence is more relevant to problems with excreta treatment than excreta collection, and understanding it is central to making the excreta safe for use.

Persistence, or survival in the environment, is only meaningful in relation to data on the minimal infective dose of the pathogen. This is often imprecisely known and also subject to extreme variability. For example, a dose of sodium bicarbonate taken shortly before cholera bacilli are ingested reduces the median dose by a factor of a thousand in healthy volunteers. The malnourished communities who suffer most from these diseases are likely to differ again in susceptibility whilst being unavailable for direct study. It is extremely unusual to be able to measure both the dose of an infecting agent to which a community is exposed, and also the infection rate and intensity in the population that result. This is because most 'common source' outbreaks are due to transient events: by the time a clinical outbreak occurs, the peak pollution has passed. It is more feasible in the highly polluted situation, and with endemic infections, to assess the level of contamination of the environment and the level of infection in people, but these two are open to so many other determinants that a precise relation is unlikely. Much of the environmental contamination is not relevant to subsequent infection, and the endemic pattern in man depends on the host response as well as the exposure to pathogens.

Immunity and age

Among the many factors which influence response to infection, acquired immunity and a person's age are of particular importance for predicting the effects of sanitation. At one extreme would be a short-lived helminthic parasite to which little immunity developed and in which the relation between infection and disease was not age-dependent. Then a nearly linear relation between exposure and disease might be expected, with improvements in the appropriate aspects of sanitation giving health improvements proportionate to effort—Figure 2.2(a). Possibly the helminth *Ascaris* approaches this situation.

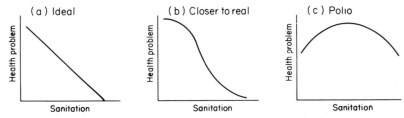

Figure 2.2   The reduction of health problems with improvements in sanitation: (a) the ideal solution: (b) what usually happens — initial small improvements in sanitation have little effect; (c) poliomyelitis — sanitation reduces transmission of the virus, but does not reduce the health problem.

At the other extreme are viral or bacterial infections which give rise to long-lasting immunity, and where the chance of overt disease in those infected rises with increasing age. A clear example is infection with poliomyelitis virus. Under very bad sanitary conditions, everybody is infected at a very young age, so older children and adults are immune. Disease is thus limited to a few of the youngest children, though disability persists (and is more common than was once believed). If hygiene greatly improves, infection is deferred to later childhood and adult life, when the frequency and severity of pathological consequences are increased—Figure 2.2(c). Thus although poliovirus transmission may be reduced by improving sanitation, reduction of disease is in practice achieved by immunization. Does this situation apply to any other faecal infections? Possibly it does with some, but the epidemiology is more complex.

What may be more frequent is that human immunity is of some importance in regulating the amount of infection and disease. This will tend to reduce the health benefits of moderate sanitary improvements, and may be a partial explanation of the rather limited disease reductions that so often follow sanitation programmes.

The processes by which infections spread

The way in which the preceding mechanisms operate in relation to sanitation will depend on the pattern of transmission from faeces. Where no latency exists, a very direct cycle from anus to mouth is possible, and where this is the main route, personal cleanliness, dependent largely on water usage, attains greater importance than does excreta disposal. But with many infections, the extent to which transmission is by this direct route or by other routes is notably unclear.

Where latency is great, it is often accompanied by a multiplicative stage (in water snails with schistosomiasis infection), or by very persistent stages, as with such geohelminths as *Ascaris*, the roundworm. There will thus tend to be a separation in both space and time between the escape of the infection in the faeces and any illness caused in other people. The extent of this separation will greatly depend on the 'social geometry' of the people—their patterns of movement and behaviour. So far as sanitation systems are concerned, these infections, where independent of a second host, can build up in any regularly used but unclean site, whether a patch of banana trees or an unhygienically maintained latrine. Even where an individual family improves its sanitation standards, infections of this type may spread to them from neighbouring families because of the way these infections may be diffused during their long persistence in the environment. The extreme consequence of latency and persistence is seen in the raised hazard to sewage farm workers from the persistent parasites, as compared with the general population of the same locality.

On this basis, it may be helpful to consider the infections that are faecally excreted as being transmitted by three progressively longer cycles. The 'tightest' cycle is directly faecal-oral; it involves the organisms with no latency and is specially important among those with a low persistence in the environment. Improvements in personal cleanliness even more than faecal disposal are the key to reducing these infections. Adequate water supplies are a pre-requisite for such improvements. The next larger cycle concerns organisms with some degree of environmental persistence and often, though not necessarily, a latent period of development on the ground. The local or family level transmission of these depends on an unhygienic defecation facility. Improvements depend on the way latrines are maintained. With further persistence in the environment, the transmission cycle becomes wider still and hazards to those outside the family increase. The site of final disposal of the faeces becomes of greater importance than the earlier stages of defecation and excreta removal.

It is with the more persistent infections, involving the longer cycles, that this chapter mainly deals, because they are less frequently considered than the diarrhoeal infections most notoriously associated with insanitary conditions. Very often, too, it is these more persistent infections that will be most effectively diminished by programmes for the improvement of latrines and excreta disposal.

The next part of the chapter presents a classification of helminth infections based on ideas related to the suggestions made above; the infections transmitted by the tightest cycle of transmission are designated 'direct faecal-oral'; those transmitted by a longer cycle are designated 'indirect faecal-oral'; and those with larval development or multiplicative stages in the environment are subdivided according to whether they are transmitted mainly in water, or on the ground, or via the flesh of animals used as food.

The categorization of some infections in terms of the main cycle of transmission is easy. Some are too fragile to survive beyond the directly faecal-oral route, and others, depending on the intermediate hosts, are clearly transmitted wholly via the widest cycle. But many of the geohelminths and persistent viruses spread across the above three categories and this serves to show up the limits to our epidemiological understanding of their spread. Almost certainly the patterns vary with culture, environment, and economy.

What then is the significance of any analysis of this type? It may clarify thought on the likely health consequences of a new type of sanitary facility; it may remind us of our epidemiological ignorance of many topics, and spur us into further work; and it should serve to remind us that personal cleanliness and maintenance of facilities is of central importance: that human behaviour dominates the scene.

2.2 AN ENGINEERING VIEW OF CERTAIN HELMINTH (WORM) INFECTIONS

Peter Hawkins and Richard Feachem[2]

Basic helminthology

Helminths are the parasitic worms which live in many species of animals. Here we are concerned only with helminths which cause illness in man, and they belong to three biological categories: the nematodes (roundworms), trematodes (flukes), and cestodes (tapeworms).

Unlike other classes of human pathogens (such as bacteria or viruses)[3], which may multiply within the human body, sometimes causing an acute infection to develop from a small infecting dose, most helminths cannot reproduce within the human host, but must distribute their eggs into the outside environment. The severity of a helminth infection therefore depends on the number of worms which have invaded the body from outside. This 'worm load' also determines the rate at which the infection is propagated by transmission of eggs in the faeces, urine, or sputum of the human host.

The helminths are relatively long-lived (from a few months up to about thirty years), and often give rise to only limited acquired resistance by the human body. Hence the typical pattern of infection is one of chronic rather than transient illness, with a gradual increase in worm load over time maintaining a long-term debilitating infection.

We may consider four stages of the helminth life cycle — escape of eggs or larvae into the environment, development and survival in the environment (sometimes in another animal, referred to as the 'intermediate host'), the infection of another human host, and the adult life within the human body, when eggs are produced to restart the cycle. If any one of these stages can be effectively blocked, the continuous transmission of the parasites is interrupted, and human infestations fall to lower levels or may even disappear. As with many endemic diseases, attacking the parasites inside the human host may yield an immediate fall in infection levels. But infection often increases again more or less slowly to the original level of equilibrium with the environment. Hence any lasting effects will be wrought mainly by changes in the environment. It is in the planning, design, and implementation of the environmental changes that the public health engineer has a key role to play.

The prevalence[4] (total number of infected people) and geographical distribution of some of these parasites is summarized in Table 2.1, which also lists relevant environmental control measures.

Environmental taxonomy

To the biologist, species are differentiated by form and structure, but for the public health engineer, a different taxonomy is needed. Engineering methods are aimed at the external stages of the helminth life cycles, and these have been chosen as a suitable basis for classification.

Seven kinds of life cycle can be distinguished, and they provide the categories for our proposed classification. To begin with, there are three *water-based* categories, so called because helminths of these kinds develop in aquatic animals[5]. Then there are two types of *faecal-oral* life cycle, in which transmission of the helminth occurs when material from faeces contaminates food or drink. These latter categories must be distinguished from the *meat-based* helminths, where an essential development stage in the helminth life cycle takes place within the muscles of infected cows or pigs; the infection is passed on to people who eat the uncooked meat from these animals. Then finally, there are the *soil-based* helminths, which comprise the hookworms; these develop in warm, moist soil rather than in another animal, and infect people by producing larvae which can penetrate the skin, most often of bare feet.

This method of characterizing the helminths according to their life cycles thus gives rise to the following seven categories:

(a) *Water-based* (cutaneous-oral) life cycles, represented by guineaworm.
(b) *Water-based* (percutaneous) life cycles, as typified by the schistosome worms.
(c) *Water-based* (raw food transmitted) life cycles, of which the intestinal and lung flukes are examples.
(d) *Soil-based* (percutaneous) life cycles (the hookworms).
(e) *Indirect faecal-oral* life cycles (e.g. *Ascaris*).
(f) *Direct faecal-oral* life cycles (e.g. pinworm).
(g) *meat-based* life cycles (the tapeworms).

The most important helminths belonging to each of these seven categories is most easily seen in Table 2.1. As already noted, among the water-based helminths,

Table 2.1 Prevalence of disease caused by helminths and an environmental classification of the helminths concerned

Latin Name of Helminth	Common Name	Prevalence of disease (million cases)	Category	Control Methods
1. Dracunculus medinensis	Guineaworm	48 (c)	water based (cutaneous-oral)	protect water supply / intermediate host control / purify drinking water
2. Schistosoma mansoni / „ haematobium / „ japonicum	Bilharzia	114 (c)	water based (percutaneous)	sanitation / intermediate host control / prevent exposure to polluted water
3. Fasciolopsis buski	Intestinal fluke	10 (d)	water based (raw food transmitted)	sanitation / health education (food) / intermediate host control
4. Paragonimus westermani	Lung fluke	3 (d)		
5. Clonorchis sinensis	—	19 (d)		
6. Diphyllobothrium latum	Broad tapeworm	10 (b)		
7. Necator americanus / Ancylostoma duodenale	Hookworm	457 (a)	soil-based percutaneous	sanitation / wear shoes
Strongyloides stercoralis		35 (a)		
8. Ascaris lumbricoides	Roundworm	644 (a)	indirect faecal – oral	sanitation / composting / hygiene
9. Trichuris trichiura	Whipworm	355 (a)		
Ancylostoma duodenale	Hookworm	(f)		
10. Toxocara canis	—			
11. Enterobius vermicularis	Pinworm	209 (a)	direct faecal–oral	hygiene
12. Hymenolepis nana	Dwarf tapeworm	20 (a)		
13. Echinococcus granulosus	Hydatid			
14. Taenia saginata	Beef tapeworm	39 (a)	meat – based	sanitation / health education (food)
15. Taenia solium	Pork tapeworm	3 (a)		

KEY:
(a) cases dispersed throughout the world
(b) occurs throughout the world at foci associated with water
(c) occurs in Africa, Asia and Latin America at foci associated with water
(d) occurs only in Asia at foci associated with water
(e) occurs in Oceania, Asia, Latin America and Africa at foci associated with water
(f) this helminth occurs also in line (7); it is transmitted by the indirect faecal-oral route as well as like the soil-based percutaneous helminths

guineaworm is placed in a cutaneous-oral subdivision which reflects its unique method of transmitting eggs to the environment through the ruptured skin of the infected person. The percutaneous subdivision includes the *Schistosoma* species, which are the only medically important water-based helminths infecting humans by skin penetration. Finally, the raw food transmitted helminths in the water-based category include those which infect people who ingest water, fish or crab containing their larvae.

The faecal-oral helminths have been split into two subdivisions, namely, indirect, which are those requiring some time outside the host for their larvae to develop to the infective stage; and direct, whose eggs are already infective on reaching the external environment.

As already explained, these categories are related to control measures which come within the sphere of the public health engineer. Some control measures affect more than one category of helminth. This is particularly true of modifications in the water supply. For instance, a piped water supply laid on to every house might affect schistosomiasis by *reducing contact* with infected water among people bathing and laundering, while it might also affect the faecal-oral helminths by making *more water available* for washing and thereby improving personal hygiene.

If a water supply or any other engineering measure is to have the required impact on a particular helminth disease, its exact role in interrupting transmission must be understood, and this understanding must influence the detailed engineering design. It should be emphasised, though, that a combination of control measures (including medical ones not shown in Table 2.1), will prove most effective, and close collaboration between engineers and medical personnel is required at all stages in a preventive campaign.

Reference to Table 2.1 emphasizes the paramount importance of sanitation and hygiene in preventing helminth infections, and this is amply supported by Stoll's data.[6]

2.3 ENVIRONMENTAL CONTROL OF CERTAIN HELMINTHS

Peter Hawkins and Richard Feachem[7]

Breaking helminth life cycles

For the purposes of discussing environmental engineering techniques, three ways of controlling helminths by interrupting the life cycle can be considered:

(a) blocking transmission of helminth eggs to the environment;
(b) controlling the helminth within the environment;
(c) blocking transmission of the helminth's eggs or larvae back to man.

Transmission of helminth eggs to the environment can be blocked by drug therapy which kills the worms within the human body. Although the effect of one mass dosage is small in the long run, the slow approach to a new ecological equilibrium by a community whose environment has been altered (e.g. by improved sanitation), can be greatly accelerated by the administration of drugs.

In the case of guineaworm (water-based, cutaneous-oral according to Table 2.1), which emerges from the human body through the skin into water, simple protection of the water source can substantially reduce transmission. This protection can take the form of hard standing and an outward draining parapet round a well, or the boxing of a spring. Ponds should be filled in and replaced by other sources.

Control within the environment

Intermediate host control is one of the two main ways of controlling helminths in the environment, sanitation being the other. One strategy is to apply chemicals to stagnant ponds and slow streams or rivers which harbour the intermediate hosts of water-based helminths.[8] The other strategy is to redesign water courses and provide canal linings to increase flow velocities, discourage aquatic vegetation, and generally deprive the intermediate host of its habitat.

The hydraulic design techniques are being slowly introduced on some new irrigation schemes and should yield positive results, when combined with other methods of control. The lining of canals will not only help to reduce snail populations, and thus schistosomiasis transmission, but will also greatly reduce seepage losses and maintenance work. Thus, the relatively large expense of such work can be discounted not only against health benefits but also against the operating costs of these irrigation schemes.

In *sanitation systems*, helminth ova survive for varying but quite long periods. They are only killed with certainty if fermentation, causing thermal death, occurs. Hence, for the faecal-oral helminths (which comprise the great majority), scattered defecation in the open, especially when the environment is damp, leads to a wide dispersal of infective ova, particularly in the shaded areas near human habitations.

For many of the water-based helminths, particularly where snails are the intermediate hosts, the ova must reach water quickly if they are to survive. This gives rise to two patterns of transmission. In the dry season, only the occasional pool will contain infected snails, usually because children have defecated in the water. The provision of latrines would not change this. In the wet season, however, the surface run-off containing fresh faecal material is taken straight to rivers and pools, thus infecting the snails. This type of pollution is much more susceptible to sanitation, which isolates the ova from the environment.

With the fish-transmitted helminths (water-based, raw food transmitted), two kinds of faecal pollution are important. The first applies to fish culture in East Asia, where faeces are deliberately fed into the village fish pond, often by building latrines to overhang the pond. Any alternative method of excreta disposal would displace the valuable method of food production, so the most effective engineering measure is to kill the ova before depositing night soil in the pond. This might be done by treating the excreta in a holding tank for 12-24 hours with 0.07 per cent ammonium sulphate, provided this was found to be non-toxic for the fish.[9] Alternatively, the night soil may be aerobically composted for a few days to allow the whole mass to reach 55-65°C, a temperature which will quickly destroy helminth ova.

The second type of pollution may occur wherever lakeside or riverside settlements discharge raw sewage into the water, or where people defecate at the water's edge or use overhang latrines. If raw fish is commonly eaten, the conditions exist for a transmission focus to build up. This cycle can be broken by providing latrines from which sewage is not discharged into the water, possibly because it is diverted to other uses.

The meat-based tapeworms have ample opportunity to thrive when excreta is placed on ground where cows and pigs may wander, and ingest infective tapeworm proglottids. This may be the result of casual defecation, or of deliberately disposing of night soil into pig pens (which is done in parts of Asia). Use of waste-water for irrigating pasture may transmit *Taenia saginata* to cattle, and suitable precautions against this are discussed in Section 12.4.

The hookworms require only moisture and shade to develop into infective larvae, and where favoured defecation sites provide these conditions, people become infected while using them. Latrines can prevent the larvae reaching the soil where they can infect people, but unless they are very clean, the latrines themselves may easily become efficient foci for transmission.

The most prevalent group of all, the indirect faecal-oral helminths, are those requiring some development outside the host before the ova or larvae become infective. Subsequent infection is via food and hands, so personal hygiene is obviously very important. However, the most salient biological feature is the longevity and toughness of some ova, notably *Ascaris lumbricoides*. If latrines are not kept scrupulously clean, the longevity of these ova means that large numbers will accumulate over time. Indeed, the higher incidence of *Ascaris* among urban latrines users as compared with rural non-users has been attributed to dirty latrines forming very intensive foci for transmission.[10]

The direct faecal-oral helminths, whose eggs are infective immediately on reaching the environment and are relatively short-lived, are thought to be transmitted by the direct contact between members of a family, or indirect contact via dirty clothes: latrines that are not clean may be a source of indirect contacts.

Thus, *improved excreta disposal can be seen to have great potential benefits, but equally great potential dangers.* On the one hand, it can isolate ova from the environment, and may include a sewage digestion process which kills many of them. But on the other hand, latrines may easily become a focus from which faecal-oral helminth diseases are spread, unless special care is taken to promote hygiene and good maintenance of the latrine. Even if all excreta are hygienically collected, proper steps must be taken to ensure the destruction of pathogens during the treatment process.

It can be concluded, then, that health benefits will not follow from the construction of latrines unless thought is also given to their proper use, regular cleaning, and effective maintenance.

Blocking transmissions to man

There are three processes in standard water purification practice which will have an effect on the survival of helminths. These are storage-sedimentation processes, filtration processes, and the addition of disinfectant chemicals, all of which may sometimes be used in combination.

With guineaworm, infection is by ingesting infected cyclops in water. Their relatively large size (about 1mm) allows them to be easily moved by any type of filter. Cyclops are also susceptible to (pot) chlorination, which has proved quite successful in reducing the disease in India.[11]

The infective agents of schistosomiasis are the cercariae released from infected snails. For the 24 hours of their infective life, they are highly motile[12] so any filter to remove them must be rather fine (sand less than 0.35mm) which may explain why some workers have observed cercariae to be penetrating sand filters.[13] An experiment on *Schistosoma mansoni* cercariae showed that, although they remain motile for longer, they become non-infective after 24-30 hours' storage in water. Hence, storage of water in a snail-free tank for 30 hours should be an effective barrier against this (and possibly other) schistosome species. Chlorination at the concentrations and contact times generally used for domestic water supplies is effective against cercariae.

In contrast, the water-based helminths transmitted by raw food such as *Clonorchis sinensis* produce cysts which are not susceptible to chlorination, but which are large and heavy enough to be removed by filtration or sedimentation.[14]

It must be stressed that the only helminth infection likely to be much reduced by *water treatment alone* is *guineaworm*. It should also be noted that old polluted sources of water should be blocked off when a new supply is installed, and steps should be taken to ensure adequate, long term maintenance of the improved supply, otherwise the health benefits expected will not be achieved.

Preventing the exposure of people to percutaneous infection by hookworms and schistosomes is a control measure beset by cultural and social problems. With schistosomes, exposure is by contact with infected waters. Attempts can be made to fence these off, site villages away from them, and provide a piped water supply. Bridges can be built over streams and irrigation canals, and bathing people can be supplied with purified water. A project in St. Lucia which provided reticulated water supplies, bathing pools, and communal washing places did manage to reduce the transmission of schistosomiasis.[15] Thus the provision of a comprehensive and comparable alternative to the use of unpurified water does seem able to acquire the necessary social acceptance. It should be noted that the prevention of contact with polluted water implies the availability of 'clean' water.

The larvae of the soil-based, percutaneous helminths (predominantly *Necator americanus*) are transmitted by skin contact with faecally contaminated soil. This can be avoided by wearing shoes (especially when visiting communal defecation grounds). However, cost and lack of cultural acceptability will often make this strategy impracticable.

Composting is important as a means of blocking transmission of helminths to man because it is a reliable means of killing helminth ova and larvae. Without exception, all helminth stages will die quickly (in minutes or, at most, hours) at 55°C, and within days at 45°C, which are temperatures usually exceeded in the composting process. A detailed discussion of this method of excreta treatment is given in Section 12.1.

Personal cleanliness represents yet another means of blocking helminth transmission to man. It is notable that the faecal-oral helminth diseases tend to concentrate in particular families, emphasizing the importance of domestic hygiene, especially with regard to cooking and eating utensils, and the kitchen area. It appears that the biggest factor is the provision of water *inside* the home[16], backed up by some excreta disposal measures. It has been suggested that the best "value for money" in hygiene and disease prevention terms is piped water to one tap, and possibly a shower, in every home,[17] when between three and five times as much water may be used as compared with homes lacking a supply[18]. The bulk of this extra water use is probably for washing and cleaning purposes. But such provision of water is probably only practicable in a nucleated or dense settlement. In dispersed rural communities, the greater amounts of pipework necessary for a complete reticulation system may be prohibitively expensive, so domestic cleanliness can only be promoted by the provision of more standpipes or wells, or by health education.

Discussion

From the preceding sections, it is clear that there are many strategies for the control of helminths, and it would be wrong to think of any particular method in isolation from the others. Within any particular community it is likely that several helminth transmission cycles are proceeding simultaneously along their various routes, and again, the need for composite control strategies is clear. Within an integrated control programme, however, each control method has its own role, which is set out below and summarized in Table 2.1.

Sanitation is a blanket measure reducing environmental pollution by all the helminths considered, apart from guineaworm, *Toxocara canis*, and the direct faecal-oral species. It is a first line of defence, and can never be completely effective, but must form the backbone of any control programme. It is important to ensure that the latrines and excreta disposal systems are properly used and maintained and this will usually require a high degree of community involvement in the sanitation programme. The disappointing results obtained from many previous sanitation programmes can often be attributed to the lack of community involvement and understanding. The social acceptance of sanitation is equally as important as the basic engineering provisions.

A second important general measure is the promotion of personal and domestic hygiene, effective against the largest group of helminthiases, the faecal-oral species. Again, this is a combination of engineering (the provision of plentiful water) and social (health education) measures. The prevention of contamination of growing fruit and vegetables with fresh excreta (used as a fertiliser) is also important, and the use of composting latrines will not only decrease contamination, but also improve crop yields.

Intermediate host control, effective against the water-based helminths, is unlikely to have a large impact by itself, but is important in an integrated control programme. Engineering methods, concerned with the design of irrigation systems, should be incorporated from the start of such projects.

The provision of water supplies can act in various ways. Improvement of water quality is highly effective only against guineaworm. In schistosomiasis foci, prevention of exposure to the infected waters may have a large impact on transmission of the parasite. This demands comprehensive alternative supplies of purified water to taps, and washing and bathing areas. Where personal hygiene is poor, and the faecal-oral helminths are common, the provision of plentiful, reliable water supplies is an important measure, and water quality is a secondary consideration to quantity.

2.4 EFFECTS OF LEAKY SANITATION ON HOOKWORMS AND OTHER GEOHELMINTHS

Gerhard Schad[20]

An enigmatic observation

'The erroneousness of judging hookworm infection by the percentage of people infected is nowhere better demonstrated than in Bengal, where an average of at least 80% of the 46,000,000 inhabitants are infected, a condition which some years ago was spoken of as "staggering." But egg counts show that in 90% of the area of Bengal the average number of worms harbored per person is less than 20, and not more than 1% of the people are estimated to have over 160 worms and almost none over 400.'

...Asa C. Chandler & Clark P. Read, 1961

The quotation presented above is based on Chandler's surveys conducted in India in the 1920's, in which he showed that in rural Gangetic Bengal there was an enigmatic high prevalence of low grade, generally well-tolerated, hookworm infections.[21] Although advances in technique demonstrate that Chandler's estimates were low, our data and those of others indicate that, in general, his conclusions were correct. This is contrary to the expected pattern for most unsanitated tropical areas where mean worm burdens vary directly with prevalence. The high prevalence-low intensity relationship has persisted in rural Gangetic Bengal for approximately 40 years, although neither anthelmintic treatment nor sanitary facilities are widely used. These facts suggested that, in this part of India, the hookworm population was naturally regulated to low, tolerable levels.

To understand how hookworm populations might be naturally regulated, a multidisciplinary investigation of the ecology and epidemiology of ancylostomiasis in a rural area 40 miles north of Calcutta was conducted.[22] The dynamics of hookworm infection in two sample populations of Bengali villagers was studies by monitoring changes in their faecal output of hookworm eggs during a period of two years.

Of the two groups, one consisted entirely of children, because in a community where 90 per cent of the population is infected, the exceptional individuals who are not infected are found mostly among children, and it is in these individuals that the result of any single exposure to infection can be most clearly seen. The other sample consisted of people of all ages, and was more representative of the whole community. Mean faecal egg counts were made on stool samples taken at bimonthly intervals.

A clear pattern emerged in which there was a marked dry season decline in the worm burden in both groups. Among the children, there was evidence also of an overall gain in worms from one year of age to the next up to age 19. However, it is evident that the dry season decline in worm burdens can produce a net loss of worms for some children in some years. In our survey, the 8-year-olds showed such a loss.

It appears from our studies that in Gangetic Bengal, the average villager gains worms throughout most of the first two decades of life. Then from the age of 20, the worm burden remains roughly constant, or declines, until in old age it starts to rise again. It appears, then, that the natural control mechanism which constrains the intensity of infection to a low level is also effective in holding it constant in adults. The seasonal decline in worm populations is clearly an important part of the control mechanism.

However, two other inter-related factors also play a part in controlling the worm burden, namely, the community's defecation habits, and the way these interact with the human body's ability to resist infection. The body's resistance probably depends on the rate of invasion, which in turn depends on abundance of larvae on the soil. Sampling the soil surface on defecation grounds for infective larvae regularly discovered larvae during the monsoon season, but failed to do so once the soil dried out in November or December. The soil sampling was done in a radial pattern around a freshly passed stool, including the area where feet were placed during defecation. It was evident from this that people coming to defecate made contact with very few larvae; they rarely placed their feet on places where faeces had been deposited until the faeces were so old that few larvae survived. In the monsoon season, feet might encounter larvae fairly frequently, but only a few at a time.

These investigations suggested that ecological and human behavioural factors, peculiar to Gangetic Bengal, combine so that villagers are exposed to frequent invasions with only a few larvae per infective contact. This postulated rate of infection (i.e. trickle infection) is known to elicit an effective acquired resistance to other hookworm species, and therefore, is thought to provoke an effective host response to Bengali villagers.

Repeated small doses have been shown to stimulate resistance to infection in numerous host-parasite associations involving nematodes. Therefore, the main thrust of rural sanitation with regard to control of the geohelminths could be the elimination of those foci of soil infestation which lead to heavy invasions of single exposures. Co-operative investigations involving soil ecologists, behaviourists, and sanitary engineers may be able to evolve programmes for incomplete (i.e. 'leaky') systems of rural sanitation, which intentionally allow some infection so that the populations gain a naturally acquired resistance. This limited objective may be an economically desirable interim goal.

2.5 THE IMPACT OF SANITATION IN BANGLADESH

John D. Skoda[23], *J. Bertrand Mendis*[24],
and Michael Chia[25]

Water supplies

In November and December 1976, a country-wide survey was made throughout Bangladesh covering water usage and sanitary habits, diarrhoeal morbidity, and related factors. The purpose of this study was to assess whether there have been any health benefits from the rural water supply construction projects which have been undertaken in Bangladesh with UNICEF and WHO assistance. The survey was also meant to assist planners in preparing future programmes.

Survey methods were decided in discussion involving staff members of both UNICEF and WHO stationed in Bangladesh. The survey was supervised in the field by UNICEF District representatives, and was carried out by field staff from the Ministries of Health, Social Welfare, Local Government, Rural Development, and Co-operatives.[26] The total population covered by the survey was 68 155 people living in 11 489 households in 120 randomly selected villages. A special effort was made to include women on as many teams as possible so as to contact the wife of the head of each household regarding the family's habits and morbidity.

A great majority of people (79 per cent) were found to be obtaining drinking water supplies from groundwater sources. Over half (52 per cent) of the households surveyed used tubewells with hand-pumps as the source of drinking water and 27 per cent used dug wells. The remainder used surface water.

The diarrhoeal attack rate in the week preceding the survey showed that those using groundwater had a diarrhoeal attack rate 48 per cent lower than the surface water drinkers (3.9 as against 7.5 per cent).

Excreta disposal

The survey investigated the availability of latrines and the use made of them, with the result already quoted in Chapter 1 (Table 1.1). Less than 2 per cent of households use sanitary water seal latrines. Open latrines and pit latrines are used by about half the adults, but most children do not use any type of latrine.

Significant factors with regard to health are the socio-economic status of the villagers and the availability of water (drier zones, with a higher water deficit, were found to have significantly higher morbidity rates). In every socio-economic group, tubewell water users have a lower morbidity than others, but the better-off also have significantly less morbidity, even though their tubewell water usage is only marginally greater.

Urban influence (apparently related to high population density) is associated with diarrhoeal morbidity, and so are areas where there is a high iron content in the groundwater. Villagers living in the latter areas are lagging behind their neighbours in use of well water and in health because the taste of the water deters full use being made of tubewells. Another general conclusion is that the children in the 1 to 10 years age group have a higher rate of diarrhoeal morbidity than those of other age groups, irrespective of the source of water. This appears to be because the children do not follow a disciplined pattern in the use of water or of latrines.

Very few people are using tubewells for anything other than drinking water, and there is good reason to believe that the diarrhoeal morbidity could be reduced if more people, especially children, would use a protected source such as tubewell water for all domestic purposes. Preventive health measures (water, sanitation, and hygiene practices) appropriate to rural areas need to be developed and provided. In this respect, rural Bangladesh, with population densities approaching or exceeding urban densities in some countries, has a special need.

2.6 THE IMPACT OF SANITATION IN TEN INDIAN VILLAGES

B.K. Handa[26], *P.V.R.C. Panicker, S.W. Kulkarni*[27],
A.S. Gadkari, and V. Raman

Pilot project

Health surveys conducted in different regions of India show that about 70 per cent of mortality and morbidity among the rural population can be attributed to the direct or indirect effects of poor environmental conditions in the villages. Lack of protected water supplies and indiscriminate defecation are the two most important of these conditions. Thus the transmission and spread of gastro-intestinal diseases is encouraged and helminthic infestation is also very heavy. Safe water supply and excreta disposal are therefore primary requirements for improving rural health.

A pilot project aimed at assessing the impact on people's health of various improvements in sanitation has been set up by the National Environmental Engineering Research Institute (NEERI)[28] in collaboration with the District authority (Zilla Parishad). In this joint venture, the provision of individual family latrines and the protection of water supplies have been undertaken in ten villages around Nagpur. But before these improvements were started, a base-line health survey was carried out, mainly aimed at estimating the parasite load from stool samples. A similar survey will be undertaken after the improved sanitation arrangements have been in use for three or four years, to see whether the parasite load in the human population has been reduced.

Four different sanitation measures are being applied in different combinations in the ten villages, as indicated in Table 2.2. One village is being used as a control, with health data being collected but no improvements made. The other nine villages are each the subject of one or more of the following measures:

(a) provision of individual hand-flushed latrines;
(b) provision of sanitary latrine blocks in village schools;
(c) protection or improvement of the water supply;
(d) chemotherapy for people with parasites.

Table 2.2 Summary of the sanitary measures taken in ten project villages. (X denotes application of the relevant measures)

Village	Control: no improvements	Health data collected	Chemotherapy for affected people	Disinfected well water or standpost water supply	Sanitary latrines at homes and schools
Asoli	X	X			
Avandi		X	X		
Khursapar		X			X
Mahalgaon		X		X	X
Burjwada		X			X
Fetri		X	X	X	X
Mahadula		X			X
Ajni					X
Wadoda					X
Wadi					X

In eight of the project villages, an individual hand-flushed latrine is being constructed for every household. It consists of a privy hut with a water closet pan which discharges into a soak pit (Figure 2.3); the pan provides a 13 mm water seal.

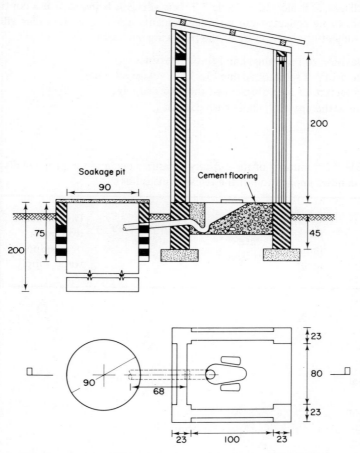

Figure 2.3   Hand-flushed, water seal latrine with off-set pit designed by NEERI, Nagpur, India (dimensions in centimetres)

Construction materials are supplied to each household, and technical assistance is available to help villagers who build their own latrines. The cost of the materials used, up to plinth level, is Rs. 125/- (US $14), and grants are available from the district authority and other local authorities to help villagers who build their own latrines. Low-cost superstructures designed by NEERI require materials costing up to Rs. 150/- ($17) which the villagers are expected to contribute themselves. School latrine blocks consist of two of these units, one for boys and one for girls, with a standing urinal for boys in addition.

Improvements in water supplies take the form of public standpost water distribution in one village (Fetri), and disinfected wells in another (Mahalgaon). Pot chlorinators are used to disinfect the well water. These are filled with a 1:4 mixture of bleaching powder and sand, and are lowered into the wells. The pots are recharged from time to time so that the residual chlorine in the water is never less than 01. mg/1.

The response to the latrine-building programme has not been good, and people's habits have persisted with regard to defecating on open land. The majority of the people are so poor and so low on the social scale that they have come to assume that the benefits of technology are not for them.[29] However, people are slowly realizing that latrines are of some value, and the rate of latrine construction is increasing.[30]

A log book is kept in each village in which problems arising from the latrines are recorded by a social worker whose job it is to encourage latrine usage. Observations are also being made on the rate of filling of soak pits. In some instances, users of a latrine mark a chart after each use, so that the capacity and rate of filling of the pit can be related to the amount it is used. Samples of material are being extracted from different depths in the pits for analysis, in order to study the digestion process and the distribution of helminths in the pit. When the pits are full, they will have to be emptied as there is not usually space to build a second one to serve each latrine. Knowledge of the survival of helminths in the pit will be used to devise safe emptying and disposal procedure.

The health survey

A base-line health survey has been completed in seven out of the ten villages. Three villages that are receiving latrines but no other improvements were not included. The main components of the survey were:

(a) stool examination of 25 per cent of the village populations, selected as a random sample;

(b) haemoglobin and eosinophil counts on blood samples;

(c) recording clinical histories of individuals.

People's co-operation in collecting stool samples was satisfactory, except in a few families where the people felt an aesthetic revulsion in collecting the sample in the specimen tube. The morning after the stool samples were gathered, the people concerned were interviewed about their clinical history. Their blood was examined for haemoglobin, and a peripheral blood smear for eosinophil count was taken. The stool samples were examined for parasites immediately by the smear and concentration methods.

Some of the data from the base-line survey is shown in Table 2.3, which also shows the number of people covered by the survey in the villages indicated. At Mahadula and Khursapar, more people were examined than had been proposed because of their active co-operation, but in the control village, Asoli, the people were less co-operative.

Table 2.3 Selected health data from four of the project villages

	Mahalgaon	Khursapar	Fetri	Asoli
Population in 1971	850	827	676	380
Number of households	170	183	130	72
Source of water supply	open well	open well	open well; tubewell	open well
Number of latrines in use	40	15	30	nil
Number of people under 16 covered by survey	105	117	80	99
Number with parasites	80	75	51	81
Number with multiple parasite infections	27	40	18	48
Number of adults covered by survey	101	155	94	100
Number with parasites	78	115	71	82
Number with multiple parasite infections	34	62	27	44
Parasites most often found (in order of occurrence)	1. *Ascaris* 2. Hookworm 3. *Entamoeba coli*	1. *Entamoeba coli* 2. *Entamoeba hystolitica* 3. Hookworm	1. Hookworm 2. *Entamoeba coli* 3. *Entamoeba hystolitica*	1. *Ascaris* 2. Hookworm 3. *Entamoeba coli*

In Figure 2.4 parasite infestation in different age groups among the population is shown. The way in which infestation increases with age is evident, and this can be compared with the observations on hookworm in West Bengal mentioned in Section 2.4. Parasitic infestation in the villages ranges between 74 and 82 per cent, which is exceptionally high, though it is comparable with the infestation rate revealed by a study in Uttar Pradesh.[31]

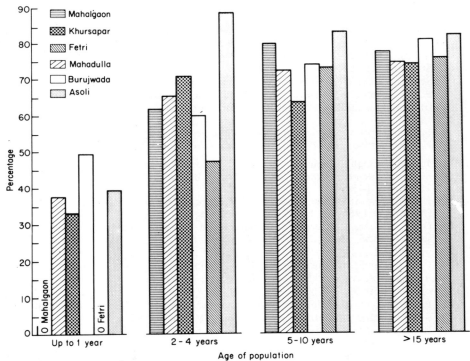

Figure 2.4 Prevalence rate or parasite infestation in six villages near Nagpur, India

Table 2.3 also shows which parasites were observed most frequently in the different villages. In Mahalogaon and Asoli, *Ascaria* affects more people than any other parasite; in Fetri, hookworm occupies this position; and in Khursapa, *Entamoeba coli*, a non-pathogenic parasite is most common.

In his studies of worm load in Egyptian villages, Chandler[32] found that the incidence of *Ascaria* was reduced by the provision of bored hole latrines, improved water supply, and better refuse disposal. Parallel results have been found by other workers[33]. Similarly, we shall hope to find some reduction in the worm load when a second health survey is taken in three or four years. Furthermore, by comparing the cost per capita of the sanitary measures taken in each village, we shall hope to form some tentative conclusions about which is the most cost-effective combination of measures.

40

NOTES AND REFERENCES

1. D.J. Bradley is Professor of Tropical Hygiene and Director, The Ross Institute of Tropical Hygiene, Keppel Street, (Gower Street), London WClE 7HT, England.

2. Peter Hawkins and Richard Feachem are from the Ross Institute of Tropical Hygiene, Keppel Street, (Gower Street), London, WClE 7HT, England.

3. G. Macdonald *Transactions of the Royal Society of Tropical Medicine and Hygiene* 59 (5), (1965), pp 489-506.

4. N.R. Stoll, 'This wormy world', *Journal of Parasitology,* 33 (1), (1947), pp. 1-18.

5. R.G.A. Feachem, 'Water supplies for low-income communities in developing countries', *Journal of the Environmental Engineering Division, ASCE,* 101 (EE5), (October 1975), pp 687-702.

6. Stoll, *op. cit.,* note 4.

7. See note, 2; this is the second part of the paper by Hawkins and Feachem.

8. P.L. Rosenfield, 'Development and verification of a schistosomiasis transmission model', Ph.D. Dissertation, Johns Hopkins University, Baltimore, 1975.

9. E.C. Faust *et al., American Journal of Hygiene, Monograph Series,* (8), 1927.

10. N.J. Richardson, *et. al., South African Medical Journal,* 42 (1968), pp. 46-9.

11. Jaswant Singh, Raghavan N.G.S., 'Dracontiasis in India', *Bulletin of the National Society of India for Malaria and Mosquito-borne Diseases,* 5(3), (May 1957), pp. 141-60.

12. L. Olivier, *American Journal of Tropical Medicine and Hygiene* 15 (6), (November 1966, pp. 882-5).

13. G.R. Mijares, 'Influence of water and sewage treatment processes on schistosomes', *Medical Bulletin (Standard Oil Co.),* 27 (3) (November 1967), pp. 280-93.

14. C.H. Barlow, 'The life cycle of the human intestinal fluke, *Fasciolopsis buski',* *American Journal of Hygiene, Monograph Series,* 1925; see also Faust *et. al., op. cit.,* note 9.

15. P. Jordan, *et. al.,* 'Control of *Schistosoma mansoni* by provision of domestic water supplies', *Bulletin of WHO,* 52 (1), (1975), pp. 9-20.

16. R.G.A. Feachem, 'The rational allocation of water resources for the domestic needs of rural communities in developing countries', *Proceedings of the 2nd World Congress, International Water Resources Association,* 2, (December 1975), pp. 539-47.

17. G.F. White, D.J. Bradley, and A.U. White, *Drawers of Water: Domestic Water Use in East Africa,* Chicago U.P., 1972.

18. 'Community water supply and sewage disposal in developing countries', *WHO Statistical Reports,* 26 (11), (1973), pp. 720-83; see also White, Bradley and White, *op. cit.,* note 17.

19. W.H. Wright, 'A consideration of the economic impact of schistosomiasis', *Bulletin of WHO,* 47 (5), (1972), pp. 559-66.

20. Gerhard Schad is from the School of Veterinary Medicine, University of Pennsylvania, 3800 Spruce Street, Philadelphia, Penn. 19104, U.S.A.

21. A.C. Chandler, 'The prevalence of hookworm and other helminthic infections in India', (in 12 parts), *Indian Journal of Medical Research,* 14 (1926), p. 185 to 15 (1927), p. 695.

22. G. Schad *et al.,* 'Arrested development of human hookworm infections', *Science,* 180 (1973), pp. 502-4.

23. John D. Skoda is Chief of the Water Section, UNICEF, GPO Box 58, Dacca, Bangladesh.
24. J. Bertrand Mendis is Assistant Programme Officer, UNICEF, GPO Box 58, Dacca-5, Bangladesh.
25. Michael Chia is Medical Statistician, WHO, Dacca, Bangladesh.
26. B.K. Handa, P.V.R.C. Panicker, A.S. Gadkari, and V. Raman are Scientists, National Environmental Engineering Research Institute, Nehru Marg, Nagpur 440020, India.
27. S.W. Kulkarni is Reader, Grant Medical College, Bombay, and was formerly at the Government Medical College, Nagpur.
28. The authors are greatly indebted to Professor N. Majumder, former Director of NEERI, and to Shir J.M. Dave, Deputy Director, for initiation of this project and for their guidance.
29. T.R. Bhaskaran and M.A. Sampatkumaran, 'Review of work done on rural latrine in India', Indian Council of Medical Research, 1966.
30. V. Raman, 'Rural sanitation and eco-development', *Khadi Gramodyog,* October 1975, pp. 83-5
31. Planning, Research and Action Institute (PRAI), Lucknow, 1962.
32. A.C. Chandler, *American Journal of Tropical Medicine and Hygiene*, 3 (1954), p. 59.
33. S.C. Bagchi, 'Study of some socio-environmental factors of hookworm infection', *Indian Journal of Medical Research,* 52 (1964); also, D.P. Agrawal, *Indian Journal of Preventive and Social Medicine.* 3 (1972), pp. 230-3.

3

Choice of Technology

3.1 INTRODUCTION

Criteria and data needed for choice

The choice of a sanitation technology depends on the *criteria* used for comparing one method with another, and on the availability of *knowledge* about each method. This chapter is concerned with these two issues, putting forward criteria for the selection of a sanitation technology in Section 3.2, and discussing the available information on the range of techniques in Sections 3.3 and 3.4.

It is of considerable value to have a checklist of criteria by which to evaluate sanitation systems, but it will be found that many items in that list have to be defined in terms of local conditions and needs, and have to be interpreted in the light of what people want. Choices about technology cannot therefore be made in general terms for all developing countries, but must be made separately and locally by each community or nation. Perhaps the most important part of this chapter is an account of the methods being used and the processes involved in making such a choice within four towns in Botswana (Section 3.5).

The selection of appropriate sanitation techniques is made particularly difficult by the fact that for several decades, there has been only one kind of excreta disposal accepted for general use in Western industrialized countries. This is, of course, the cistern-flushed latrine or water closet used in conjunction with what this book will call 'conventional sewerage' — the network of underground pipes needed to carry sewage to a treatment works. This system is so much taken for granted that many people have assumed that it is the only satisfactory method of excreta disposal. But on considering the widely varying circumstances of developing countries, it becomes clear that no one system is likely to be appropriate to the needs of all communities over all time.

It is vital, therefore, that a wider range of options should be considered, and if every possibility is included, the options vary between simple techniques used by remote rural communities, to the most specialized of recent innovations. In between these extremes, there are several intermediate technologies. For the purposes of this book, the whole range is subdivided as follows:

(a) cistern-flushed latrines with conventional sewerage (discussed in Chapter 4);

(b) specialized techniques (packing toilets, chemical latrines, etc., discussed later in this chapter);

(c) aqua-privies and related systems (Chapter 5);

(d) pit latrines and derivatives (Chapter 6);

(e) composting latrines (Chapter 7);

(f) bucket latrines or conservancy vaults with cartage of excreta off the site (Chapter 8);

(g) simple techniques (burial, trench latrines, open latrines, furrowed defecation grounds, etc., discussed at several points in Chapters 6 and 10).

This large range of excreta disposal methods and latrine technologies has inspired several attempts at a systematic classification. One key distinction is between dry systems, of which the composting latrine is the best example, and wet systems, where water is mixed with the excreta, usually by a flushing mechanism. Another distinction is between systems in which excreta is carried off-site by cartage, or by water flow in sewers, and systems which treat the excreta and dispose of it on site. Given these broad categories, the list above might be re-arranged as follows:

Wet systems, off-site treatment and disposal:
— conventional sewerage.

Wet systems, on-site treatment:
— aqua-privies, septic tanks, wet pit latrines,
most biogas plants.

Dry systems, off-site treatment and disposal:
— bucket latrines with cartage.

Dry systems, on-site treatment:
— composting latrines; dry pit latrines.

There are, inevitably, some techniques which fall between two of these classes. Pit latrines cover a wide range, some of which are wet and function somewhat like an aqua-privy, and some of which are dry and are used as composting latrines. Sewered aqua-privies, to be discussed in Chapter 4, are intermediate between the first two classes. And the great variety of 'specialized techniques' to be discussed at the end of Section 3.2 covers all categories but the first.

3.2 CRITERIA FOR EVALUATING EXCRETA DISPOSAL TECHNIQUES

Krisno Nimpuno[1]

Lists of criteria

Existing waste disposal technologies within the industrialized countries aim to achieve a good environmental and physiological hygiene in sewage treatment by two main steps:

(a) reduction of organic matter, measured by BOD (biochemical oxygen demand), in order to limit water pollution;

(b) reduction and control of pathogens.

There are many obstacles to the general application of sewage treatment which will perform these functions in developing countries, one of the most important of which is cost. Even the most primitive adaptation of the Western 'wet' system of excreta treatment in aqua-privies and septic tanks is too costly. In Tanzania, an aqua-privy costs at least U.S. $300 for a household model, whereas a family has on average only $900 at its disposal to spend on housing[2].

But it is not only for economic reasons that these methods do not offer a solution. It is almost impossible to dig a complete system of drainage pipes into an existing, unplanned residential area. In some countries, too, scarcity of water hampers the development of urban water-borne excreta disposal. And apart from these problems, one should remember that although the sewage treatment proceses developed in the West are very effective in reducing BOD, they rarely destroy pathogens at all efficiently. So a septic tank is very useful for BOD reduction, but its effluent can be very dangerous, and is usually just allowed to infiltrate into the soil, where it may pollute groundwater supplies which people are using.

All these considerations are pointers to the environmental and economic criteria which need to be used in evaluating excreta disposal technologies, and the World Health Organization has suggested others[3]. They point to 'a direct as well as an indirect relationship between the disposal of excreta and the state of health of the population'[4]. The *direct* relationship refers to the spread of excreta-related diseases, including cholera, typhoid, schistosomiasis, diarrhoea, enteritis, and hookworm. The *indirect* health hazards arise from the breeding of insects and other disease vectors in decaying excreta.

These two considerations, plus the need to reduce BOD, and to have low-cost systems which it is feasible to install in developing countries provide some initial criteria. Other people[5], culminating in the WHO study made by Wagner and Lanoix[6], have added to the list.

Most of these attempts to draw up criteria for the evaluation or design of sanitation systems concentrate on health matters — they stress that it is preferable if excreta do not need to be directly handled, and that access by flies and other insects should be prevented. And in the list compiled for WHO by Wagner and Lanoix, there are six such criteria. These are accepted as the basis for discussion here, but the seventh WHO criterion, which refers to the cost and feasibility of the proposed technique, needs considerable expansion. In fact, five additional criteria referring to costs, skills, use of local materials, maintenance requirements, and feasibility in dense urban areas, are added to the list, giving the following eleven criteria:

1. The surface soil should not be contaminated.
2. There should be no contamination of ground water that may enter springs or wells.

3. There should be no contamination of surface water.
4. Excreta should not be accessible to flies or animals.
5. There should be no handling of fresh excreta, or when this is indispensable, it should be kept to a strict minimum.
6. There should be freedom from odours or unsightly conditions.
7. The daily operation of the system should only require a simple and safe toilet routine.
8. The construction costs should not exceed 10 per cent of the total investment in housing.
9. The facilities should mainly be made of local materials and require minimal maintenance.
10. The use of water to dilute and transport excreta, should, if possible, be avoided.
11. Application in existing high density areas should be possible.

These eleven criteria are, of course, additional to the two basic criteria for the functioning of an excreta treatment system previously mentioned, namely, reduction of BOD and reduction or elimination of pathogens. In Table 3.1, this whole range of criteria is expressed in a somewhat different way, and is applied to some of the sanitation techniques currently available. Thus the list given above is subdivided between health criteria and cost criteria. Health criteria comprise items 1 — 6 in the list; cost criteria are related also to questions of social organization affecting operation and maintenance, and include items 7 — 11.

It will be noted from this table that water closet systems with treatment plant are capable of meeting all the health criteria but none of the cost criteria for a developing country. The techniques which meet all the cost criteria are the very basic ones, such as the pit latrine, but these satisfy only some of the health criteria. Composting latrines stand out as meeting many of the criteria of both kinds, and this type of technology seems to have considerable potential, especially in tropical climates where conditions favour the composting process.

Existing methods in developing countries

In the cities of the developing countries, those who can afford it will frequently acquire water closets. Such people are a privileged minority, not least because very few households have the necessary water connection. In Dar es Salaam, for example, only 18.7 per cent of all households have water laid on. A central sewerage system is very rare, so water closets usually discharge into septic tanks. Very large institutions such as schools and hospitals sometimes have their own oxidation ponds to treat the sewage. In some countries, the aqua-privy has become the common solution. These systems all produce an effluent which is still pathogenic and virulent, and which is frequently infiltrated into the ground or discharged into nearby streams where it can pollute water sources used for supply purposes.

Table 3.1 The suggested criteria applied to four types of excreta disposal system

Criteria (numbered as in text)	Conventional W.C. with sewerage & treatment plant	Aqua-privies	Pit latrines	Composting latrines (e.g. Vietnamese double bin)
HEALTH CRITERIA				
—* No pathogen survival	XXX†	—†	XXX†	XX†
—+ Full BOD digestion	XXX	XXX	XXX	XXX
1. No pollution of soil	XXX	XX	X	XX
2. No groundwater pollution	XX	—	X	XX
3. No surface water pollution	X	XX	XX	XX
4. No access by insects	XX	XX	X	XX
5. No handling of fresh excreta	XXX	XXX	XXX	XX
6. No odours	XXX	XX	—	—
SOCIO-ECONOMIC CRITERIA				
7. Simple toilet routine	XXX	XX	XXX	X
8. Cost less than 10 per cent house	—	XX	XXX	XX
9. Local materials and technology	—	X	XXX	XX
10. Minimal use of water	—	—	XXX	XXX
11. Applicable in high density areas	X	X	XX	XX
—≠ Valuable by-product	—	—	X	XXX

Notes
* Basic health criterion taken for granted in the WHO list.
+ Basic environmental/health criterion.
≠ Additional criterion.
† Weightings will differ according to circumstances, but for a typical developing country may be as follows:
XXX : criterion fulfilled
XX : criterion fulfilled under certain conditions
X   : criterion only fulfilled under most stringent controls

One problem which contributes to these hazards is that very few installations received the maintenance required for effective operation. Many oxidation ponds and septic tanks get completely clogged with sludge without anybody feeling the need to get them emptied. In neglected sewage treatment works, insects are allowed to breed freely so that the treatment process becomes a focus for these vectors of disease. H. H. Leich[7] has summarized these 'sanitation errors', which he sees as intrinsic to the 'wet' systems of excreta disposal by means of the following list:

(a) large amounts of water from the public supply are needed to transport small quantities of body wastes;
(b) high capital costs;
(c) adverse effects on lakes and estuaries of unwanted nutrients (phosphates and nitrates) in the effluent from treatment plants;
(d) build-up of large amounts of sewage sludge;
(e) hazards which arise from failure of large treatment works, or from neglected maintenance;
(f) health hazards where effluent affects drinking water supplies — bacteria can be controlled by chlorination, but there is some doubt about viruses.

Conventional sewerage, of course, does have many advantages for those who can afford it and who can control its unwanted effects, and an attempt to arrive at a more balanced view will be made in Chapter 4. The point to be stressed here is that most households in developing countries can neither afford to pay for water closets, nor do they have the water with which to operate them. If adequately operated, conventional sewerage *can* be satisfactory in terms of health criteria, but can rarely meet the cost criteria.

The majority of town dwellers for whom 'wet' systems of excreta disposal are ruled out make use of pit latrines or bucket latrines. The pit latrine is a very simple device, but has environmental and hygienic advantages. Apart from any fouling of the squatting plate, all infections are contained, because all excreta are concentrated in one place without any dilution, and are decomposted by microbiological action. Disadvantages of pit latrines are possible pollution of groundwater, risk of insect breeding, and smell.

Specialized techniques from industrial countries

Growing awareness of environmental pollution and resource depletion in the industrialized countries, has led some people, especially in Scandinavia, to recognize the disadvantages of conventional sewerage enumerated above, and has stimulated research on alternative waste disposal methods. Of particular interest are some simple latrines which have been tried out in remote areas where accommodation is required for recreational purposes. These latrines include the following types:

(a) water-saving flushers,
(b) composting and mouldering latrines,
(c) packing toilets

Water-saving flushers are toilets which can easily be connected to the existing system for dealing with water-borne excreta such as a septic tank. A special type is the Electrolux vacuum toilet which does not use conventional treatment but applies a massive lime dosage to precipitate and sterilize BOD matter. This technique might also offer a suitable solution for small communities.

The most interesting solution, however, has taken place in the field of composting and mouldering. Composting latrines have been introduced as a suitable solution for isolated cottages in Scandinavia. In some cases, the excreta are mixed with household wastes. The detailed operation of the treatment process varies with the temperature and carbon/nitrogen ratio. It should also be noted that composting latrines were developed independently in Asia many years ago, and have recently come to be very widely used in Vietnam. All the indications from these very varied applications are that the principle of the composting toilet has a very considerable potential which has not yet been fully exploited.

Another recent device is the packing toilet. In this system the fresh excreta are collected in a plastic tube, a short length of which is sealed off with excreta inside it every time the toilet is used. The long 'sausage' tube is collected in a sub-floor container and the fresh excreta are not exposed any more and are safe in handling. No decomposition takes place and each load of forty bags is taken elsewhere for treatment.

Chemical toilets have found a wide application for remote areas and in transport systems. The chemical prevents decomposition and odours, so that excreta can be stored until treatment can be arranged. Chemical toilets have become quite acceptable in boats, buses, aeroplanes, and holiday cottages, but there are considerable environmental disadvantages connected with these systems. Some chemicals are dangerous and can easily cause allergic skin reactions. The chemicals make the ultimate treatment process difficult, and can themselves cause considerable pollution problems. The system is definitely not recommended for remote areas with difficult communications.

Many of the above techniques are indeed specialized, depending as they do on supplies of particular materials (chemicals, plastic tubes). They are thus not widely applicable in developing countries. But recent innovations in composting and mouldering latrines do seem to have considerable potential, and will be discussed more fully in Chapter 7. Before that, it is necessary to consider in general terms the availability of information on some of the other alternatives to conventional sewerage — the data needed for an informed choice of technology.

3.3 APPROPRIATE TECHNOLOGY FOR SANITATION: A WORLD BANK RESEARCH PROJECT

J. M. Kalbermatten[8] *and D. C. Gunnerson*[9]

Water supply and wastes in developing countries

There is an increasing number of commitments to provide safe water for people in the developing world, at a cost which might even reach $60 billion. Proper waste disposal could cost up to $200 billion more. Technological options for providing this water range from communal wells in rural villages, to integrated community systems for water supply and waste disposal. Options which are economically feasible are fewer, because they must satisfy financial, institutional, public health, social, and environmental constraints. Conventional solutions based upon capital-intensive and waste-intensive practice in North America and Europe result in three times as much being spent on the disposal of water as it costs to provide it. The emphasis in developing countries has consequently been on supplying water without provision of adequate waste disposal, and this has led to serious water pollution and public health hazards in many countries.

A two-year study of appropriate technology for water supply and waste disposal is under way at the World Bank in order to analyse:

(a) the technical and economic feasibility of various options available for water supply and waste disposal in developing countries;
(b) the effects of technologies which provide for conservation of water and other resources and for reclamation of wastes;
(c) the scope for designing technical improvement of existing intermediate technologies to improve their efficiency or enhance their transferability and acceptance.

Considerable urgency attaches to the project because of decisions now being made by officials of developing countries, lending institutions, development agencies, and by their engineering and economic advisers. These decisions are characteristically made on the basis of short-term financial considerations, but they result in long-term commitments with significant social and economic impacts. Even when long-range planning is attempted, the lack of information on low-cost alternatives to conventional systems of waste disposal frustrates effective decision making.

Objectives and scope

The objective of the research is to identify the appropriate technology for providing the urban poor and rural communities with socially and environmentally acceptable water supply and waste disposal services at a cost they can afford.

A total of 22 countries are scheduled for study. Of these, 11 have been selected for detailed field studies. The balance are included to provide specialized information or locations for pilot projects. Collectively, the countries include a variety of stages of development, technologies, cultural and institutional forms, and environmental features.

Planned geographic coverage includes (1) Japan, Taiwan, and Korea; (2) Indonesia, Malaysia, Bangladesh, India, and China; (3) Afghanistan, Egypt, Yemen, and Sudan; (4) Botswana, Ghana, Nigeria, Tanzania, and Zambia; and (5) Colombia, Guatemala, Mexico, Nicaragua, and Haiti. Principal investigators and supporting consultants ordinarily are selected from host country specialists. Technological options to be considered include the following either singly or in combinations:

(a) water service levels of 10 to 500 litres per capita per day obtained from streams, wells, vendors, community standpipes, yard spigots, or high-volume plumbing;

(b) low-cost options for waste disposal by privies, vaults, composting toilets, aqua-privies or cess-pools, septic tanks, removal by cart, vacuum truck, or low-flow sewers;

(c) traditional, advanced, or exotic waste treatment based on composting, digestion, fermentation, oxidation, or spreading of night soil, sewage, agricultural manures, or food wastes;

(d) reclamation schemes including biogas, fertilizer, aquaculture, pig-raising, stock and garden watering, and irrigation.

Approach

Information is to be collected on the whole range of factors that relate to the choice of the appropriate water supply and waste disposal technology. Economic data being collected include costs of construction and operation; costs of collection, transportation, treatment, and disposal systems; public health and reclamation benefits; costs and availability of construction materials and labour; foreign exchange requirements; and market distortions due to exchange rates and statutory wage rates, interest, import duty, subsidy. Public health information being collected includes morbidity, mortality, health services and education, and anecdotal data. Institutional and behavioural data collection includes anthropological and sociological enquiries into how decisions are made, implemented and maintained at the local level.

For each technology studied at the community level by the field consultants, a technical evaluation of the system's construction and operation is first carried out with special reference to any problems associated with the performance or community acceptance of the existing system. Using standard cost-benefit techniques (including shadow pricing where appropriate) each technology's economic feasibility is then analysed, and average household costs are computed. Special emphasis is given to the ability and willingness of consumers to pay for the system, their experience of real or perceived improvements in health and living conditions, and any obstacles to adaptation of the technology for other communities.

Early results

The first phase of the research involved a detailed bibliographical search for literature relevant to low-cost waste disposal technologies (described more fully in Section 3.4). This exposed as invalid the conventional engineering wisdom that there are no viable technological alternatives lying between pit privies and conventional sewerage. It demonstrated that much information exists on treatment of dilute wastes by oxidation ponds but little on treatment of night soil or sludge by composting or aquaculture; and it showed that information on septic tanks is plentiful, but little is available on pit privies.

Field studies of night soil collection and/or disposal confirm the findings of the literature review. Studies were conducted in eleven communities in Japan, Taiwan, and Korea, with populations varying from 285 to 1.5 millions. Annual per capita income ranges from about $6000 in Japan to $700 in Korea. Climate in the communities studied varies from humid sub-tropical to sub-humid temperate. Water service levels vary from 100 to 437 litres per capita per day. The annuitized capital and annual operating costs per household for storage, collection and disposal of night soil ranged from about $30 per year in the villages to $185 per year in a city with a high-technology system where night soil is diluted for treatment by conventional activated sludge. Reported costs for a complete sewerage system ranged from about $330 to $500 per household per year including the cost of water used for flushing. Reclamation practices include household biogas units in Taiwan and Korea, commercial aquaculture in Taiwan, and some use of night soil as humus and fertilizer in all three countries. Re-use aspects were reported to be more sensitive to convenience and economic factors such as changes in relative prices of chemical fertilizer or labour costs than to concern over public health or aesthetics.

Co-operation, co-ordination and liaison

Co-ordination and liaison of research activities are maintained with on-going programmes of operating departments of the World Bank, the World Health Organization, the United Nations Environmental Programme, and various national research, development, advisory, or operating agencies Co-operative research programmes are under way with the International Development Research Centre (IDRC), Ottawa, and the Ross Institute of Tropical Hygiene, London. Principal investigators for country specific studies include local sanitary engineers, economists, urban planners, and public health workers.

Products of the research

An early product of the research will be annotated bibliographies and state-of-the-art reports on appropriate waste disposal technology and health effects prepared by the Bank, IDRC, and the Ross Institute. Final publications will include books, field manuals or guidelines, and instructional materials prepared for decision makers in development agencies, developing countries, consulting engineering organizations, and universities. These will aid in both the technical and economic evaluation of alternative water supply and waste disposal projects and urban projects with a water supply component. Conceptual and final designs will be developed for improved mechanical devices; for pilot studies of alternative storage, collection, and transportation systems; for composting and land application systems; and for final disposal systems.

3.4 DATA ON NON-CONVENTIONAL WASTE DISPOSAL OPTIONS

Witold Rybczynski[10]

The literature search

Although the inappropriateness of conventional waste-water technologies is beginning to be realized by many national governments and international organizations trying to deal with the sanitation conditions of the urban and rural poor, and though there is interest in non-conventional options, these are, by definition, less well known and less well documented. It was the purpose of the work described here to present an over-view of the options, and to identify specific literature that could form the basis for a planner, engineer, and researcher in a developing country to understand, evaluate, and implement specific technologies.

The basis of the work was an intensive literature search recently completed at the International Development Research Centre in Ottawa, and closely connected with the World Bank study described in the previous part of this chapter. A computer-aided search of fourteen North American data bases yielded 18 546 references dealing with waste-water. Out of these, only 187 were found to have some bearing on the problems of developing countries. The balance dealt with expensive and sophisticated technologies geared to the problems and resources of the industrialized countries. One of the reasons that so little information is contained in these data bases is that by and large their sources of information are scientific and technical journals published in Europe and North America, and much of the literature identified during the search turned out to be either unpublished, or published only for limited, local circulation.

Another limitation of the computerized data bases is that they are not indexed for the needs of the developing country. These data bases, after all are enterprises that reflect the information requirements of their clientele — universities, engineering firms and government agencies in the United States, Canada, and more recently Europe.

Quite clearly, one should not look for literature on non-conventional technologies in conventional places.

The result of the computer search, a manual search carried out in local information centres in several countries, and additional material provided by the World Bank and other organizations, yielded a selected bibliography of 483 references. Despite limitations of time, personnel, and budget, this represents probably the most comprehensive collection of documents on the subject of sanitation technologies for developing countries that has been available to date.

Specific technologies

It might be useful to review the literature with respect to a limited number of specific technologies. The *pit latrine*, for example, remains to date the most widely used technique for excreta disposal in the developing countries, in the urban as well as in the rural areas. Most of the scientific work on pit latrines, however, was done in the 1930s (e.g. by Caldwell[11] and Yeager[12]), and little has been reported since. Nevertheless, pit latrines are often erroneously referred to as a 'well-known technique'. It is by no means clear, for instance, that pit latrines are unsuited to higher density applications. Most work has shown that dry pits pollute an extremely restricted area[13] except where intercepted by the water table. Improvements to ventilation and an off-set squatting plate are part of the ROEC latrine (Figure 3.3), developed in South Africa[14], which overcomes smell and fly problems without using a water-seal.

The *composting latrine* (sometimes referred to as the mouldering toilet) is one of the few 'new' on-site excreta disposal technologies reported in the literature. It has been used in Vietnam since 1956 with apparent success[15]. A programme is currently under way in Tanzania testing a number of mouldering aerobic toilets in rural and urban installations (Winblad[16]); pilot installations have also been carried out in a squatter settlement in Manila (Rybczynski[17], Figure 7.3), and there are other latrines on trial in Botswana (Figure 3.1). Most of the other data on these aerobic 'Multrum' type mouldering toilets are from temperate climates (Nichols[18], Lindstrom[19]).

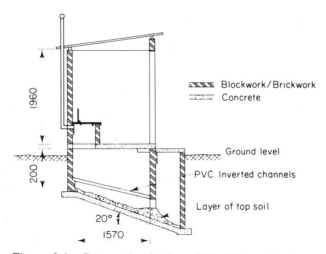

Figure 3.1   Composting latrine of the Multrum type as used in the Botswana Low Cost Sanitation Project (dimensions in millimetres). Illustration by permission of the International Development Research Centre (IDRC)

Aqua-privies, invented in India in 1917 (Williams[20]), are proposed in recent literature (Mann[21], Oluwande[22]) as an appropriate low-cost solution. There is a great deal of American literature dealing with *septic tanks*, though little of this seems relevant to developing countries because of high costs and high water usage. A variant of the septic system is reported from China[23] in which excreta and small quantities of water are passed through three tanks, with a total retention time of 50 days. A communal scale septic tank has been designed in England for disaster relief situations[24] (Figure 9.3).

Cartage systems for excreta removal from urban areas are widely reported from Asia. Large areas of Tokyo are reported to be serviced by vacuum trucks and conservancy vaults[25], and night soil is collected in Tainan[26]. In Jakarta, vacuum trucks are used to maintain existing cess-pools, even though soil conditions are poor. A number of engineering studies have proposed vacuum trucks and vaults for cities in Afghanistan[27] and Bangladesh[28]. Most of the literature on cartage is based on the Japanese experience, and little is reported on low-cost adaptions for poorer economies.

Treatment and re-use of excreta

Waste stabilization ponds are dealt with extensively in the literature (e.g. by Gloyna[29] and Mara[30]) and represent a well-known and understood technology. It is unfortunate that so much work has been done on the treatment of sewage while the problem of getting the excreta to the pond is unsolved. Since such a small fraction of the population of developing countries has access to sewers, sewage treatment, by ponds or otherwise, remains a side issue.

Composting is a method of treatment more suited to a sewerless society. Although proposed some time ago as a suitable method for waste treatment in tropical regions[31], there seems to be renewed interest in Scandinavia[32] and the United States[33] as well as in Nigeria[34]. Night soil composting is reported on a large scale in China[35], and also in India[36].

Aquatic weeds are used to purify sewage in ponds in Germany[37] and Holland[38] and are reported to be used in rural areas throughout south-east Asia.

Most of the work that is reported on *irrigation* with waste-water, and it is considerable, deals with treated sewage or stabilization pond effluent[39] and is hence of only minor relevance to developing country conditions. The fact that so much scientific work has been done on waste-water irrigation in many of the developing countries is more a reflection of Western-influenced engineering education than of a real need. There are a number of reports dealing with the use of *untreated sewage* for irrigation in India[40] and recently from Israel[41].

The combination of *aquaculture* with waste treatment has been widely studied[42], and the use of night soil for fish-pond fertilization is widely practised in south-east Asia[43]. The production of *algae* in high-rate ponds could play a useful role in developing country agriculture[44], but the work reported in this field has only been on pilot scale so far.

The use of human excreta as a fertilizer in agriculture is practised throughout south east Asia, but unfortunately, there have been very few scientific studies. The current attitude of condemnation of this practice without offering any alternatives or improvements has tended to discourage investigation in this field.

There is considerable literature dealing with the design and construction of *biogas* plants for the digestion of animal and human wastes[45]. In China, considerable progress has been made in reducing construction costs of the plants[46].

Wet and dry systems

Two general conclusions can be drawn as a result of this review of waste disposal options for developing countries. Firstly, the bulk of the literature deals with the *waste-water* problem rather than the *excreta* problem. Secondly, there is rather little literature that describes in detail the current waste disposal practices and problems of the 93 per cent of the populations of developing countries that are not served by a sewerage system.

The distinction between *excreta* and *waste-water* is critical in understanding the needs of the urban and rural poor in developing countries. Virtually all of the literature that originates in the industrially developed countries begins with waste-water (i.e. excreta and large amounts of water) as the basic problem, whether with respect to transport, treatment, or re-use. The technologies that result often have limited application in most developing countries where excreta disposal is the first priority. The transport, treatment, and re-use of excreta with little or no water poses a new problem, and very little literature exists on the subject. As a result, a proposed solution to excreta disposal is often based on the addition of water to turn it into waste-water disposal (aqua-privies, septic tanks), a subject with which most engineers are more familiar (see also Section 4.3 on this topic). Much work needs to be done on the 'dry' waste disposal/re-use technologies — pit latrines, composting latrines, and night soil re-use.

The differences in climate, resources, and the sheer scale of the problem make it difficult, if not impossible to apply technical data from an industrial country directly to conditions in a developing country. The successful examples of developing country sanitation described in the literature are neither imported Western industrial technologies (which are too expensive), nor are they rehashed nineteenth century colonial sanitation solutions (which generally represent 'top-down' improvements that integrate with difficulty into a popular-based development process). The successful examples, such as the double-vault composting latrine, or the biogas plant, have been developed locally to suit local conditions and maximize local resources. Nevertheless, the influence of research in conventional waste-water collection and treatment cannot be over estimated. Much of the research on sanitation, even when it is going on in a developing country, follows Western models and turns its back on local traditions and practices; as a result, *very little is reported about what is actually going on.* Indigenous methods for excreta disposal are ignored since it is assumed that these would be replaced by sewerage 'in the near future'. If a step-by-step upgrading of the existing situation is to be implemented, and this is the only strategy with any chance of success, it must be based on sound understanding of existing resources, limitations, and possibilities.

3.5 CHOICE OF TECHNOLOGY IN BOTSWANA

Michael D. Blackmore, Robert A. Boydell and Nomtuse Mbere[4][7]

Background

Occupying some 582 000 km^2 of arid land in southern Africa, Botswana supports a population of 750 000 people. Their livelihood and prosperity, until recently, were tied to an agricultural tradition — largely cattle raising — but mushrooming urbanization has been stimulated by the discovery and exploitation of minerals, including copper, nickel, coal, and diamonds, during the post-independence decade.

With low overall population density and relative geographic isolation, Botswana's health problems have, in the past, been less severe than those of many developing countries. However, with burgeoning urbanization, the incidence of environment-related disease has risen. Affecting a population engaged in a variety of productive undertakings, this has the usual depressing implication for the indices of national output. In 1975, for example, the number of man-days lost as a result of water-related diseases was approximately 387 000, reflecting a growing incidence of enteritis and diarrhoeal infection.

One disquieting aspect of environmental health in Botswana, and one which would very likely respond to a widespread improvement in the level of latrine technology, is the prevalence of unacceptably high levels of nitrate pollution. In the Francistown area, an analysis of sampled well-points indicated diminishing nitrate concentration away from centres of population, and lent support to the claim that the source of pollution was human, the vehicle for its transmission being the pit latrines abounding in the town's low-cost housing areas. Nationally, levels as high as 663 mg/1 have been recorded with alarming implications for the health of very young children.

While a complete water-borne excreta removal system based on conventional sewerage is a desirable ultimate objective for all dwellings in towns, the cost for the 10 000 or so additional low-cost housing plots now being provided or actively planned would be in excess of P 8 millions (1 Pula = $1.20). On a non-subsidized basis, it would be quite impossible for the low-income families to meet the extra service charges, and in Botswana's situation of very limited water resources which are costly to exploit, the levies needed to pay for the water would also be excessively high. What the government is seeking is a relatively low-cost sanitation system which operates with little water and is at the same time hygienic, efficient in operation, and socially acceptable to the users. This quest is the reason for the research study into all aspects of low cost sanitation now being carried out in conjunction with the International Development Research Centre.

The question of social acceptability has been emphasized by strongly adverse reactions to an unsatisfactory aqua-privy made of fibre glass — the apec privy — whose further installation has been officially banned. It suffered from many defects, including flexing of the floor under load, an ill-designed sitting pedestal, and a superstructure which was uncomfortably confining while not offering sufficient privacy, because of the large ventilation gaps at top and bottom of the door. Much significance was also attached to the argument that the need to carry water to the latrine militated against the traditional secrecy of the act of defecation in Botswana.

Physical and sociological surveys

A physical survey of existing latrines were carried out in the four major towns of Botswana, covering low-cost housing and squatter areas, and also areas where people are being housed on a site-and-service basis. The object was to determine the type and extent of toilet facilities, and to record their design, construction, associated health hazards, misuse, and nuisance factors.

Of the latrines surveyed, the majority (81 per cent) were conventional pit latrines, of which four out of five had pedestal seating rather than squatting plates. The remainder were conventional aqua-privies, apec aqua-privies, Reed Odourless Earth Closets (ROECs), and flushing toilets used with septic or conservancy tanks.

Nuisances associated with all systems, but especially with the pit latrine and apec aqua-privy, are fly breeding, offensive odours, and fouling of the toilet. The causes are many, but include lack of hole covers, poor ventilation, poor toilet design, and construction using hard-to-clean materials such as rough-cast concrete. Little or no water is used in operating any latrine, the average distance from a water source being 1 km. This may be one reason why the apec aqua-privy was rejected. Common ways in which latrines are misused are by people neglecting to close hole covers, where these are provided, and disposing of refuse in the latrines, some of which is not biodegradable.

Parallel with the physical survey of latrines, an attitude survey was carried out. This showed that although everybody stated a preference for the flushing toilet, they recognized that its high cost was a major constraint. The second choice was the pit latrine. People were told that a levy of P 5.10 ($6.12) per month would be reasonable to pay for water-borne excreta removal; 319 out of 770 people said that they could afford this, but 389 opted for the pit latrine.

Those householders who build their own toilets choose pit latrines, which they say take two weeks to build with two people helping, and cost P11 − 20. These costs seem unreasonably low, but it may be that some pits are not of the required depth and the materials used are not good. Half of those who own pit latrines mentioned problems of smell, flies, and pits caving in.

All respondents without exception rejected communal toilets, reasons given being that no one is responsible for them, they fill in quickly, are very dirty, and are not emptied promptly by the local authorities when full. As there is no recognized owner, everybody does as he or she pleases and cannot be reprimanded by anyone.

Duration of stay in urban areas has a strong influence on preferences. The longer people have lived in a town, the more likely it is that they will eventually put up some toilet. This may partly be due to the influence of recent health education efforts, or it may reflect the influence of site-and-service schemes, one of whose requirements is that would-be owners should put up a toilet first. This is certainly the case in Lobatse, where one sees pit latrines in most of the plots even before the houses are built.

Design criteria for latrines

The problems and attitudes revealed by the two surveys led to the following design criteria, which supplement and reinforce the usual criteria dictated by health considerations (such as those set out in Section 3.2):

(a) Problems of fly breeding, offensive odours, and fouling must be overcome.
(b) Latrine superstructures, an important factor in social acceptability, must be roomy, ventilated, solidly constructed, and have pedestal seating and a screen wall.
(c) Large volumes of water for operating a latrine are rarely available.
(d) Complex systems, especially those involving intensive maintenance, are undesirable, especially in 'self-help' applications.
(e) The disposal of washing water and domestic garbage should be catered for, either as part of the latrine technology, or separately.
(f) Re-use of wastes is not traditional, and its introduction would require back-up from an educational programme.

In addition to these criteria, severe constraints on design are imposed by ground conditions in many places. Solid rock, outcropping or near the surface, causes problems with excavations and limits soakaway facilities. Coarse-grained 'running' sand is common, and is a major cause of Botswana's chronic problems with collapsing pit latrines. Laterite soils, interspersed with layers of impermeable stiff clay, make excavation difficult in places and impede the infiltration of liquid wastes.

The latter situation is associated with groundwater at shallow depths perched above the bedrock. This water is frequently used for domestic water supplies, and is very vulnerable to pollution.

·The constraints imposed by the above factors made apparent the need for more than one type of latrine, including a shallow, dry, self-sufficient unit not requiring a soakaway, and an improved, structurally stable pit latrine, a design for which appears in Figure 3.6. However, it was also decided to retain an option for use of a 'wet' system in areas where there is a suitable subsoil for a soakaway facility; this led to the inclusion in the project of the 'type B' aqua-privy.

Composting latrines

The requirement for a latrine not needing any type of soakaway, and capable of being built partly or entirely above ground in rocky areas, seemed likely to be met by the use of some kind of composting latrine. Four types were chosen for trial:

two kinds of Multrum toilet, a modified ROEC latrine, and a double vault system. The working of such latrines is discussed in detail in Chapter 7.

A visit was made to Tanzania to see the composting latrines at Uno Winblad's project there[48], and a study was made of other composting toilet designs, notably those from McGill University[49]. From this it seemed that composting toilets could be acceptable to the Botswana people. Two designs were evolved, a basic unit similar to Winblad's (Figure 3.1), and a modified unit where the composting chamber is located to the rear of the superstructure with the cover slab exposed to solar heat gain, thereby raising the internal temperature (Figure 3.2).

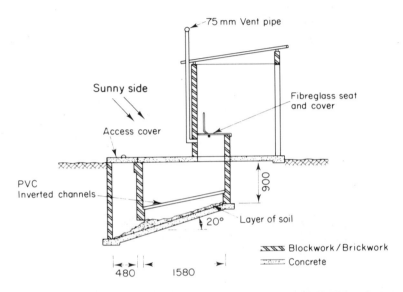

Figure 3.2 Modified Multrum latrine designed for use in Botswana; the latrine is oriented so that the temperature in the composting chamber is raised slightly by the heat of the sun (dimensions in millimetres). Illustration by permission of IDRC

The Reed Odourless Earth Closet (ROEC)

Originally developed in South Africa, the ROEC has been used in Botswana around the Molepolole area for over twenty years. During the physical survey, ROEC latrines were inspected and found to be operating with less nuisance than pit latrines and apec aqua-privies. They were also accepted and well liked by the users, and so were worth further investigation under the terms of the project.

Nuisance is reduced because of the configuration of a chute which funnels excreta and urine into a chamber to the rear of the superstructure (Figure 3.3). The chute, in conjunction with a ventilation stack, encourages vigorous air circulation down the latrine, thereby removing odours and discouraging flies.

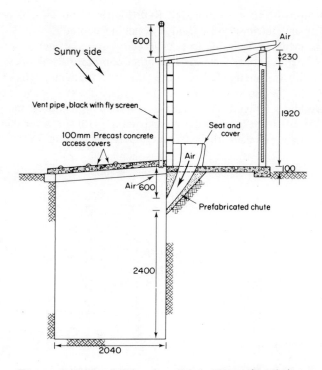

Figure 3.3   Reed Odourless Earth Closet (ROEC) as used in Botswana (dimension in millimetres). Illustration by permission of IDRC

As the standard unit has the disadvantage of pit filling and causing groundwater pollution, similar to the conventional pit latrine, a modified version was evolved (Figure 3.4). This unit retained the ROEC chute, but the rear pit is in the form of a composting chamber similar to a multrum.

Double vault composting latrine

Because of the project team's view that composting could be a viable answer to Botswana's sanitation problems, it was considered prudent to include the double vault latrine in the trials. This system plays a crucial role in certain Asian countries (Chapter 7), where it clearly works well. It is simple to construct and operate, and provides a suitable disposal point for biodegradable garbage (Figure 3.5).

The 'type B' aqua-privy

Although aqua-privies have gained a poor reputation in Africa, and particularly so in Botswana, we feel that a good design would answer many problems posed in

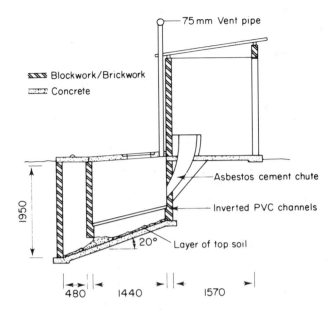

Figure 3.4 Modified ROEC latrine (dimensions in millimetres). Illustration by permission of IDRC

low-cost sanitation technology. Hence the 'type B' was evolved. The unit incorporates a special spiral flow flushing action in the toilet pan, which is operated by waste water from either an internal wash hand basin, or an external washing trough (Figure 5.3). Two purposes are served by this, namely to maintain the water seal, and to dispose of sullage water.

A great advantage of the unit is its suitability for being up-graded at a later date. If the householder can afford a water connection, a conventional (although low volume) flushing cistern may be plumbed into the pan. In addition, the overflow from the tank can be connected to a piped drainage system if main drainage subsequently becomes available. This is likely to happen in Botswana's site-and-service areas.

The disadvantages of the aqua-privy are its dependence on a water supply, and the need for soil conditions in which a soakaway can be safely and satisfactorily used.

Organizing the prototype and pilot studies

It was decided at an early stage of project planning that it would be impossible to design and construct a latrine that would be immediately successful. This, together with the social acceptance problem, dictated that the design and building should be organized in two phases.

Firstly, there would be a prototype phase where a number of different units

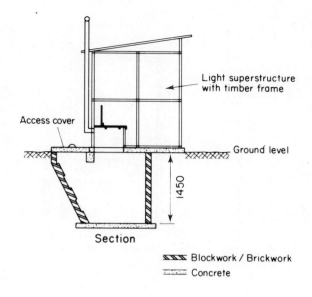

Light superstructure with timber frame

Access cover

Ground level

1450

Section

Blockwork / Brickwork
Concrete

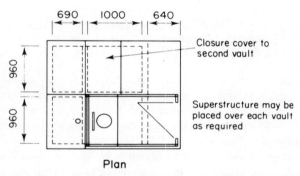

690   1000   640

960

960

Closure cover to second vault

Superstructure may be placed over each vault as required

Plan

Figure 3.5   Double vault composting latrine on trial in Botswana (dimensions in millimetres). Illustration by permission of IDRC

would be constructed with the intention of substantial modification to achieve optimum performance during the monitoring period, and also to test their relative performance and acceptability.

Secondly, a pilot phase would come into operation, with two or three of the better units from the previous phase introduced in greater numbers. Possibly 150 latrines would be built in this phase, and careful attention would be paid to their economic viability.

After long deliberation, the seven types of latrine already mentioned were selected for the prototype phase, and construction estimates were obtained from the Public Works Departments (PWDs) in the four towns concerned (Table 3.2).

Between one and three examples of each type were then to be built in each of the four towns — Gaberone, Lobatse, Francistown, and Selebi-Phikwe. The intention was that each town should have 13 prototype latrines, so there would be 52 prototypes in all (Table 3.2). Construction of many of these is already complete in Lobatse and Gaberone.

Table 3.2   Latrines forming part of the prototype phase of the Botswana project

Latrine Type	Number Planned*	Lowest Cost Estimate (Lobatse PWD)	Highest Cost Estimate (Selebi-Phikwe PWD)
		(pula)†	(pula)†
COMPOSTING LATRINES			
Multrum	8	325‡	576
Modified Multrum	4	332‡	656
Double vault	8	328‡	661
Modified ROEC	4	367‡	564
PIT LATRINE DERIVATIVES			
ROEC latrine	4	257‡	429
Improved pit latrine	12	284‡	455
AQUA-PRIVY			
Type B Aqua-privy	12	421‡	715

Notes

* : The numbers given are equally divided between the four towns of Lobatse, Gaberone, Francistown, and Selebi-Phikwe.

† : 1 pula = $1.20

‡ : Actual costs have shown a substantial saving on these figures.

The limited time period available for the project (24 months) dictated that the planning and programming of the construction phases was critical if adequate monitoring was to be carried out. Thus only 12 weeks could be allowed for design and 12 weeks for construction in the prototype phase. Parallel with the design process, the problem of allocating latrines to specific households was tackled. Town Council officials suggested families which the sociologist then visited. Criteria used in selecting the 13 households in each town which would receive latrines were willingness of people to assist during the monitoring stage and the question of whether the family was big enough to use the latrine intensively. Preference was also given to those who could not otherwise afford a latrine, and soil conditions were taken into account.

In the prototype phase, householders did not have to contribute at all to the cost of their latrine. In the next phase, however, they will be requested to paint the superstructure and to put up the screen wall around the entrance if they want one.

Participation of users in the project is important, because during the monitoring stage, we rely on them to report their experience in operating the latrine. This will be done through weekly visits, interviews by the project sociologist, questionnaires, and sampling of latrine contents. Householders have also been given a pamphlet — a *users' guide* — to help them understand how the toilets work.

Long-term prospects

The systems described in this paper, presently under trial in Botswana, have been selected with local needs and constraints in mind, and they should be technically appropriate. However, if the technology is to be permanently successful, it is appreciated that some form of organizational input will be necessary. Even with the basic ROEC, long used at Molepolole, people have not managed to surmount the emptying difficulty, and few of these latrines remain in use for a second cycle of operation. Yet so many of the systems which could serve the needs of the future rely on emptying as a regular, if not frequent operation, and one for which the mechanized systems used with septic tanks cannot be used.

Our attitude is basically that if performance and general acceptability justify the adoption of one or more of the latrines described, then the outstanding problem of eventual waste removal must be solved by making it a community responsibility. The opportunity to realize the productive value of much of the material which constitute 'waste' has so far been neglected. Traditional attitudes militate against re-use of human waste on an individual basis, but urban sanitation planning which casts re-use in a *municipal* role could go further, and through the improved cultivation of park and grassland, create urban amenities which would return to the civic population a measure of the value of their own waste contributions.

So much, of course, is comment and perspective; the terms of reference of the Botswana Low Cost Sanitation Project do not charge it with responsibility for planning policy. All the same, it is unarguable that for the long-term success of this undertaking, such planning is precisely what is needed, and equally precisely what is lacking at present.

Initial results

At the time of writing, monitoring the prototype units in Gaberone and Lobatse has just commenced, and it is difficult to see the outcome. The most popular unit at this early stage is the double vault latrine. The way its alternating vaults avoid the need for repeatedly excavating new pits is very much appreciated by people accustomed to pit latrines. The 'type B' aqua-privy is popular because its porcelain toilet pan makes it look like a conventional flush latrine. The Multrum concept is not fully understood. but people are happy to use it.

Apart from these preliminary reactions, our chief conclusions concern the methodology of the project, which may be of help to any other organization wishing to mount a similar evaluation of different technologies. The problems encountered are complex from both the engineering and sociological points of view, and we have found it especially valuable to have in our team a planner, an engineer, a sociologist, and a health assistant. Consultants in microbiology and economics will also be involved. A second point is that the time allowed for the project (24 months) was unrealistic, and during our.longest monitoring period of six months, the composting latrines will not complete one cycle.

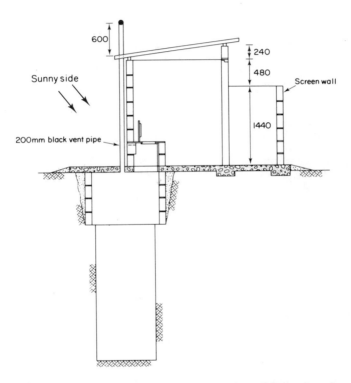

Figure 3.6 Modified pit latrine in Botswana (dimensions in millimetres). Illustration by permission of IDRC

Throughout the project, we have sought the help and interest of Town Council officials, Councillors, and Ward Officers, officers of the self-help Housing Agencies, and government officials. But there still lingers a doubt that at the end of the project, its findings may be lost because of the absence of any official body to take over the work.

66

NOTES AND REFERENCES

1. Krisno Nimpuno works with the United Nations Development Programme, Avenue Kenneth Kaunda, 931, Maputo, Mozambique.
2. Building Research Unit, Dar es Salaam, 1973.
3. WHO Expert Committee on Environmental Sanitation, 1954.
4. E. C. Wagner and J. N. Lanoix, *Excreta Disposal for Rural Areas and Small Communities*, WHO, Geneva, 1958.
5. For example, criteria put forward by the Swedish Road and Water Board, *Sma avloppsanlaggningar*, 1962.
6. Wagner and Lanoix, *op. cit.* note 4.
7. Conference paper submitted by H. H. Leich of Environment Forum, 5606 Vernon Place, Bethesda, Maryland 20034, U.S.A.
8. J. M. Kalbermatten is Water and Wastes Adviser, in the Energy, Water and Telecommunications Department, The World Bank, 1818 H Street, N.W., Washington, D.C. 20433, U.S.A.
9. D. C. Gunnerson is a Consultant to the World Bank.
10. Witold Rybczynski is Director, Minimum Cost Housing Group, McGill University, 3480 University Street, Montreal H3A 2A7, Canada. This paper summarises work published by Witold Rybczynski, Chongrak Polprasert and Michael G. McGarry, in *Stop the Fecal Peril: a Technology Review*, preliminary report, International Development Research Centra, Ottawa, 1977.
11. E. L. Caldwell, *Journal of Infectious Diseases*, 62 (1938)
12. C. H. Yeager, *Malayan Medical Journal*, 4 (4), (December 1929).
13. J. K. Baars, *Bulletin of WHO*, 16 (1957).
14. Bestobell Engineering, *ROEC Sanitation*, South African Patent No. 991/1944.
15. *Double Septic Tanks*, translation of booklet published by the Department of Hygiene and Epidemiology, Ministry of Health, Democratic Republic of Vietnam.
16. U. Winblad, *Compost Latrines − A Review of Existing Systems*, unpublished report, Environmental Sanitation Research Project, Tanzania, July 1975.
17. Witold Rybczynski, *The Minimus Composting Toilet... An inexpensive Sanitation Solution for the Philippines,* unpublished report to UNEP Manila, September 1976.
18. H. W. Nichols, *Analysis of Bacterial Populations in the final product of the Clivus Multrum*, Report of the Center for the Biology of Natural Systems, Washington University, St. Louis, December 1976.
19. C. R. Lindstrom. *Multrum Undersokning av Driftsforhallanden Hos en Formultsnings*, report issued by Clivus AB, Sweden, 1969.
20. G. B. Williams, *Sewage disposal in India and the Far East*, Thacker, Spink and Co., India, 1924.
21. H. T. Mann, *Sanitation without Sewers − the Aqua Privy*, Building Research Establishment, Overseas Building Note 168, U.K.
22. P. A. Oluwande, *Appropriate Technology*, 3 (3), (November 1976).
23. *The Two-partitions, Three-tanks Hygiene Toilet*, in M.G.McGarry and J. Stainforth, *Compost, Fertilizer and Biogas Production from Human and Farm Wastes in China*, Ottawa, IDRC, 1978.
24. J. Howard, B. Lloyd and D. Webber, *Oxfam's Sanitation Unit*, Oxfam Technical Paper, U.K., 1975.
25. Camp, Dresser & McKee, *Sewerage Planning in the Greater Taipei Area, A Master Plan Report*, prepared for WHO as Executive Agency for UNDP, 1970.
26. M. G. McGarry, *Sewage as a Natural Resource*, proceedings of a symposium on the Role of the Engineering in Environmental Pollution Control, Malaysia, 1972.

27. World Bank, *Appraisal of the Kabul Water Supply and Sanitation Project Afghanistan*, IBRD unpublished report no. 746-AF, 1975.
28. P. V. Hennessy, W. F. Langer, Y. S. Lin and F. Rhodes, *Master Plan for Development of Water Supply, Sewerage and Drainage for Khulna*, unpublished report to Directorate of Public Health Engineering, Government of East Pakistan, Section IV, April 1965.
29. E. F. Gloyna, *Waste Stabilization Ponds*, WHO, Geneva, 1971.
30. D. Mara, *Sewage Treatment in Hot Climates*, London, John Wiley & Sons, 1976.
31. H. B. Gotaas, *Composting*, WHO, Geneva, 1956.
32. G. Hovsenius, *Kompostering af Hushhall Savfall Tillsammans med Slam*, Avfall, Sweden, 1976.
33. G. B. Wilson and J. M. Walker, *Compost Science*, 14 (5), 1973.
34. C. Peel, in *Planning for Water and Waste in Hot Countries*, Loughborough University of Technology, U.K., 1976.
35. M. G. McGarry and J. Stainforth, *op. cit.* note 23.
36. T. R. Bhaskaran, R. Ghosh, B. K. Roy, M. A. Sampathkumaran, I. Radharkrisnan, and D. B. Mukerjee, *Indian Journal of Agricultural Science*, 27 (1), March 1957.
37. K. Seidel, in *Biological Control of Water Pollution*, University of Pennsylvania Press, 1976.
38. J. de Jong, in *Biological Control of Water Pollution, op. cit.* note 37.
39. H. I. Shuval, in *Water, Wastes and Health in Hot Climates*, ed. R. Feachem, M. G. McGarry, and D. Mara, London, John Wiley & Sons, 1977.
40. G. B. Shende, *Indian Farming*, 23 (11), February 1974.
41. S. D. Goldberg, *New Techniques in the Re-use of Effluents*, report prepared for the World Bank, November 1976.
42. G. H. Allen and B. Hepher, *FAO Technical Conference on Aquaculture*, Japan, Paper No. FIR: AQ/Cont/76/R.19, 1976.
43. D. D. Tapiador, 'A preliminary review of the possibility of commercial fish meal production from sewage fish farming', draft paper prepared for FAO Technical Conference on Fisheries Products, Japan, 1973.
44. M. G. McGarry, *Thai Journal of Agricultural Science*, 4 (October 1971).
45. R. B. Singh, *Biogas Plant — Generating Methane from Organic Wastes*, Gobar Gas Research Station, India, 1974.
46. M.G.McGarry and J. Stainforth, *op. cit.* note 23.
47. Michael D. Blackmore, Robert A. Boydell and Nomtuse Mbere are from the Botswana Low Cost Sanitation Study, Ministry of Local Government and Lands, Private Bag 6, Gaberones, Botswana.
48. For Winblad's work, see note 16 above.
49. For the McGill University work, see the latrine on trial in Manila, note 17 above, and Figure 7.3.

4

Conventional Sewerage

4.1 THE CASE FOR AND AGAINST

John Pickford[1]

Merits of water-carried excreta removal

The advantages of using water to transport excreta and other wastes in sewers have been a recurring theme in sanitary engineering for a century. Public health, it is claimed, can only be adequately served by an underground piped system. There can be no doubt that if funds are unlimited, conventional sewerage satisfies all the criteria laid down for satisfactory excreta disposal by Wagner and Lanoix[2], Winblad[3], and Marais[4], and all the health criteria set out in Section 3.2 above. In a system that is properly designed and constructed, and is completely separate from storm-water drains to avoid the obnoxious overflows characteristic of combined sewerage, there is no possibility of pollution of soil, surface water, or groundwater. All excreta, and all pathogens, are transported away from the household to the treatment plant. The system is 'out of sight', and therefore aesthetically satisfactory, and the excreta is 'untouched by hand'.

If slopes permit a sewerage system to be actuated by gravity without pumping, there is virtually no need for maintenance apart from very occasional removal of grit from the inverts. Many sewerage systems in the cities of developing as well as industrial countries have functioned perfectly for a century or more. The loans raised to pay for their construction have been repaid long ago, and now they do not cost the communities they serve a penny.

In addition to the efficient removal of excreta, the sewerage reticulation system deals with many other wastes. All the water which has been used for bathing, for laundry, and for cleaning pots and pans disappears down the drain. By using under-sink grinders solid kitchen waste can be removed without difficulty. Industrial wastewater, too, can be safely conveyed in the same system provided its volume, concentration of pollutants and temperature are not too great and it contains little that is dangerous to the sewers or men working in them.

In some developing countries the old imperial powers of the nineteenth and early twentieth centuries installed sewerage systems as a matter of course. Although built-up zones now extend far beyond the extremities of the sewers, and although in many places there is little or no treatment of sewage, these old systems are still proving of great value. Where there is adequate treatment or satisfactory discharge of sewage, and where the community has been educated (or forced) to use the system properly and to abstain from using monsoon drains as receptacles for sullage and excreta, the system seems perfect.

What is more, since sewerage is the 'norm' for industrial country sanitation, there exists a vast expertise. Indigenous engineers, trained at home or in Europe or North America, are familiar with sewer design and have plenty of textbooks to consult if in doubt. Not that there are many doubts because the technology is so well-known and so simple. In places with a shortage of local designers, or for big schemes beyond the capacity of the stay-at-home team, it is easy enough to enlist the services of international consultants. So it would seem logical to continue a system which is proved beyond any doubt. In the tropics there are even greater health advantages than in temperate zones. New sewerage systems will improve the prospects for tourism and industrialization. They may improve property values beyond the cost involved. They may initiate an upward spiral of improved health and social/economic development leading to more effective education, increased productivity, higher standards of living and improved quality of life[5].

But . . . .

Such rosy-coloured speculation totally ignores the magnitude of the sanitation deficiency compared with the available resources in poor developing countries.

Even if the total net savings of a developing country in Africa were used to provide the urban population with water supply and sanitation the funds would be insufficient[6]. In large sections of innumerable towns and cities the cost of providing a water-carried sewage system and the necessary water supply would far exceed the value of the buildings. Sewerage may cost US$ 500 or more per household.

Solutions are urgently needed. There is a need for haste to overcome the total inadequacy of existing sanitation. Mention has already been made of how great the deficiency is, according to the returns made to WHO[7]. These returns are suspect anyway. As an example, only 953 000 people in the whole of Africa south of the Sahara were reported as served by bucket latrines. Several countries submitted nil returns for this category whereas the form-filling bureaucrat needed only to leave his car and walk round the back-alleys to see dozens of little doors and trickles of foetid spillage.

Even if the supply of internal and external funds could be stepped up by an order of magnitude — adding a nought at the end of the number of dollars available — there would hardly be enough money to provide *all* the present urban population with sewers and the corollaries of sewerage — plenteous water into the house, household sanitary fittings and sufficient treatment of the discharged sewage to make it innocuous. And the 'present' urban population is only current for a day. Cities with the greatest need have the greatest growth rate — population doubling in twenty, ten, five or even three years. Around cities the people with the greatest need for sanitation, the dwellers of 'transitional urban settlements'[8] proliferate at the greatest rate.

One of the requirements for sewerage is an adequate water supply. Water supply and sanitation are inextricably linked. Provision of safe drinking water has a high priority in the plans of most developing countries and there is just a glimpse of hope that the Mar del Plato target of safe water for all by 1990 can be achieved. However, sewerage and water supply have two contrary interactions. On the one hand in some cases, owing to the lack of adequate facilities for excreta disposal, an increased water supply may even cause the spread of disease[9]. On the other hand, quite a substantial volume of water is required simply as an excreta-carrier in sewerage systems.

In exceptional places there is a dual supply so that scarce drinking water is not wasted in this carrier-function. Hong Kong's use of sea-water for latrine flushing is an obvious example. In general water used for sewerage is the same as that which is drunk. In many places it has to be stored, treated and distributed at enormous cost.

For the 1970 WHO survey developing country governments reported that less than half their urban population had house connections to water supply, and over 30 per cent had no access to the supply at all. More than half the public supplies were intermittent. So a great effort and vast expenditure is needed to provide continuous water for all. Even so a single house connection or a nearby standpipe is no use for water-carried sewerage, and the report did not differentiate between single-tap and multiple-outlet connections. Although the report did not list water consumption, it is certain that a large proportion of the 'served' population had less than enough for WC flushing. A total daily consumption of 75 litres per person may be the minimum requirement where WCs are installed[10].

In any čase, whatever the present consumption without WCs, a substantial extra volume is needed to activate conventional sewerage. In many cities such addition to the demand can only be satisfied by expensive works. The marginal cost of increased supplies is almost always more than the cost of existing provision, as less accessible or less pure sources have to be tapped. Apart from cost, increased abstraction for domestic purposes may deprive other functions of much-needed water. Municipal supply often decreases the availability of water for irrigation.

Looked at in this way, it is absurd to use thirty or more litres of precious treated water each day for every inhabitant of a town simply to add to a litre of excreta — and then go to a great deal of trouble in attempts to take out the excreta from the water.

Where sewerage systems in developing countries follow the pattern of industrial countries, there are two factors which make the developing country sewerage less satisfactory. The first is septicity and the second is increased blockage. High temperatures accelerate biological degradation in the pipes and so deplete the dissolved oxygen. Because air-saturated warm water can hold less oxygen than cool water, tropical sewage often becomes anaerobic. Such septic conditions, especially where the natural water has a high sulphate content, result in corrosion[11]. The problem is particularly troublesome in areas where the natural fall of the land is slight so that sewers are laid at flat gradients for economy and pumping is necessary to avoid deep excavation. Blockage is common in some areas because of abuse of the system due to ignorance, or because of traditional methods of anal cleaning. In the Middle East and the Indian sub-continent ablution is customary, but in parts of Africa and the Caribbean the use of leaves, rags, stones and hard paper (eg newspaper) results in increased chance of blockage.

In many cities of the Third World the streets are laid out in a grid-iron pattern which is ideal for installation of sewers. Elsewhere, often in the same cities, buildings have been erected in congested unplanned disarray. In this second category come the old centres, where gradual reconstruction of traditionally-built properties has often followed the original pattern on small plots separated by narrow tortuous alleys. Equally unplanned are the 'transitional urban settlements — the bustees, squatter-areas and shanty-towns. Here the construction of sewers with straight runs between well-spaced manholes becomes virtually impossible without the demolition of obstructing property.

Appropriate sewerage

All engineering should be appropriate[12]; having seen the case for sewerage and some of the evidence against it, we can consider where conventional sewers are appropriate, where some modification of the system should be looked at, and where some completely different method of excreta disposal should be used. A table is perhaps the best means of sorting out ideas on this — one suggestion is given in Table 4.1

One of the most absurd features of international aid efforts for sanitation has been the proportion of resources devoted to sewerage feasibility studies. There are reasons for this, of course. Expertise and manpower are available from international consultants; a master-plan gives the appearance of helping the whole community; awkward political decisions can be shelved. And so for a score of years and more a succession of master-plans covering whole cities and their suburbs have filled the cupboards of government offices — I believe Bangkok has at least five. Sometimes, after years of waiting, part of the system is constructed with sewer sizes based on 'ultimate flows'. Only the well-off connect; flows are inadequate for proper operation; and recently-built septic tanks are abandoned.

At the root of the trouble is the assumption that only conventional sewerage can be satisfactory. However, the first priority should be decisions on what form of sanitation is appropriate for different areas. Then resources and engineering effort can be concentrated on the districts with greatest need, using the most appropriate method, whether community latrines, composting latrines, pit latrines or sewerage. As Pineo and Subrahmanyam[13] commented, 'ways must be explored of making current investment go further and serve more people'.

Table 4.1 Suggested selection of appropriate excreta removal, treatment, and disposal systems. In addition to the points made in the table, the selection depends on the availability and cost of water supplies, the lie of the land (flat, undulating or sloping), and in the 'standard of living' as measured by GNP

Category	Appropriate districts	Reasons for appropriateness	
conventional sewerage	commercial part of city centre	high-density building (many multi-storied) and high property values	Owners/occupiers can afford to pay for total cost of sewerage and ample water supply
	industrial estates	sewers most convenient means of removing industrial wastewater	
	high-class residential	high-class buildings justify high-class sewerage	
	new medium-class residential*		
modified sewerage (e.g. aqua-privy sewerage)†	new low-cost high-density authority-built housing	simultaneous construction of houses and sewers is economical	
	new medium-class residential*		
on-site household facility (pit latrine, compost latrine, septic tank)	scattered rural	'dead' lengths make sewerage unsuitable	
	low density transitional‡	temporary occupation requires tempoary solution	
	new medium-class residential*	septic tanks may be best if building is scattered	
communal unsewered sanitation (e.g. aqua-privy 'comfort sations')	congested residential parts of city centre	high density adds to difficulties of sewerage construction; small plot-size eliminates on-site facility	
	high-density transitional‡		
	nucleated rural (villages)		

* The appropriate method depends on the plot-size and the rate of building (many such areas develop fully over thirty or forty years).
† Other modified sewerage systems may evolve – e.g. small catchments draining to waste stabilization ponds.
‡ Transitional urban settlements – bustees, shanty-towns, squatter settlements etc.

4.2 CONVENTIONAL SEWERAGE IN BRAZIL

Salomao A. Silva [14]

Financing a National Plan

In the context of this book, Brazil is of interest as a country with a commitment to conventional sewerage, and effective programmes for providing it. In 1971, the Federal Government of Brazil initiated the *Plano Nacional de Saneamento* (PLANASA) which is designed to supply treated water to 80 per cent of the urban population by 1980, and provide conventional sewerage facilities for 50 per cent in the same period.

This compares with a proportion of only 30 per cent connected to conventional sewerage in 1967. Under the plan, each state was required to establish a water and sewerage company to cover both urban and rural areas throughout its territory. An important part of the duty of each Company was to study the water resources of its State, and to ensure that every town was equally served, even if this meant some towns subsidizing others.

The money required to implement PLANASA comes from two sources — loans from the Federal Bank, and an investment by each State of 5 per cent of its taxation revenue. Normally, these two sources of funds play an equal part in supporting each project, but in any State unable to pay its half share, the Bank may make an extra loan, or the Federal Government may give a grant.

In Brazil there are 3954 municipalities and by 1975 approximately 1500 were supplied with mains water under the PLANASA programme, leaving some 1700 to receive a supply by 1980 in order to meet the PLANASA sewerage target. Lack of finance delayed the implementation of the full sewerage programme. Even so the Government invested Cr 6.2 billion (US $ 443 million) during 1968-76 to solve the more acute sanitation problems. However, by 1976 only 34 per cent of the urban population, that is 21 million people, were served by a sewerage system, compared with 70 per cent (43 million people) supplied with mains water.

In order for each state water and sewage company to be able to repay its loan to the Bank, it has to make as economic a charge as possible for the services it supplies within the ability of its public to pay. These charges are related to the official minimum salary payable to all workers, as follows:

Water: 5 per cent of minimum salary
Sewerage: 80-100 per cent of water charges

The basic water charge is for a minimum volume of 10-20 m^3 per household per month with quantities above this amount charged for at the rate appropriate to the consumption.

Sewage treatment

In order to be able to implement the PLANASA programme the Federal Government recognized that considerable research and development was necessary to minimize its capital and operational costs, and allocated funds to its specialised agencies for this purpose. The Centro de Ciencias e Tecnologia of the Universidade Federal da Paraiba has received grants from Brazilian agencies and the Canadian International Development Agency so far totalling Cr 9 million (US $ 0.64 million) for research into sewage treatment. The most suitable and economic site for this research was the former sewage treatment works in the city of Campina Grande which had been out of operation for several years. This has now been converted into an experimental station; sewage is taken from the new interceptor sewer running through the site and metered into the following waste stabilization ponds:

4 independent facultative stabilization ponds

5 ponds connected in series (1 anaerobic, 1 facultative and 3 maturation ponds)

2 anaerobic ponds, each discharging into a facultative pond, with facility for recirculating the facultative pond effluent.

1 high rate pond.

These facilities have been in operation since February 1977 and a regular monitoring programme has been established. The results from the four independently loaded facultative ponds have already yielded 'controversial' results which have extended our knowledge of pond behaviour at high temperatures[15].

It is intended to expand these facilities to include other methods of sewage treatment, including: aerated lagoons, oxidation ditches, upflow filters (for septic tank effluent), bio-filtration and activated sludge including the ANOX process for nutrient removal. As this work is developed over the next few years, much emphasis will be placed on the agricultural and aquacultural re-use of treated effluents in order that the full economic potential of domestic sewage may be realised.

It is perhaps useful to make one comparison between Brazil and other developing countries. In Brazil we have in the water and sewage companies a highly developed institutional infrastructure which in many other countries does not exist, with consequent severe restraints on the implementation of urban sanitation programmes. However, in common with many other developing countries there is in Brazil an acute data shortage on local parameters for certain treatment processes, for example, waste stabilization ponds which have hitherto often been designed on the basis of American experience. This is clearly inappropriate for a tropical developing region such as the north-east of Brazil. The development of experimental stations in different climatic zones in Brazil is of the utmost importance if we are to be able to design full-scale treatment plants meaningfully and at minimum cost.

4.3 THE INFLUENCE OF CONVENTIONAL PRACTICE ON DESIGN CAPABILITIES

Duncan Mara[1 6]

The bias in engineering training

The large-scale provision of sanitary services has historically been work for the civil engineer; and today in tropical countries where sanitation is often at best imperfect and at worst entirely absent, it is to civil engineers that national and municipal authorities delegate the responsibility for the planning, design, and implementation of sanitary facilities.

But too few civil engineers working in tropical climates have received any training in tropical sanitation. Expatriate engineers have been trained in their own temperate countries where sanitation is synonymous with conventional sewerage; and local engineers are either trained abroad where they receive the same prejudice, or at home where, because the engineering curriculum at most tropical universities is western-urban oriented, they are similarly indoctrinated. *There is thus an overwhelming prejudice of training in favour of conventional sewerage as the only realistic system of sanitation.* This attitude of mind, although perhaps understandable, is most regrettable; it is the principal reason why so few people in tropical countries have adequate facilities for the disposal of their excreta and why in consequence morbidity and mortality in these countries are so alarmingly high. Conventional training in sanitary engineering has thus provided tropical developing countries with many hundreds of engineers with severe 'tunnel vision' — the result has been unimaginative designers producing unimaginative designs which few communities can afford to implement. It is rather as if all the world's automobile engineers were to design only Rolls Royces, when what is needed is Volkswagens — or even bicycles.

In this paper I wish to consider two different areas of sanitary engineering — waste stabilization ponds and aqua-privies — both not too far removed from the mainstream of conventional sanitary engineering. They will serve well to illustrate current design capabilities in tropical sanitation technology.

Waste stabilization ponds

Ponds are not only the cheapest method of sewage treatment in hot climates but also potentially the most powerful. This is because (a) the reduction of faecal bacteria in a properly designed series of maturation ponds can be greater than 99.9999 per cent — that is, a reduction from 10^8 faecal coliforms to less than 10^2 per ml of effluent; and (b) algal harvesting, either in the form of fish or the algae themselves, can make a substantial contribution to the food supply of a community. However, much needs to be done in both these respects. For example, there is the problem — I think an alarming one but one which is often played down

— of drug resistance and its transfer between intestinal commensals and intestinal pathogens. Recent work[17] has suggested that both raw and treated wastes may serve as major reservoirs for the spread of resistant bacteria and transferable resistance in the environment. We should not need to be reminded that drug resistance is one of the more serious threats to tropical public health after the shigellosis pandemic in Central America during 1968-71 caused by a multi-resistant strain of *Shigella dysenteria*. In January — October 1969 this killed 8200 people in Guatemala alone where the main vehicle of the disease was contaminated water[18].

Perhaps therefore we should be designing maturation ponds, not on the basis of the removal of faecal coliforms, but rather on the removal of drug-resistant coliforms (either faecal or non-faecal) or indeed of salmonellae; but we have very little design data on the decay rates in ponds of either of these bacterial groups. This may possibly seem unduly esoteric to design engineers, and indeed it probably is, especially when we consider that we do not really know how to design ponds even for faecal coliform removal. For example, it is commonly stated[19] that at temperatures above 21°C faecal coliform die-off in ponds decreases because conditions in the pond become more anaerobic and faecal die-off is less — even nil — under anaerobic conditions. Regrowth of faecal bacteria is a current problem in sanitary bacteriology — especially in tropical water bacteriology — but recent work in Brazil has uncovered an 'unusual' phenomenon. At our experimental station, described above in Section 4.2, we found that during April 1977, not only were faecal coliform decay rates at 27°C much higher than current knowledge predicted but that the rate increased linearly with the applied organic load, i.e. as the pond became *more* anaerobic (Figure 4.1). Admittedly this represents only one month's results but nevertheless we now have valid grounds for questioning the whole of current pond design criteria for faecal coliform removal in hot climates. Given that in these climates, faecal bacterial removal is of much greater public health significance than mere BOD removal, we would appear to be back at 'square one'

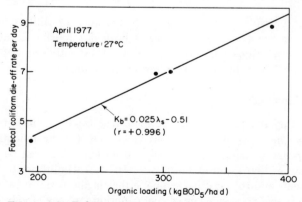

Figure 4.1 Relationship between faecal coliform die-off rate (K_b) and applied organic loading in facultative ponds at 27°C

regarding pond design. But perhaps not; perhaps even by the mere realization that faecal bacterial removal is important, that 'the removal of BOD without regard to the destruction of disease-causing bacteria is inadequate'[20], we have made some progress.

Sanitary engineers have for so long been dazzled by the virtue of BOD removal — in order to prevent deoxygenation in the receiving river — that it is not really surprising that the other potential major benefit of waste stabilization ponds — algal harvesting — has been seen only from the point of view of preventing river pollution. The suspended solids concentration in pond effluents is generally much too high for permissible discharge into temperate rivers. Apparently blinded by 'The' standard of 'The' Royal Commission (British, of course) of less than 20 mg $BOD_5/1$ and less than 30 mg $SS/1$, regulatory agencies have been the power behind algal removal from pond effluents.

T. S. Eliot wrote that 'the greatest treason is to do the right deed for the wrong reason'. And perhaps as mere engineers we should apply the poet's wisdom to ponds: we should not be removing algae from pond effluents just to prevent river pollution, as the agencies would have us do, but rather removing them for use as food: food for animals and food for man. Yet algal harvesting is still much too complex, even in its simplest form of pisciculture. We do not yet really know how to design a series of waste stabilization ponds to treat sewage or night soil and at the same time maximize fish yields, although some recent work on this is described briefly in Chapter 12. Algal removal by flocculation and sedimentation is of course technically feasible, but these processes are highly complex, and are beyond the maintenance capabilities of most communities. There are impressive results of feeding trials in which algae are used to provide up to 50 per cent of the diet of cows, poultry, or pigs, but where are the African or Indian farmers who use these techniques?

Alternatives to conventional sewerage

There are a number of socio-environmental factors which militate against the use of conventional sewerage systems in tropical developing countries; for example: an on-lot water supply is essential; relatively complex skills are required for both the design and installation of the pipe network; blockage due to 'unconventional' anal cleaning materials and other household waste objects is a frequent occurrence and, more importantly perhaps, conventional sewerage is entirely inappropriate for use in squatter settlements[21]. To this list can be added the enormous problem of sewer crown corrosion in hot climates (page 70). Conventional sewerage therefore has severe limitations on its use in developing countries. Moreover it is so expensive that it is most unlikely that the proportion of the urban population connected to a sewerage system will increase by any significant degree, at least over the next decade.

What then are the alternatives to conventional sewerage? It appears that there are only four realistic sanitation systems which are applicable to the urban tropics:

(a) The improved pit latrine and related types (Chapter 6 below);

(b) The compost toilet (Chapter 7);

(c) The aqua-privy, including sewered aqua-privies and septic tanks (Chapter 5);

(d) Night soil cartage systems (Chapter 8).

These systems have been fully described by McGarry[22] and elsewhere in this book. It is not my intention to duplicate this material, but to highlight certain gross shortcomings in current design and to remark on the extreme lack of progress we, as sanitary engineers, have made this century. Of the four alternatives listed above, the aqua-privy serves well to illustrate current design limitations, the more so as it is closely related to two systems − septic tanks and conventional sewerage − the design of which sanitary engineers are familiar with. Thus it might be expected to be the one system, of the four listed above, with which conventionally trained design engineers should have least difficulty. How then has conventional sanitary engineering wisdom been applied to the design of aqua-privies?

Aqua-privy design

The principles of the aqua-privy are discussed in the next chapter. On paper, this type of latrine is of very simple construction, and is cheaper to build than a septic tank or an equivalent provision in conventional sewerage. In practice, however, there are a number of problems. The foremost of these is centred on the maintenance of the water seal: with the simple drop-pipe, additional water must be poured into the tank to maintain the seal; this elementary task has to be done at least every other day, and commonly daily. In practice, of course, it is not done with any such regularity, with the consequent development of odour and fly nuisance. Such nuisance can be devastating and is the reason for the aqua-privy's considerable unpopularity; in Botswana, the installation of aqua-privies has been officially banned since 1975 just for this reason[23]. If a woman lives on a large low-income, high-density housing estate where each house has its own aqua-privy, but shares a standpipe with 79 others, is it realistic to expect her to carry considerable quantities of water just to maintain the seal in her aqua-privy? I think not, but one such estate has actually been designed for use in central Africa.

One solution to the problem of water seal maintenance has been to divert the household sullage into the tank. But even this (the so-called 'self-topping' aqua-privy) has not always been successful. The next developmental step was to link several aqua-privies in series; provided the water seal in the first aqua-privy was maintained (and this could be achieved by installing a communal washing station immediately above it), the water seal in all the downstream aqua-privies would be automatically maintained. These were good solutions[24] as they introduced the concept of discharging the tank effluent into small bore (100 mm) sewers. Since these sewers do not carry large solids, they do not need to be designed to achieve self-cleansing velocities and so can be laid at very flat gradients (1 in 300) with a consequent reduction in material and excavation costs.

So we have an example of conventional wisdom cunningly applied to an alternative sanitation technology. But there are still some problems. The cost reduction is not large enough; for example in N'Djamena, Chad, it was estimated that the cost of sewered aqua-privies was as much as 90 per cent of that of conventional sewerage[25]. And, in spite of assertations to the contrary, blockages do occur, and have proved so troublesome in Zambia in recent years that the sewered aqua-privy is regarded in that country as a failure.

One more problem is that associated with the design of the squatting plate which has to incorporate either a water seal or a drop-pipe. The very simple approach to the latter described by Oluwande[26] — basically a flat slab with a central 150 mm drop-pipe — is simple enough for construction purposes, but hygienically it seems too simple: there is little guarantee that the user, especially if a child, can deposit all his excreta with sufficient precision and the flatness of the slab makes its cleansing an unpleasant task. In urban areas, at least, a more sophisticated approach would seem not only desirable but also viable; for example, some suitable modification of the squatting plate from the Oxfam emergency sanitation unit.

It is of course so easy to criticise; to develop new ideas is more difficult. Professor Wolman in Chapter 1 stated that "a profitable area for inquiry is to search out the technology used in developed countries 50 to 75 years ago". Consider, therefore, the septic closet which was in widespread use in the southern states of the U.S.A. earlier this century. As described by Hardenburgh[27] the septic closet is nothing more than an aqua-privy, but with a raised, covered seat in place of a squatting plate. The designs shown have several "novel" features: the use of multi-compartmented tanks (Figures 4.2, and 4.4); a simple access point for

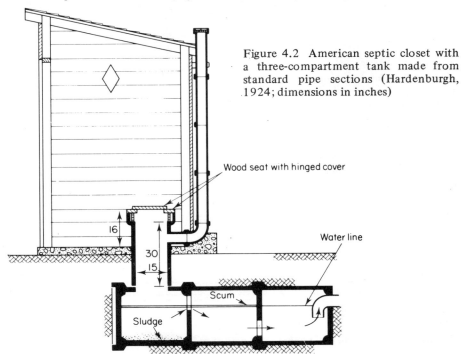

Figure 4.2 American septic closet with a three-compartment tank made from standard pipe sections (Hardenburgh, 1924; dimensions in inches)

Wood seat with hinged cover

Water line

16

30

15

Scum

Sludge

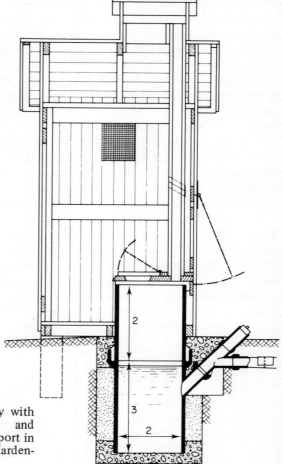

Figure 4.3 American aqua-privy with a good, simple desludging and (dimensions in feet) deblocking port in the effluent overflow pipe (Hardenburg 1924; dimensions in feet)

desludging and deblocking (Figure 4.3) and the use of standard pipe sections for construction of the tank (Figure 4.2). Of course there is room for improvement in all of these designs, especially for use in the urban tropics today. But these old American designs pose important questions: for example, why don't we incorporate a second chamber in modern aqua-privies? After all, they are now standard practice

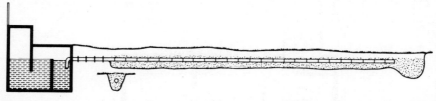

Figure 4.4 American aqua-privy with very simple soakaway (Hardenburgh, 1924)

for septic tanks; perhaps we would then avoid the blockages which were so troublesome in Zambia; but the design of the second chamber has to be very clever in order to minimize costs.

Concluding remarks

Enough has been said to indicate the current limitations of modern design capabilities via-a-vis aqua-privies. Similar considerations of the other three sanitation systems listed above lead to broadly similar conclusions, that as sanitary engineers, our record in attempting to solve the problems of tropical insanitation is really less than perfect. This is not to deny the real advances that have been made; my purpose has been to highlight some of our shortcomings. Such observations are perhaps painful, but they should be salutary. At least there is now a growing number of sanitary engineers who recognise these shortcomings and this is indeed the new spirit of our times. One of our problems is that we are still suffering from a dearth of technology transfer, not only of traditional practices and natural phenomena in one country to another, but also from research and development to design. Admittedly a consultant engineer's job is much more than just design, but the magnitude of the problem is such that innovative design is needed *now* and needs to be implemented *soon*. I believe we are working towards good solutions; but we need to accelerate our progress very rapidly.

NOTES AND REFERENCES

1. John Pickford is Leader of the Water and Waste Engineering for Developing Countries Group, Department of Civil Engineering, Loughborough University of Technology, Leicestershire, LE11 3TU, England.
2. E. G. Wagner and J. N. Lanoix, *Excreta Disposal for Rural Areas and Small Communities*, WHO Monograph Series No 39, Geneva, 1958.
3. Uno Winblad, *Evaluation of Waste Disposal Systems for urban low income communities in Africa*, Scan Plan Coordinator, Copenhagen, 1972.
4. G. v R. Marais, 'Sanitation and low cost housing', in *Water Quality, Management, and Pollution Control Problems*, Pergamon, Oxford, 1973, pp. 115-25.
5. D. A. Okun and G. Ponghis, *Community waste-water collection and disposal*, WHO, Geneva, 1975.
6. World Bank, *Urbanization: sector working paper*, World Bank, Washington D.C., 1972.
7. C. S. Pineo and D. V. Subrahmanyam, *Community water supply and excreta disposal in the developing countries – a commentary*, WHO Offset Publication No. 15, Geneva, 1975; see also the World Bank document noted in the previous reference.
8. United Nations, *Research and development activities of the Centre for Housing, Building, and Planning*, E/C 6/115, New York, 1971.
9. M. G. McGarry, 'Waste collection in hot climates: a technical and economic appraisal', in *Water, Wastes and Health in Hot Climates*, Wiley, London, 1977, pp. 239-63.
10. Richard Feachem, 'Appropriate sanitation', *New Scientist*, 69 (982), (8 January 1976), pp. 68-9.

11. Brian Appleton, 'Acid test for Middle East brain drain', *New Civil Engineer*, 19 February 1975, pp. 20-3.

12 John Pickford, 'Appropriate technology for Third World water supply and sanitation', *Environmental Pollution Management*, 7 (2), (March/April 1977), pp. 50-1.

13. Pineo and Subrahmanyam, *op. cit.* note 7.

14. Salomao A. Silva is from the Universidade Federal da Paraiba; address — Rua Monteirp Lobato 207, Alto Branco, 58.100 Campina Grande, Paraiba, Brasil.

15. See Duncan Mara's article, Section 4.3

16. Duncan Mara is from the University of Dundee, Scotland, and the Universidade Federal da Paraiba, Brasil; address — Department of Civil Engineering, The University, Dundee, DD1 4HN, Scotland.

17. T. D. Fontaine and A. W. Hoadley, *Health Laboratory Science*, 13 (4), 238 (1976).

18. E. J. Gangarose *et al.*, *Journal of Infectious Diseases*, 122 (1970), p. 181; W. E. Farran and M. Edison, *Journal of Infectious Diseases*, 124 (1971), p. 327.

19. G. v R. Marais, *Journal of the Environmental Engineering Division, ASCE*, 100-(EE1), (1974), p. 119.

20. E. F. Gloyna, *Waste Stabilization Ponds*, WHO, Geneva, 1971.

21. Richard Feachem, *op. cit.* note 10.

22. M. G. McGarry, *op. cit.*, note 9.

23. *Daily News*, Gaberone, Botswana, (218), 13 November 1975, p. 1.

24. L. J. Vincent, W. E. Algie, and G. v R. Marais, in *Proceedings of a Symposium on Hygiene and Sanitation in relation to Housing, Niamey, 1961*, Commission for Technical Co-operation in Africa, London, (Publication No. 84); also see WHO *Technical Report Series*, No. 541.

25. Black and Veatch International, *Storm Drains and Sanitary Sewerage Master Plan Report for the City of N'Djamena, Chad*. African Development Bank, 1975.

26. P. A. Oluwande, *Appropriate Technology*, 3 (3), (1976), p. 26.

27. W. A. Hardenburgh *Home Sewage Disposal*, Lippincott, Philadelphia, 1924.

5

Aqua-Privies

5.1 THE APPLICABILITY OF AQUA-PRIVIES IN DEVELOPING COUNTRIES

Conference Working Group[1]

Definitions and distinctions

The aqua-privy can be regarded as a simplified septic tank system — excreta are deposited directly into a tank, rather than being flushed along a short length of pipe before reaching it. The distinction between the two devices, and the simpler construction of the aqua-privy, is made clear by Figure 5.1. This distinction needs to be emphasized because in some countries, notably India, terminology is different, and the term 'septic tank' is consistently used to describe what this book calls an 'aqua-privy'. The two systems use the same principle — anaerobic fermentation or digestion of excreta in a tank of water — but an aqua-privy costs less than a septic tank, and requires less water for its operation.

Deposition of faeces into an aqua-privy tank from above the squatting plate can be via a vertical drop pipe, or alternatively, via a simple low volume 'pour flush' water seal. The latter is more sophisticated and hygienically superior, but more expensive, and, depending on the type of anal cleaning material, more prone to blockages. Where the simple drop pipe is used, it needs to have its lower end below the water level in the tank to form a water seal. In both cases, a vent-pipe should be provided to exhaust the gaseous products of the anaerobic fermentation occurring in the tank (which principally consist of methane or 'biogas'). Disposal of the liquid effluent from the tank can, depending on the housing density and soil characteristics, be achieved by subsurface percolation into the ground via a soakaway, or by small-bore sewers connected to waste stabilization ponds. The use of aqua-privies with sewer connections has been tried extensively in Zambia, and has been discussed as a possibility for Botswana (Section 3.5) and Chad. This technique is described in the previous chapter (Section 4.3) and not here.

It should be stressed that the liquid effluent is liable to carry many of the pathogens originally present in the excreta. It can be highly dangerous, and soakaways must be designed with great care so that there is no danger of a surface overflow of effluent during wet weather, and no danger of wells in the vicinity being polluted.

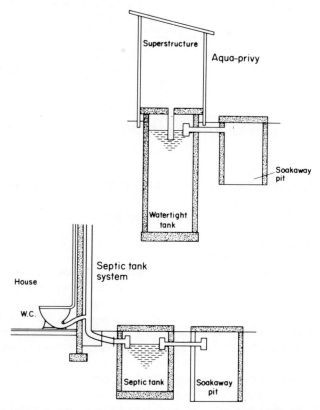

Figure 5.1 Comparison of the principle of the aqua-privy and the principle of the septic tank. The aqua-privy shown has a simple drop pipe as used in rural areas of Nigeria (see Section 5.2)

The process whereby excreta are digested anaerobically under water is also used in a number of other low-cost 'wet' systems for excreta disposal, including pit latrines designed to hold standing water (Figure 6.4), and biogas plants (Figure 12.2).

The distinctive features of the aqua-privy and septic tank system which are not used in either of these other applications of the same principle are the constant maintenance of a fixed water level in the tank, and the way in which the solid residue of digestion — the sludge — is periodically removed from the aqua-privy tank. Biogas systems are usually designed for a much greater throughput of sewage; the sludge is not allowed to settle, but is continuously removed by the movement of water through the tank. In wet pit latrines, on the other hand, there is little control of the water level, and there is often no desludging at all — as the pit fills up, solid matter may pile up above the initial water level so that decomposition ceases to be wholly anaerobic.

The distinctive feature of aqua-privy and septic tank systems, therefore, is the separation they achieve between a solid sludge and a liquid effluent. The effluent carries in solution many of the products of decomposition, so that the sludge left behind in the bottom of the tank is much less in volume than the original excreta.

Septic tanks, aqua-privies, wet pit latrines, and biogas plants all belong to the family of 'wet' systems providing on-site treatment of excreta. In contrast, cess-pits and conservancy vaults are merely places where excreta are stored until they can be disposed of, and should not be confused with aqua-privies.

Applicability

The key difference in the applicability of septic tanks and aqua-privies has to do with the different volumes of waste and water with which they can deal. A septic tank is appropriate to houses or other buildings with piped water supply, multiple taps, and large quantities of sullage water to be disposed of. In contrast, the aqua-privy is most appropriate where the quantity of water to be dealt with is much less, as in houses whose water supply is limited to a single tap. However, aqua-privies are not really suitable in circumstances where all water has to be carried to the home; they need a regular supply.

These differences can be summed up by saying that aqua-privies and septic tanks, though similar in principle, represent two quite different levels of application of technology. The aqua-privy is a low-cost technology, intermediate between the pit latrine and the flush toilet. The septic tank is suited to a high technology lifestyle, with cistern-flushed toilets and high level of water usage — it provides a disposal system for modern water-borne excreta removal practice, though on a small scale, suited to rural areas where isolated houses cannot be connected to a main sewer.

In bracketing septic tanks with conventional sewerage, we need to note exceptions such as the Oxfam sanitation unit, which uses the septic tank principle in a very unconventional guise, and there are other instances where a septic tank treats the sewage from communal latrines serving very poor communities. However, these exceptions apart, septic tanks are limited in use to:

(a) isolated rural houses;
(b) urban areas without sewers where water is piped into houses;
(c) multiple house schemes, blocks of flats, schools, health centres and clinics, and other public institutions.

In contrast, the aqua-privy is more widely applicable. Examples of its use in urban conditions are to be found in Pakistan, Thailand, India (there are 30 000 in Calcutta — see Chapter 9), and on a small scale in Botswana (Chapter 3). The range of applications for aqua-privies can be summarized as:

(a) semi-urban and urban communities where water is not piped into houses;
(b) rural communities where the pit latrine is not appropriate;
(c) communities where the water table is high;

(d) communities where per capita income is not sufficient to pay for a septic tank;

(e) public toilets and comfort stations in urban and rural areas (e.g. Ibadan, where they have proved very successful).

Construction and materials

Tanks can be constructed of either concrete or brick. Concrete tanks are very durable but are comparatively expensive and require considerable skill to build. Brick and concrete blocks are cheaper and easier to use, but are not so suitable where water tables are high. Units built from precast concrete panels made under factory conditions may be of more consistent quality, but transport to site can be difficult. In parts of India where water tables are high, tanks are built in very shallow excavations so that users have to climb steps to get to the latrine on top. Aqua-privy tanks may be cylindrical, but septic tanks are usually box-shaped, or take the form of two cylindrical tanks in series.

The volume needed in an aqua-privy tank depends on the number of users, the amount of water entering the system, and the frequency of desludging. With water used only for anal cleaning and hand-flushing, a tank used by ten people with a capacity of 1.5 m^3 below the water line might need desludging once in two years; with only 0.8 m^3 capacity, it might need desludging every nine months. The tank in Figure 5.3 has a capacity of 0.85 m^3 below water level.

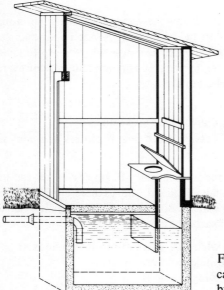

Figure 5.2. The septic closet, an early American version of the aqua-privy (from Hardenburgh, 1924 — see Section 4.3)

The two kinds of squatting plates which can be used in aqua-privies have already been mentioned. One has a drop pipe (Figure 5.1); the other has a pan with water seal (as in the Calcutta aqua-privy, Figure 9.2). The two other aqua-privies illustrated in this chapter have raised seats rather than squatting plates. The Botswana design (Figure 5.3) is altogether more elaborate than the very basic aqua-privy recommended for rural areas (Figure 5.1); it has a trough where people can wash after using the latrine, waste water from which flushes the pan and tops up the water in the tank.

An important purpose of the drop pipe in the simplest type of aqua-privy is to provide a water seal by penetrating below the water level in the tank. The optimum diameter of this pipe is found to be 15 cm because with larger diameters, users may

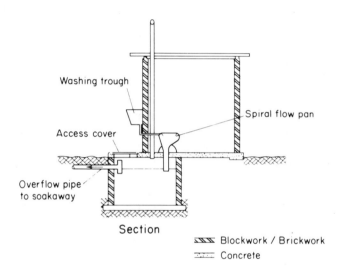

Section

Blockwork / Brickwork
Concrete

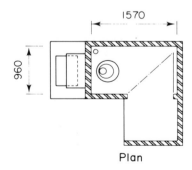

Plan

Figure 5.3 The Botswana 'type B' aqua-privy (measurements in millimetres). By permission of IDRC

feel splashes from the tank. Some fouling of the pipe is inevitable, but a pipe wide enough to avoid this would be impracticable, and could be a danger to children.

Concrete is the cheapest material for the squatting plate, but unless it is carefully finished, such slabs are not easy to keep clean. Glass fibre squat plates are expensive (US \$20-\$40 each) and must usually be imported, but are durable and effective; PVC is less durable, but about half the price of glass fibre.

Construction costs vary between countries and according to the sophistication of the design. Costs quoted in this book vary from US \$150 for very simple aqua-privies in Nigeria (Section 5.2) to \$220 in Calcutta (Section 9.2). These figures ignore the additional investment needed to equip a municipality with vacuum trucks for desludging the tanks, and the plant needed to treat and dispose of the sludge. Although there are obvious hazards in comparing costs between one country and another, Table 5.1 attempts some comparisons. It would be unwise to take this as a guide to absolute costs, but in general it can be said that the cost of an aqua-privy is about *twice* the cost of a pit latrine.

Maintenance and operation

The maintenance of aqua-privies is possibly more demanding than the maintenance of most other low-cost excreta disposal systems (apart from some composting privies). The large number of failures in aqua-privy systems which have now been recorded usually arises from neglect of this aspect, and the notoriety of the problem has caused it to be discussed in several other parts of this book (Sections 4.3 and 10.2). Little need be added here, therefore, but to stress the importance of the subject.

The two key points are the maintenance of water levels in aqua-privy tanks (Section 4.3) and desludging. Desludging must be organized on a regular basis by the municipality, who should also be responsible for the disposal of the sludge, either for composting, or for treatment in an oxidation pond. But the responsibilities of the municipality should not end there; they should have some oversight of the maintenance of the aqua-privies also. For example, the desludging operatives could be trained to inspect installations (particularly communal ones) for breakages, they could identify latrines in an insanitary state, and they could generally help maintain a high standard of cleanliness. They should not be regarded as people of a low social status, but should be trained technicians, able to advise householders on repairs, or do the job themselves.

5.2 THE POTENTIAL OF THE AQUA-PRIVY: NIGERIAN EXPERIENCE

P. A. Oluwande[2]

Comparison of the pit latrine and the aqua-privy

In many developing countries, the pit latrine is the only excreta disposal method which is within reach of a majority of the people. In favourable circumstances, the

Table 5.1 Construction costs of aqua-privies and septic tanks compared with other latrines

Latrine type, country, and section reference for this book.	Approximate construction cost of latrine plus superstructure, U.S. dollars, 1977 prices.		
	Cost of materials only.	Total cost, materials plus labour.	Cost of experimental models at Lobatse (Table 3.2)
SEPTIC TANKS			
Nigeria (sec. 5.2)	—	315+	—
Taiwan (sec. 11.3)	—	160≠	—
AQUA-PRIVIES			
Nigeria (sec. 5.2)	90*	150+	—
Calcutta (sec. 9.2)	—	220	—
Tanzania (sec. 3.2)	—	300	—
Botswana (sec. 3.5)	—	—	505
PIT LATRINES			
Nigeria (sec. 5.2) (slab only	1.20	—	—
(all materials	39.20*	69+	—
Zimbabwe (sec. 6.3)	30-40*	—	—
India (off-set wet pit, sec. 2.5)	25-31	—	—
" " " " sec. 10.1)	—	78≠	—
Botswana (sec. 3.5)	13-24	—	340
COMPOSTING LATRINES (MULTRUM TYPE)			
Philippines (sec. 7.4)	—	55≠	—
Tanzania (sec. 3.5)	30-40*	—	—
Botswana (sec. 3.5)	—	—	390

*   figures quoted during the conference from which this book originated, but not otherwise discussed in the book
+   1973 costs
≠   quoted costs may not cover whole installation, e.g. they may exclude superstructures

only item on which money need be spent is the floor slab, which should be made of reinforced concrete. This can be made from one-third of a 50 kg bag of Portland cement, so families need to spend as little as 80p or $1.20 to have a pit latrine. The hole can be dug and lined, and the superstructure can be provided wholly by the householders's own labour, and using local materials.

Unfortunately, though, the pit latrine is not popular in many areas of the developing countries. Although most of the causes of its unpopularity can be removed by judicious siting, correct construction, good maintenance, and by incorporating a water seal device in the floor slab, many people still do not like the pit latrine. Since such people can rarely afford the flushing toilet as represented by the septic tank system, the aqua-privy can be recommended as intermediate between the pit latrine and the septic tank, from the point of view of cost, construction technology, and maintenance requirements.

The two features which differentiate the aqua-privy from the pit latrine constitute a constraint on its construction and use in Nigeria and other developing countries. These features are the watertight tank and the inlet drop pipe in the floor slab illustrated by the aqua-privy in Figure 5.1. Two methods have been employed to construct the tanks in Nigeria. Wide tanks are constructed with reinforced concrete, while narrow tanks are built up from solid cement blocks. The latter method is simpler and cheaper. It has been found to be very convenient for family size aqua-privies, and for those with many compartments.

It is important to supervise the plastering of the inner wall of the tank to ensure that it is watertight. One way of achieving this is to plaster with 1:3 cement:sand mix to a thickness of 12.5 mm. The tank may also be made of metal protected against corrosion, or wood coated with preservative. In places where the groundwater level makes excavation difficult, the aqua-privy tanks may be constructed above the ground level. Such tanks are then provided with steps for access to the tops of the tanks, where the privy compartment is located.

Simplified methods for constructing the floor slab[3] make it possible for the aqua-privy to be provided in rural areas where sophisticated technology is lacking.

The cost of an aqua-privy in Nigeria depends on many factors, including the cost of labour and materials (especially cement), and the method used in construction. The type of superstructure chosen will also affect the overall cost. In 1973, the average cost for family size units with separate superstructures of planks and corrugated iron sheets was about US $150, 17 per cent of this being spent on the superstructure. The corresponding costs for the pit latrine and septic tank were $69 and $315 respectively, although the pit latrine could cost much less if the family used its own labour and local materials.

Maintenance

To ensure that the water level is maintained sufficiently to submerge the end of the drop pipe, water is added daily to replace liquid displaced or evaporated. The inside of the drop pipe also needs to be cleaned once or twice daily to prevent fly breeding, preferably in the morning and again in the afternoon.

The aqua-privy works particularly well where people use water for anal cleaning. Any other material may be used, but solid material will reduce the time which the tank can be left before desludging. Aqua-privies in Moslem communities where water is used in personal hygiene operate without trouble for long periods. But where people use tough qualities of paper for anal cleaning, the paper tends to stick in the drop,pipe, particularly in public latrines, and this prevents faeces from reaching water in the tank, and offers a site where flies will lay eggs. To prevent this, paper must be in small pieces, and maintenance must be effective in clearing any blockages in the drop pipe.

Special applications of aqua-privies

As can be observed from the foregoing comments, the aqua-privy may be used for excreta disposal almost anywhere. In some places, it may be necessary to employ aqua-privies in special applications, for example, in towns where they are connected to sewers for effluent disposal.

Another specialized application is the use of aqua-privies in comfort stations, which are a type of communal facility owned by a compound of many houses, Each comfort station consists of latrine compartments of aqua-privy type, showers, and clothes-washing ·facilities. In Ibadan, comfort stations of this type were introduced to solve the sanitation problems of highly congested built-up areas where there were neither private nor public sanitary facilities, and there was neither the space nor the resources to introduce them[4]. The idea of a communal facility in such situations is sound, but it is essential that maintenance and operation are carefully planned during the design stage. In Ibadan, the comfort stations have run into maintenance problems arising from the fact that the local people cannot afford to pay the operation and maintenance costs.

We may conclude, then, that the aqua-privy is a widely applicable, and highly adaptable excreta disposal system. It avoids the high costs associated with conventional systems, whether involving sewers or septic tanks, and at the same time, it avoids some of the drawbacks of the pit latrine.

NOTES AND REFERENCES

1. Working group members: P. A. Oluwande (chairman), M. Ballard (rapporteur), Michael D. Blackmore, D. J. Bradley, R. Cezayirlioglu, E. L. P. Hessing, Henry Mann, S. A. Silva, and Henning Therkelsen.
2. P. A. Oluwande is from the Department of Preventive and Social Medicine, University of Ibadan, Ibadan, Nigeria.
3. P. A. Oluwande gives fuller details of his simplified techniques of aqua-privy construction in *Appropriate Technology*, 3 (3), November 1976, pp. 25-8.
4. Maclaren International, *Immediate Measures Report on Master Plans for Wastes Disposal and Drainage in Ibadan,* Ibadan Wastes Disposal Board, 1970; see also P. A. Oluwande in *Proceedings of 2nd International Conference on Water, Wastes, and Health in Hot Climates*, Loughborough University of Technology, U.K., 1975, pp. 110-12.

6

Pit Latrines

6.1 THE NEEDS OF RURAL AREAS

B. Z. Diamant[1]

The urgency of the problem

The data on excreta disposal facilities in rural areas presented in Chapter 1 demonstrated that the problem of rural sanitation is urgent and serious. The World Health Organization (WHO) has set targets for improvement in this sector, but even if the target for 1980 is met, three-quarters of the rural population in developing countries will still be without facilities, and therefore exposed to serious health hazards.

A word of caution against assuming organized sanitation always to be necessary is sounded in the next section of this chapter, where it is pointed out that the lack of latrines in some sparsely populated areas or nomadic communities may not be a disadvantage. However, as populations grow, and large, permanent villages become the norm even in areas where they have not previously existed, so the dangers to health due to lack of sanitation facilities increase quite rapidly. Populations have increased ten-fold in parts of Africa since the turn of the century[2], with the result that practices which were once harmless now pollute rivers significantly or create health risks for people working in the fields.

A programme for the safe disposal of human wastes involves many aspects of people's lives − personal attitudes, social relationships, their economy and technology. The technological aspect should, as a rule, follow and be based upon the other aspects. The people themselves should have started the process of change before the technology is introduced.

The problem to be discussed here is therefore the design and construction of a suitable latrine which can be produced in very large numbers[3], is durable and works well, and is suited to community self-help programmes. Aqua-privies might be effective in some areas, but we have found them too costly and too sophisticated for the rural areas in our part of Nigeria. The pit latrine is the simplest excreta disposal system, and the most efficient for existing rural conditions. It is economical, simple, and if properly installed, it can prevent the pollution of water supplies which is currently widespread. An alternative version in areas with deep soil free of stones is the bored hole latrine (Figure 6.1), where the hole is made using an auger, instead of being dug by hand.

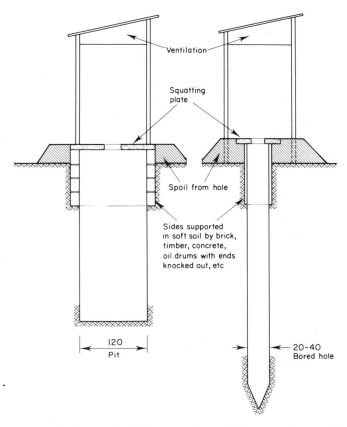

Figure 6.1 The basic features of a pit latrine and a bored hole latrine (dimensions in centimetres)

The pit latrine consists of three main parts: the dug pit, the superstructure, and the squatting plate, or slab floor, which is usually made of concrete. A pit measuring 1 x 1 x 4 metres (4 m^3) will accommodate the wastes from a family of five people during a 3-4 year period. The pit is usually dug by the householder himself, and does not involve any special problems or costs if it is sited at an adequate distance downhill from any water source. Superstructures can be made from local materials, which leaves the floor slab as the most difficult part of the latrine to construct.

The pit-latrine slab

The proper design and construction of the floor slab will determine whether the latrine will be satisfactory in use. The best material for the slab is concrete, and the main cost is the cement needed, and the steel bars used for reinforcement[4]. The quality of the slab depends on many factors, but notably on the mould used for casting the concrete. The provision of a suitable mould will not be the responsibility of the user, but that of the local authority which organizes the campaign, as will be discussed later. The user can have for the same expense a good slab or a bad one, according to the casting shape. What is a good slab?

A satisfactory pit-latrine slab must have the following qualities:

(a) *Easy cleaning*. The upper surface should be smooth and have a slope towards the centre hole, so as to enable a quick rinsing with a small quantity of water.

(b) *Comfortable use*. The slab should have elevated foot rests so that the user will automatically stand in the correct position, minimizing the contamination of the slab. For the same purpose, the hole opening into the pit should have the shape of a key-hole, preventing excreta and urine from reaching the slab.

(c) *Fly control*. Flies tend to breed in human wastes, but they do so in the light mainly. The hole in the slab should be provided with a wooden cover which must be placed over it after use. In order to ensure the cover's presence, it should be chained, with the end of the chain connected to a hook anchored in the concrete slab.

(d) *Easy handling*. A concrete slab is quite heavy and might be cracked when moved or placed on a new pit, after the previous one has been filled. The slab should therefore be cast in two halves, connected by means of a tongue and groove (Figure 6.2).

(e) *Support for superstructure*. Since the superstructure is made of light materials such as mats, it can easily be blown away in any storm. By anchoring it at the four corners of the slab by four iron holders, this can be prevented.

(f) *Lime*. The slabs used in the Ishara area of Nigeria also have a small depression to hold a tin of lime, which is often sprinkled inside the pit to control smells. Not all authorities would agree about the desirability of using lime, and later in the chapter, other methods of preventing smells are discussed, by ventilation of the pit or by a water seal. This is a recurring problem.

Concrete slabs containing these features were cast in large numbers and successfully installed on pit latrines in the rural district of Ishara. The key to this operation was the use of steel moulds provided by the local authority; the moulds were each in two parts, for the two sections of the slab.

For any similar pit latrine campaign which aims to benefit a large population, several moulds will be needed, each of which is successively borrowed by many

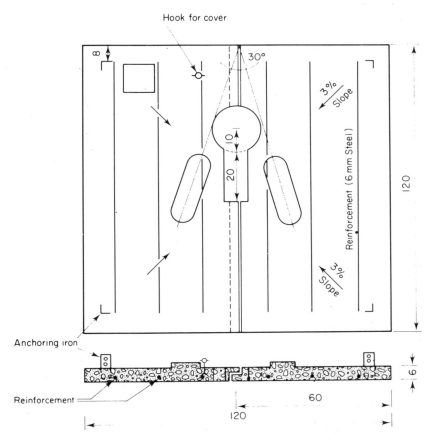

Figure 6.2 Concrete pit-latrine slab made in two interlocking parts, as used is the Ishara district of Nigeria (dimensions in centimetres)

householders building their own latrines. A suitable provision would be at least ten moulds for every thousand people in the area being covered. The moulds must be produced in modern workshops in the city that are equipped with the necessary machinery for a smooth and good quality product.

In the village, the health office staff, mainly health inspectors, have to organize the people for the campaign and collect the contributions for the purchase of the cement, so that it can be obtained on a wholesale basis. The leaders of the community will of course take full part in the preparation for the campaign, and it is suggested that the first pits be installed at the houses of community leaders, so that they can serve for demonstration later on. A rota will have to be formed for the use of the limited number of metal moulds. The first to dig their pit will be eligible to register first for the casting, which usually occupies the mould for at least five days. It should be kept in mind that every participant in the campaign must make his contribution in kind (labour, and provision of sand and gravel for the concrete), and in cash (purchase of the cement, approximately one half bag per slab, and iron bars where applicable).

These contributions are imperative, because they will help to give the people the feeling of sharing and participation which will guarantee the success of the campaign.

The campaign will also include meetings, demonstrations, and film shows. These activities are not included, however, in this paper, which was meant to deal mainly with technological matters.

6.2 THE APPLICABILITY OF PIT LATRINES

Conference Working Group[5]

Rural sanitation

Pit latrines can be installed under a wider variety of circumstances than any other type of sanitation; they are also usually cheaper, although comparable costings are rare (Table 5.1).

That does not mean, however, that pit latrines are always the best technique to use where low-cost, rural sanitation is required. The unthinking construction of sanitation facilities may, in some circumstances, be wasteful of resources and self-defeating, and may even be harmful to community health if it is not accompanied by intensive evaluation and adequate institutional, financial and technical arrangements for maintenance.

For instance, it may be preferable to have a few well-run latrines serving institutions such as schools, hospitals and government offices, which can have a powerful demonstration effect, than to build hundreds of village latrines which might be doomed to fouling and collapse.

One of the keynotes of this working group's discussion has been the need for sensitivity to community preferences, and adaptability to local conditions and local practice. It may be better to improve and regularize existing techniques rather than assume that pit latrines are automatically necessary.

Existing excreta disposal practices, such as excreting in small holes and then covering them may be encouraged or adapted in preference to permanent latrines in nomadic or migrating communities, where permanent facilities might not be appropriate, although the health consequences of these, as of any other rural sanitation methods, need careful evaluation.

In some rural areas, traditional excreta disposal practice may, indeed, be relatively satisfactory from a health point of view. Communities may use specified sites for defecation, which may change from season to season with the agricultural cycles. The combination of site rotation, burying method and climate may be such as to minimize health hazards, with the sun rapidly drying excreta and rendering it harmless in certain seasons. In such circumstances, the construction of latrines may mean the loss of a scarce resource (i.e. a fertilizer) with no significant health gain.

In some places, when there are high concentrations of people for a short time each year, for example cotton pickers in Sudan, it may be appropriate to dig a trench latrine for short-term use.

The problem about making judgements in all these circumstances is that the relationship between improved sanitation and health is widely variable and its details are mostly unknown. Sanitation programmes should always therefore include an evaluation component to check whether real health benefits do follow, and some ideas about how this should be done have already been put forward in Section 1.4.

Organization of programmes

One theme in this book is the necessity for adequate organization of sanitation programmes. One aspect of this is whether the latrine programme is pursued in isolation, or what is much better, whether it is part of a larger preventive health programme. In one programme, in which encouragement of latrine-building was looked at in conjunction with improvements in housing and in hygiene within the home, it was possible to get a better response to the proposals for sanitation by linking them to more acceptable measures which were implemented first.

Difficulties in motivating people to construct or use latrines should not be seen as barriers to be overcome by increased pressure or persuasion, so much as signs of particular social constraints requiring investigation and specific treatment. For example, the effect of a cash constraint may be mitigated by rotating credit associations.

The construction of pit latrines requires less expertise than other sanitation techniques, and organization is at least as important as technology, including administration by the agency concerned as well as organization at village level. Organization must cover health and health education, the digging of pits, the construction of slabs and superstructures, and the maintenance of the completed installations.

Digging pits requires little supervision except that not many people are accustomed to following plans and measurements. In St. Lucia, one way of getting over this has been to supply a wooden frame to place on the ground, outlining the section of the hole to be dug.

The construction of concrete slabs is a bigger problem, and a decision has to be made as to whether this should be organized by pre-casting them at a central point, or by casting them on site. In St. Lucia, it is found better to pre-cast them centrally. This leads to a better product as quality control is more easily arranged, but the transport of slabs to the site can present problems. However, selling or giving away complete slabs to people can be a great encouragement to them to complete the latrine.

Rural latrines should generally be built for individual households. Householders will then be responsible for maintenance, though the agency promoting the sanitation programme may need to provide some back-up and supervision to check whether maintenance and cleaning present any problems, or are being neglected. Communal village latrines are not likely to be adequately maintained, and are therefore not to be encouraged.

Location of latrines

Pit latrines are not exclusively for rural use; the major constraint on their use in urban areas, besides flies and odours, is the frequency of relocation, which may be high in constricted sites where the pits cannot be made wide or deep enough.

When choosing sites for latrines, the first factor to be considered is the wishes of the community. Latrines should not be too close to water sources, the minimum distance being dependent on local soil conditions. In limestone, for instance, pathogens may travel much further than in fine soils.

In some rural areas, consideration of latrines near to fields and field camps might be worthwhile, and the cheapness of pit latrines makes them particularly suitable for this.

Other local factors which may affect the choice of site include the point that communal latrines might have to be away from mosques and certain other places, or might be best down-wind from the village. Cultural factors may also affect the direction of facing — not toward Mecca in Muslim communities, for example.

Latrines might need to be within a certain minimum distance of houses, if they are to be used at night; but unless they are very well ventilated, they should not be inside the house structure.

Different types of pit latrine

Not enough is known about the relative merits of pit latrines and bored-hole latrines, and a third type is the Reed Odourless Earth Closet (ROEC) which has been tried out in Botswana. (More specialized types of pit latrine also exist and are discussed in the next part of this chapter.)

A bored-hole latrine (Figure 6.1) is the quickest and easiest type to construct where soil conditions are suitable; it can be several metres deep and may penetrate below the water table. This enhances the digestion of excreta, though it may induce a wider spread of groundwater pollution, and could be dangerous in some circumstances. It has a larger surface area to volume ratio than pit latrines, allowing for better percolation of water, and is cheap and quick to build. The slab does not have to span a large distance, and this may avoid users feeling insecure, but the deep hole could be dangerous to children.

A pit latrine, in contrast, can be built in relatively rocky ground where a bored hole would be impossible. It is probably easier to arrange ventilation of the pit, and there is less danger of polluting groundwater because it cannot be dug below the water table — but this limits its use in areas where water tables are high.

The *ROEC* can be regarded as an *off-set pit latrine*, with the pit alongside, but not directly underneath the privy (Figure 3.3). There is a chute to carry excreta from the latrine into the pit. This has the advantage that the pit can be dug out without disturbing the latrine (though there are no reports of this having been done in practice without outside institutional support; the pits are usually large enough to last several years without emptying).

One problem is that the chute needs regular cleaning, and although the 7.5 cm vent pipe on existing latrines may be adequate to deal with odours, doubt was expressed concerning its ability to deal with the fly problem. Studies involving fly trapping could be devised to check whether the vent is sufficient to divert flies away from the chute.

Construction of pit latrines

The pit should be as deep as possible to ensure that it has a long life, but pits of more than 3 m depth may be dangerous to diggers unless shoring is used, which increases their cost. The cross-section of the pit need not be larger than the minimum space required by the digger: 1 m diameter would be typical. A larger pit requires a much stronger slab. Support for the pit walls, if required, can be provided by old oil drums, soil-cement blocks, burnt brick, or ferrocement (concrete plastered onto wire mesh).

Slabs or squatting plates should never be made of clay, unreinforced concrete or soil-cement. They should be more than strong enough to take the necessary loads, and new materials or methods should not be tried without experienced technical advice, and thorough preliminary testing. The choice of material should also be based on considerations of hygiene and the ease with which it can be kept clean.

When pouring reinforced concrete slabs, it is best to pour a 25 mm depth of concrete before placing the reinforcing bars. These are then laid on top of the poured concrete, and the remainder is poured on top.

The choice between having a rising seat or a slab designed as a squatting plate must be left largely to users, but consideration must be given to special circumstances. Children require a smaller seat or a smaller squat hole. Pregnant women and old people may find it difficult to squat and prefer seats. Some cultural and religious groups do not use a seat, and would demand squat pans. With regard to hygiene, a seat is less likely to be fouled, but when it is, its use will be totally rejected.

The latrine superstructure must be adapted to local preferences and to the materials available. The size of the compartment and whether it should be roofed and have a door may be questions subject to strongly held preferences within the community. A heavy superstructure may have to be made quite large, especially on soft ground where it will be difficult to find a secure foundation near to the pit. A brick lining may be built around the top periphery of the pit to stabilize the edge of the pit and to carry the slab; this may also be a suitable foundation for the superstructure. Desirable fixtures may include two handles for balance while squatting, a clean shelf for clothing or the contents of pockets, and a place nearby where water is available for washing hands.

The health consequences of using pit latrines are not well understood, because the significance of several deleterious aspects is rarely evaluated. Points to watch are: casual touching of superstructure walls as a route for transmission of faecal-oral disease; fouled latrines acting as foci for excreta-related disease; and access to the latrines by flies, cockroaches and rats.

6.3 SPECIALIZED DEVELOPMENTS OF PIT LATRINES

P. R. Morgan and V. de V. Clarke[6]

Problems in rural sanitation

Although efficient means of sewage or excreta disposal have for long been available, none of the existing systems has seemed entirely suitable for rural Africa. In our country, there were three particular situations which urgently needed attention. These were (1) communities of farm labourers for whom water was available but not unlimited; (2) villages with no piped water where supplies were laboriously carried from a distant source; and (3) densely populated irrigated areas where water is unlimited but where the irrigation results in such high water tables that sewage must be diverted to ponds or sewage plants. Thus three types of latrine have been devised to suit the three situations, although the system in use in irrigation areas still requires improvement.

The watergate self-flushing toilet

The principle that a water seal is desirable has been accepted, and where water is available even if limited, the watergate toilet designed by one of us[7] has proved to be efficient. The watergate toilet is fitted with a squatting plate and it consists of a chute (Figure 6.3), the bottom of which is covered by water held in a pan. This pan is eccentrically hinged, and it is maintained in balance in the horizontal position by a weight; it is filled with water to a level to cover the bottom of the chute through the valve indicated in Figure 6.3.

When the toilet is used, the weight of faeces and urine destroys the balance, and the pan tips, ejecting its contents into the pit or tank below. The weight restores the now empty pan to the horizontal position and it again fills with water, restoring the water seal which prevents odour and flies. The watergate is commercially produced in several countries, and it has proved itself to be largely free of breakdown, and reliable under rigorous field usage. The watergate is particularly favoured by the more socially important people living in peasant communities, including teachers, foremen, and health and agricultural demonstrators.

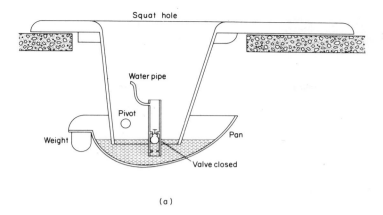

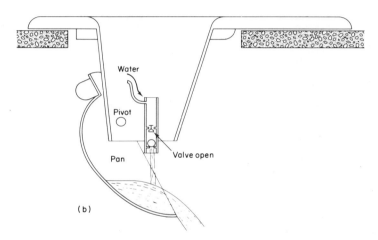

Figure 6.3   The watergate device for making a water seal in a pit-latrine: (a) with the pan in its rest position;   (b) when the deposition of faeces in the pan causes it to tip

The vented pit privy

The second system was developed by the same designer[8] for communities which are without readily available water. It is a modification of the deep pit privy, but has additional refinements to prevent the development of fly populations and to control odour, and these have proved most effective. It is considered that this system, the vented pit privy, will have a dramatic effect on rural sanitation in Zimbabwe, and it alone fully meets all the aims and objectives listed above. Already thousands of these have been installed in rural areas — on farms and in villages — and they are virtually foolproof. Because they are cheap to install, they can and are being installed for family ownership.

The vented pit privy (Figure 6.4) consists of a pit, preferably deep, on which is placed a concrete slab containing two holes — one the squatting hole, the

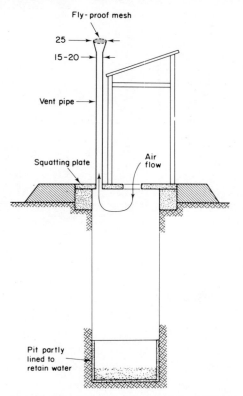

Figure 6.4   The vented pit privy. This diagram also shows a *wet* pit latrine, with a lining at the bottom of the pit to retain water (dimensions in centimetres)

immediate surrounds of which should be concave to allow easy cleaning, and the second, a hole of 20 cm diameter, to which is fitted the vent pipe, which has a diameter of not less than 15 cm. The vent pipe stands 2.5 m high, and, at the top, it bells outwards to approximately 25 cm diameter. This belled aperture is covered with glass-fibre mesh to prevent passage of flies and mosquitoes. The superstructure to the actual privy is deliberately kept small and dark — with only sufficient light for the user to see. As a result, the strongest light reaching the pit comes from the vent pipe and thus, during the day, flies in the pit are attracted to the top of the vent pipe. They tend to stay in the vent pipe until they die and drop back into the pit where they are digested with the other contents. Flies outside the system are preferentially attracted, by smell, to the top of the pipe, and they seldom enter the toilet itself. During approximately ten weeks of trapping flies, a total of 13 953 were caught in a trap fitted over the squatting hole of a privy built without a vent pipe, whereas a total of only 146 were caught during the same period in a trap fitted over the squatting hole of a privy fitted with a vent pipe. Both privies had been in use for a period of six months prior to the fitting of the traps.

Unpleasant odours in the toilet are also prevented. There is a temperature differential between the vent pipe and the pit, and this causes an up-draught in the vent pipe, removing obnoxious gases from the pit. These gases have to be replaced, and this takes place as a down-draught of fresh air through the toilet and the squatting hole into the pit. Thus no odours are noticeable in the toilet. The up-draught in the vent pipe is naturally strongest when the sun is shining on the pipe (which is usually blackened to absorb heat) but it occurs even at night and in the winter.

The pit itself is dug deep and wide so that it has a long life. However, if it is partially lined to ensure that there is always water present (Figure 6.4), the decomposition of excreta is more rapid and more complete, thus considerably extending the life of the pit.

A simple superstructure of cement plaster reinforced with metal wire and with chicken mesh has been designed for use with both the watergate and the vented pit privy, and as a result, a neat, clean, fly and odour proof latrine, highly acceptable to the user people, can be built for a total cost of US$40.

The flood trough system

The third system is working effectively in conjunction with water-borne excreta disposal by oxidation ponds within the intensely settled irrigation areas where the height of the water table prevents the use of septic tank or deep pit disposal of excreta. This flood trough system consists of a communal facility not greatly dissimilar to the Oxfam sanitation unit. It has a series of squatting plates sited over a long trough which leads to sewer pipes carrying the effluent to the oxidation ponds. The trough retains water at a depth of between 5 and 10 cm and it is automatically flushed at regular intervals by a self-tipping, eccentrically balanced drum, which in turn is fed by continuously running water. The frequency of flushing is adjusted by the rate of water flow into the drum. A suitable practice is to have a flush of approximately 100 litres of water each half-hour for a trough serving six or eight squat plates. The fact that the squat plates are sited directly over the trough, with no chute, cuts down on the degree of soiling of the surrounds used by the person, and thus the need for cleaning the toilet is kept to a minimum. Although flies are not a problem with this type of installation, some odour is present, and the system does require improvement.

These three types of toilet facilities, when appropriately used with suitable sewage or excreta disposal systems, have considerably improved the local situation in relation to rural sanitation. The results are now apparent in many ways, not the least in the improved community pride seen in many villages where the installation of acceptable toilet facilities or water supplies have led to a general improvement in hygiene, with refuse also being collected and destroyed, and with the further initiative coming entirely from the community itself. A public demand for

for improved sanitation and water supplies is also developing, even in some of the most remote communities. We believe that this is of great importance for the future health of such communities, because it shows that the first hurdle has been overcome — the ordinary people have recognized the need for sanitary improvements.

6.4 WATER SEAL PIT LATRINES

G. O. Unrau[9]

Pit latrines in schistosomiasis control

Pit latrines have gained the reputation of being ineffective as a control measure against schistosomiasis. This reputation arises mainly from efforts to evaluate latrine campaigns made some years ago in Egypt[10] and the Philippines[11]. However, in a careful review, Jordan[12] has shown that the studies do not justify the conclusions drawn. In one project, for example, when the data are looked at again, it is found that 171 individuals who were examined in the first year of the study were re-examined in two successive years, and within this group, the prevalence of infection fell from 56 to 42 per cent. This suggests that the latrines had, in fact, been of some benefit.

The Philippines project showed that *Schistosoma japonicum* infection rates among the snails which are intermediate hosts for the disease fell when latrines were installed nearby. At the same time, the trend was for infection rates to rise in snails near other houses not provided with latrines. This suggests that latrines can help reduce transmission, but long term results of this investigation were never available due to a storm which blew down many of the superstructures, causing the latrines to fall into disuse.

Even the simplest form of sanitation should be effective in breaking the life cycle of the schistosome worm if consistently used. This would be true even of the burial method mentioned in some of the oldest surviving sanitary regulations, in the Old Testament: 'you shall have a place outside the camp and you shall go out to it; and you shall have a stick with your weapon. . . you shall dig a hole with it, and turn back and cover up your excrement.'[13]

Pit latrines clearly have the capacity to break the cycle of infection, and where they are found not to do so, this if often because they are not consistently used. This may happen if they are not sufficiently attractive or acceptable. As Stoll[14] points out, the 'aesthetic affront' which many a pit latrine presents to those who are supposed to use it, 'vitiates its virtues, and drives adults as well as children back to the out-of-doors where the air is free.'

Obviously, greater efforts must be made to produce latrines that will be more acceptable to people and more fully used. On the island of St. Lucia, where at the beginning of our work, schistosomiasis affected about 30 per cent of the total population, and in some communities, as˘ many as 58 per cent, we have attempted to develop improved pit latrines, and at the same time, to improve water supplies, control snails, and provide chemotherapy for the affected people. Water supply improvement, snail control, and chemotherapy were at first tried separately, and all three methods were found to reduce the incidence of schistosomiasis dramatically in the project area. One area containing about 400 households and around 2000 people was then selected to demonstrate the effectiveness of providing a safe water supply *plus* individual household latrines, and for this project, we needed to find an acceptable pit latrine.

Water seal pit latrines

There are several ways of improving pit latrines to overcome the defects that discourage their proper use. One approach already presented in this chapter is the vented pit privy (Figure 6.4), in which air circulation removes odours and flies through a ventilation pipe.

A second approach is to introduce a water seal which entirely separates the pit and the latrine compartment, and prevents smells from getting from one into the other. The watergate device described in this chapter (Figure 6.3) is one technique for making this seal. On St. Lucia, ten watergate latrines have been obtained for trial purposes, and are functioning well. We believe this type of unit is best suited for public places like schools or community centres.

Another type of water seal latrine, widely used in India, has the pit behind the privy (Figure 2.3), not immediately below it.[15] The latrine is flushed by hand from a jug or bucket, when the excreta are washed from the pan along a short length of pipe into the pit. This has been described as a 'hand-flushed, off-set pit latrine', but it differs in many details from conventional pit latrines.

In St. Lucia, we have developed yet another type of water seal unit for use with pit latrines. Made of high density polyethylene, it is designed to cater for the local preference for a riser with a seat — a higher standard of living is associated with the 'sit down' toilet. The unit incorporates the riser, bowl and S-trap in two simple components which fit firmly together (Figure 6.5); it has the advantage of being much lighter in weight than concrete, making it easier to transport to the site. The plastic is also smoother, which makes for easier cleaning, and gives a better flushing action than the usual concrete traps which depend on the skill of the masons as to how well they flush. To date, there are nearly 400 of these units installed on St. Lutia. The community response has been very favourable, with a quite surprising lack of complaints or user problems. The people like the water seal idea due to the absence of smells and flies.

Health education

In general, community health education should accompany any provision of latrines. There should be latrines installed in schools so that children can be trained

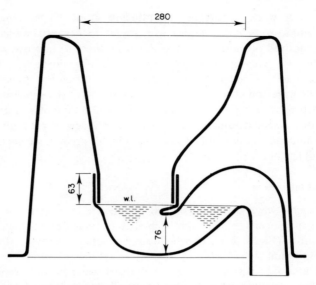

Figure 6.5 The 'TR water seal' system is used with pit
latrines in St. Lucia. Dimensions are in millimetres and
the level of the water seal is marked 'w.l.'

to use them. In this instance, it is also important that the units are well built and
well kept, since children learn through example and by doing. Furthermore,
children and teenagers are the persons that usually have the highest prevalence and
intensity of infection with schistosomiasis, and thus have the greatest
contamination potential. Great emphasis should be placed on the use of latrines by
this age group. In practice, it is found that young children are often discouraged
from using latrines through adults fearing that they may soil the units.

Another important aspect of latrine campaigns is the community attention and
interest focused on the excreta disposal problem. Getting the community and
individual involved in the programme increases the chances of the facilities being
used. In St. Lucia, we require the individual to prepare a pit and provide a
superstructure. Persons who have an investment in a latrine tend to make better use
of it.

NOTES AND REFERENCES

1. B. Z. Diamant is Professor of Public Health Engineering, Ahmadu Bello
   University, Zaria, Nigeria.
2. E.g. the population of Swaziland was about 50 000 in 1890 but had reached
   440 000 by 1973; the population of Zimbabwe was 700 000 around 1900 but
   had reached 7 millions by the mid-1970s.
3. T. W. Bendixen, *Studies on Household Sewage Disposal Systems*, U.S. Public
   Health Service, Ohio, 1950; E. G. Wagner and J. N. Lanoix *Excreta Disposal
   for Rural Areas and Small Communities*, WHO, Geneva, 1958.
4. H. E. Glenn, *Bamboo Reinforcement in Portland Cement Concrete*, Clemson
   College, South Carolina, 1950.

5. Working Group members: A. M. Cairncross (rapporteur), Ann K. Cheesmond, V. de V. Clarke, J. M. Jewsbury, P. Kelly, J. Bertrand Mendis, T. Ozmen, Gerhard Schad, G. O. Unrau, N. Greenacre.

6. P. R. Morgan and V. de V. Clarke are from the Blair Research Laboratory, Box 8105, Causeway, Salisbury, Rhodesia/Zimbabwe.

7. The invention was by P. R. Morgan, who has an account of it in preparation. Similar devices known as 'tippler' latrines were used in towns in northern England until recently, in conjunction with conventional sewerage.

8. P. R. Morgan, *Central African Journal of Medicine*, 23 (1977), p. 1.

9. G. O. Unrau is Sanitary Engineer with the Rockefeller Foundation, P.O. Box 93, Castries, St. Lucia (West Indies).

10. J. A. Scott and N. Barlow, *American Journal of Hygiene*, 27 (1938), p. 619; also J. Weir, *Journal of the Egyptian Public Health Association*, 27 (1952), p. 55.

11. T. P. Pesigan *et al.*, *Bulletin of WHO*, 19 (1958), p. 223.

12. P. Jordan, UNEP working paper, meeting of 12-14 August 1975, Nairobi.

13. Deuteronomy, *23*, 13 (Revised Standard Version).

14. N. R. Stoll, *Journal of Parasitology*, 33 (1947), pp. 1-18.

15. Material interpolated by the editor.

7

Composting Latrines

7.1 THE RANGE OF TECHNIQUES

Conference Working Group[1]

The potential of the many types

At a time when the disadvantages of using water in the transport and digestion of excreta are causing increasing concern, dry composting as a form of treatment seems especially attractive. Moreover, the principle of the composting latrine may be widely applicable in the developing countries, where climatic conditions tend to favour it. But the potential of the composting latrines is so far unrealized, and barely recognized, except in Vietnam and one or two other parts of Asia. There is probably an immense, unfulfilled promise in this technology — but there is also a lack of knowledge and a need for more research.

The various composting latrine systems can be divided into two broad groups: the single vault types (many of them originating in Scandinavia), and the double vault types (belonging to an Asian tradition). The most important *double vault* types can be listed as follows:

(a) the Vietnamese double septic bin, which collects faeces only, and has a separate arrangement for collecting urine (Figure 7.1).

(b) the Gopuri double vault, which is similar to the Vietnamese double bin, except that it has a soakaway below to drain off the urine.

(c) the WHO double vault design[2] and the comparable Botswana double vault (Figure 3.5).

(d) the Biopot, a proposed system with soakaways for urine.

(e) the Farallones composting privy, used in California by do-it-yourself house builders, but probably inspired by Asian prototypes.

(f) the BRE double vaults, designed for a continuous throughput of air to encourage aerobic composting[3].

It is worth noting that if a conventional pit latrine is kept dry, compost will form in it. If, after due time, this is used on the land (which in fact rarely happens), the pit privy can be regarded as a very basic composting latrine. One pit latrine

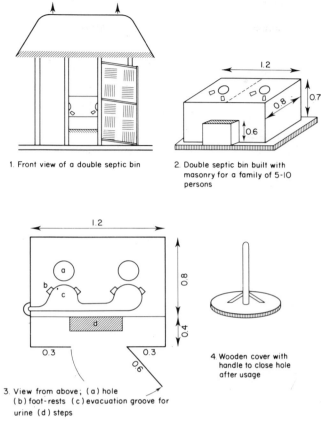

1. Front view of a double septic bin

2. Double septic bin built with masonry for a family of 5-10 persons

3. View from above; (a) hole (b) foot-rests (c) evacuation groove for urine (d) steps

4. Wooden cover with handle to close hole after usage

Figure 7.1   A double septic bin latrine as used in the countryside of northern Vietnam

designed in Bangladesh for producing compost has a lining of grass cuttings, paper, or straw at the bottom of the pit, with further vegetable matter added at weekly intervals while the latrine is in use[4]. If pit latrines used in this way may be regarded as the simplest single vault composting latrines, the most typical devices in this category are the Multrum and Clivus latrines. These are systems in which the composting chamber has a sloping floor, and originate from an invention made by Lindstrom in 1938. These composting latrines should be seen in the context of other *single vault* types, the most important of which may be listed as follows:

(a) dry pit latrines and derivatives.
(b) Multrum and Clivus composting latrines, such as the ones used in Botswana (Figure 3.1), or being tried out in the Philippines (Figure 7.3) and Tanzania (the Winblad or SCAN type).
(c) the ROEC latrine with composting chamber, currently on trial in Botswana (Figure 3.4).

(d) various small and compact latrines designed in Sweden, many of which use a fan for humidity control, and an electric heater to maintain the necessary temperature (Figure 7.4).

In some discussions of the processes used by these latrines, a distinction is made between 'composting' and 'mouldering'. There is no scientific basis for this, but it is sometimes of practical value to use the two terms with slightly different meanings. Composting is the relatively fast process of decomposition of organic matter that occurs in the garden compost heap; it achieves a relatively high temperature in the early stages of the process. Mouldering is a slower, mainly aerobic process which takes place at room temperatures; it takes two or three years to produce a 'safe' compost rather than two or three months. If this distinction is made, most Multrum-type latrines are in fact 'mouldering latrines', and are sometimes referred to as such in the literature, while in contrast, the Vietnamese double septic bin is a true composting latrine.

7.2 THE DOUBLE SEPTIC BIN IN VIETNAM

Joan K. McMichael[5]

Three aspects of rural hygiene

The first Five Year Plan (1961-65) put forward by the Ministry of Health in the Democratic Republic of Vietnam concentrated on what they called 'the three major installations for rural hygiene, namely the double septic bin, the well with a curb, and the bath-house'[6].

The problem of pure drinking water was of considerable importance. The stagnant ponds so characteristic of North Vietnam at that time were breeding grounds of disease. People and their animals used them for every purpose, including bathing and washing, and the rain washed in faecal material from men and beasts. There could be no hope in these conditions of tackling the host of gastro-intestinal diseases and parasite infections. Dr. Hoang Thuy Nguyen[7] described the efforts made in building wells as follows:

'After making a hydro-geological study of the Red River delta and drawing on popular experience, our hygiene experts have built a model well, suitable for the region. It is 6 m deep and 0.8 m in diameter. . . Other models have been studied for other hydro-geological conditions, including a filtering well to collect water from shallow pools, which is, at any rate, better than unfiltered water drawn from ponds.'

Even with the sinking of wells, adequately built with curbs to prevent the ingress of surface water, people are urged to boil all drinking water. The construction of bath-houses raises few problems — they are built of brick, with tiled floors, and each one is furnished with an enamel bowl on a stand. They are located near to wells for easy access to water. Within a few years, over 900 000 wells and close on 750 000 bath-houses have been built by peasant communities. Similar achievements were recorded in building latrines, and by 1972, there was on average one double septic bin for every 1.4 households, as compared with one well for every 3.3 households and one bath-house for every 4.7 households[8].

The double septic bin

Of all the public health measures put into operation by the Vietnamese, the latrine known as the double septic bin has been the single most important factor in the promotion of health. The idea is simple, and the latrine is easy for every family to use. It strikes at the root cause of the gastro-intestinal infections, cholera, dysentery and the typhoids, and checks the menace of fly-borne infections. Last, but no less important, it provides fertilizer in the form of sterilized organic matter at a yearly rate of about 600 000 tons.

The full name of this latrine is 'the double septic bin for on-the-spot composting of excreta'. In some reports, it has been referred to as a 'double septic tank', but this is a mistranslation of the Vietnamese word which simply means 'receptacle' or 'container'. To call it a double tank is misleading; the two receptacles are bins for containing dry material, not tanks for containing liquid.

The latrine cubicle is reached by two or three steps, as it is built on top of the two bins, which are constructed of concrete, stone, unbaked brick, or other solid material.

The two bins then serve by turns as receptacles for defecation and for composting. Both have a squat hole in their tops with a groove to channel urine to a separate vessel (Figure 7.1), but the squat hole on the bin in which composting is taking place is firmly sealed to make the bin airtight.

The urine is directed into a pitcher, or other container with a lid and a lip for pouring, and is emptied daily for use on the gardens or fields. It appears that no special steps are taken to prevent infection from this direct use of urine as fertilizer.

The bottom of the bins, often paved, is higher than ground level so as to remain quite dry, even during the rains. Before a bin is used, its floor is covered with a layer of powdered earth, or alternatively with a layer of ashes or lime. These materials absorb moisture as well as preventing the faeces from sticking to the floor when being removed. After each defecation, the paper used for anal cleaning is put in the bin, wood ashes are sprinkled over the faeces to absorb odours, and the hole is covered with a wooden lid which is usually fitted with a long handle (Figure 7.1). Experiments show that if a weight of ashes amounting to about one third of the weight of faeces is used, all smells due to hydrogen sulphide and ammonia will be absorbed[9].

When a bin is almost full, the contents are levelled with a stick and the remaining space is filled with ashes. Openings are sealed with lime cement or clay, and the adjoining compartment goes into use for defecation. The anaerobic composting process is allowed to go on for at least two months before the contents are removed by a rear access door (which is hermetically sealed during composting).

This anaerobic (or, as some would have it, micro-aerobic) composting process has now been practised for several years in place of the aerobic process formerly used[10]. The temperature in the bin during composting is typically 2-6°C higher than the ambient temperature, but it rises to 50°C in summer when ambient temperatures are 28-32°C.

Studies of the survival of pathogens in the composting process show that those which cause typhoid and dysentery are quickly destroyed. No coliform bacteria survive after 6-7 weeks from the start of composting, though small numbers of *E. coli* may survive 4 weeks[11]. Helminth ova are killed rather more slowly, and some hatch out as larvae in the compost. After 3 weeks, the compost may contain significant numbers of *Ascaris* and *Taenia* larvae, but these subsequently die, and after 7-8 weeks, 85 per cent of the *Ascaris* originally present, and a similar percentage of the total helminth population, will have been killed either as eggs or as larvae[12]. Adding kitchen ashes to the compost promotes the killing of *Ascaris*; adding soil or green leaves is less effective. Long composting periods of at least 45 days, but preferably up to 60 days are advocated to promote the killing of helminths.

After the longer composting period it is found that 98 per cent of the organic nitrogen is converted into the inorganic form. The percentage of inorganic nitrogen (mostly ammonium nitrate) rises particularly rapidly in the latter stages of the composting process, more than doubling in the last 4 weeks of an 8-week cycle. The analysis of the compost in terms of plant nutrients at the end of the cycle is typically 1.0 per cent nitrogen, 0.5 per cent phosphorus, and 0.3 per cent potassium[13].

The dimensions of two slightly different double bins, each suitable for a family of 5-10 people, is indicated in Figures 7.1 and 7.2. The *internal* volume of a single bin in either of these latrines is about 0.17 m^3, the squat holes being about 0.7 m above ground level. The actual shape of the bins depends on the method of construction, which varies from place to place according to the materials available. The walls of the bins may be made of clay compacted inside a timber shuttering, or lime mortar or concrete cast in the same type of shuttering. The walls may also be built of sun-dried bricks, fired bricks, or concrete blocks[14]. When fired bricks are used, the roof of each bin may be formed as an arched brick vault, with the squatting plate built up in brick on top of that. Concrete squatting plates are also used, but a common form of construction is to build up the squatting plates from bamboos, with a mud/lime mix (or concrete) plastered on top and smoothed to give a flat floor. Raised foot rests and a channel to carry away the urine are shaped in the floor surface, and the completed squatting plate is waterproofed by plastering with cement. The squat hole is 12-14 cm in diameter. Figure 7.2 shows a brick-built double septic bin with concrete squatting plate, but the inset illustrates the way of

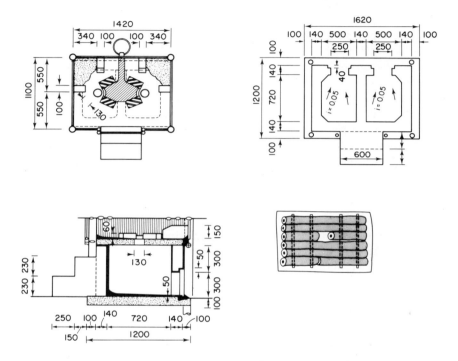

Figure 7.2 Brick-built double septic bin with concrete squatting plate. The plan at top left shows piles of ashes in two corners of the privy hut and the vessel in which urine is collected. The other two drawings show the plan and section of the bins. The section at bottom left shows te base of the walls of the privy hut, which are made of clay with lime plaster, and there are bamboo poles at the corners. The inset (bottom right) shows an alternative way of making a squatting plate from bamboo poles; the panel shown would later be plastered with mud/lime mix. (Drawings from *Ho xi hai ngan*, Hanoi 1968; all measurements are in millimetres)

making a squatting plate with bamboos. Superstructures are built of brick, compacted earth or bamboo, with ample openings for ventilation.

Implementation of septic bin programmes

Technology alone is not enough. A device of proven technical effectiveness and of obvious value in public health must be made available to the people, and must be used by them. As a Vietnamese author[15] has put it, to find an applicable formula is only a first step; 'one must also know how to get the people to accept it. Model septic bins were built to convince the peasants of their value before generalizing their use, first in pilot centres, then throughout a region, spreading like an oil stain. . . it often occurs that the backyard of one house is just in front of another house, and therefore it is necessary to consult every peasant family about the building of privies in the vicinity. Thus the large-scale construction of septic bins in rural areas has always required a patient campaign of explanation and arrangement jointly conducted by health and political workers. The good maintenance of these bins requires that the peasant overcomes his bad habits and realizes the necessity of observing the rules of hygiene. To achieve this, we carry out a series of concerted measures: regular inspection of privies by village health authorities; health education through the basic health network, at school and in evening classes, and through people's organizations; attractive prices for the farm co-ops for organic manure. . . All this means that the extremely complex problem of human faeces in our country requires a many-sided solution: social, cultural, political and even economic.'

The whole system is under the supervision of the local Community Health Centres, and in most localities, a Youth Brigade is responsible for collecting the compost and delivering it to the farms. Agricultural production has increased consistently through the use of the compost. In an area near to Hanoi, 674 tons of vegetables were produced on one piece of land in 1961 before the double septic bins were introduced. In 1965, when every family had a double bin latrine, producion had risen to 1142 tons. In Thang Loi village, Thanh Hoa province, rice yields of 4200 kg/ha were recorded when septic bin compost containing ash was used as fertilizer; the corresponding yield using similar quantities of fresh excreta was 3600 kg/ha[16]. The septic bin compost is thus very clearly the better fertilizer.

The campaign to 'build septic bins in order to increase the supply of fertilizer' has produced considerable health benefits, especially in villages which have combined it with other preventive measures against disease. Quang An village near Hanoi completed its latrine programme in 1966. In the following year, there were no cases of typhoid or polio; diarrhoea cases dropped by 85 per cent, and the incidence of worm infections fell by 50 per cent, as compared with the incidence recorded at the beginning of the latrine programme in 1962. Figures collected over a larger area show that the incidence of diarrhoeal diseases was halved between 1961 and 1965 in an area where double septic bins were being installed[17].

The double septic bin is not regarded as the ultimate solution to sanitation problems in Vietnam, but only as a means of providing family latrines in the countryside and in urban areas which lack the conditions required for the use of modern water closets. The double septic bin is not suitable for use in towns, nor in factories, schools, or hospitals, and work is in hand to develop other latrines for these situations. None of the latrines so far studied, however, is as simple or inexpensive as the double septic bin.

7.3 SCANDINAVIAN MOULDERING LATRINES AND THE BIOPOT

Krisno Nimpuno[18]

Recent Scandinavian experiences

Environmental protection laws in Norway and Sweden have forced a wide search for alternative sewage disposal techniques during the last few years, and the experience gained may be relevant to the design of latrines in developing countries.

One particular problem in Scandinavia is that of sanitation for recreational facilities in remote rural areas where soakage pits and other discharges of effluent have been banned. Mouldering latrines have developed particularly in this context, and at one time, as many as 50 commercial systems were available. Many did not work well, and at present there are fewer brands on the market. In 1975, some 22 types were tested at the Norwegian Agricultural College for the Norwegian Consumer Council. The tests studied the survival rate of various pathogens, including salmonella bacilli and the polio virus, as well as monitoring overall performance of the latrines.

The original mouldering system — Rikard Lindstrom's Multrum of 1938 — now marketed under the brand name Clivus, was not available for testing. All the other commercial systems are more or less developments of the original Multrum, or at least were initially inspired by it. The process employed consists of the aerobic decomposition of the excreta at room temperatures over a long period — sometimes as long as five years.

Excluding a small number of double vault latrines, the main commercial mouldering toilets available at the moment can be divided into two types:

(a) *Single vaults of the Multrum type*, often large and costly with big composting chambers under the floor. The composting cycle may take 3-5 years; there is no artificial heat supplied. Examples are the CLIVUS, MULTRUMMAN, and TOA-THRONE latrines, all made in Sweden, and the TOGA HYTTETOALETT from Norway. A derivative of this general type being used in the Philippines is illustrated (Figure 7.3).

(b) *Single vaults with electric heaters*; compact toilets with forced ventilation and a cycle of a few months. Examples are the BIO-LOO, the MULLBANK, and the MULL-TOA (Figure 7.4) from Sweden and the KPS MILJO-KLOSETT from Norway.

The Multrum-type systems usually also digest household wastes; inside the composting chamber, the material slides down a ramp under continuous aeration. These toilets have a large capacity, are relatively insensitive to overloading, and usually do not need mechanical ventilation to control humidity. The large sub-floor tank, and the problems of temperature control, are major disadvantages.

The compact mouldering toilets can be accommodated within a washroom or back room without any need for equipment under the floor. But because of the small size of the composting chamber, it is difficult to keep the pile sufficiently

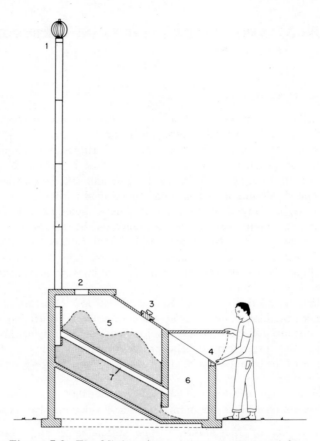

Figure 7.3 The Minimus composting toilet on trial in
Manila, Philippines. The details shown are: (1) vent
pipe, (2) squatting plate, (3) garbage hatch, (4)
fertilizer removal hatch, (5) composting chamber, (6)
fertilizer chamber, (7) air ducts. The privy
compartment at first floor level is not shown.
(Illustration by permission of Witold Rybczynski)

aerated and anaerobic conditions easily occur. The system is very sensitive to
flooding and overloading, so humidity control by forced ventilation is always an
essential part of the system. Many models have stirring devices to keep the pile
aerated, but mechanical problems are common and the systems are certainly not
yet ready for distribution and use without supervision.

Canadian trials with Scandinavian latrines

The remote areas of Northern Canada, with their isolated communities, present a
number of public health problems typical of the developing countries, though set in
an Arctic environment. Several Scandinavian sanitary products have been
introduced, including composting latrines and very small-scale sewage treatment

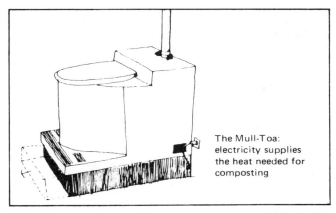

The Mull-Toa: electricity supplies the heat needed for composting

Figure 7.4 A compact, single vault composting latrine, with electricity supply, drawer access to the compost, and vent pipe (Illustration by permission of Witold Rybczynski)

plants (which have not proved to be very satisfactory). In their evaluation of the former, McKernan and Morgan[19] have indicated clearly the need for improved excreta disposal for communities in northern Manitoba by quoting figures for hospital admissions. These indicate a much higher incidence of diarrhoeal diseases in Northern areas and among communities of Canadian Indians than in the province as a whole. Hospital admissions due to bacillary dysentery are almost four times the provincial average among Indian Bands, and seven times the average elsewhere in the North. Comparable figures are recorded for enteritis and an undifferentiated group of admissions for 'diarrhoea'.

McKernan comments that, while such figures give only a crude measure, 'a fairly reasonable correlation exists' between absent or inferior sanitation and the incidence of water-borne diseases.

Where the compact mouldering toilets have been installed experimentally in this region, experience has been mixed. One weakness seems to be that the mechanical ventilation can dry out the mouldering pile and create undigested cakes. The stirring devices were often ineffective and pushed the material to the periphery of the tank where it hardened, without much aerobic action. McKernan's experiments in Northern Indian communities also revealed the effects of overloading and excess fluid accumulation in the poorly ventilated lower section of the tank. Two toilets installed in the Eskimo community of Povungnituk in 1975 had to be removed after only a few months of operation[20] due to problems with ventilation and urine overloading. This corroborates Scandinavian experience which shows that the smallest installations are very sensitive to overloading, and a toilet soon becomes inoperative when used by several beer drinkers after a Saturday night party. The larger, Clivus Multrum toilets are much more resistant to this effect, and were much more satisfactory in these trials.

A problem which has not been reported from Sweden, but which occurred in Canada concerned fly-breeding in the mouldering toilet. Although chemical sprays prove reasonably effective, it has to be noted that fly infestations can develop from the disposal of kitchen wastes and become a health hazard.

In summary, it can be said that mouldering toilets can be made to function in the remote Northern communities of Canada. Considerable advantages over water-borne systems may be noted, but the installations can only be used under constant professional supervision. The smaller type of mouldering toilet, such as the Mullbank and Mull-Toa, are not dimensioned for normal family use and are too sensitive to overloading. These systems should not be encouraged.

The Biopot

With a background which includes experience of mouldering toilets in Scandinavia and Canada, the author became involved in designing a latrine to meet urban and rural needs in Tanzania. The result was a *double vault* latrine, the Biopot[21].

The toilet cubicle is here mounted over two vaults, only one of which is in use at a time while the other is sealed by an airtight cover. The vault in operation as a latrine has a flush bowl or a drop pipe with an automatic seal, and has such dimensions that it will take 9-12 months for a family of six people to fill it.

There are two stages of biochemical treatment involved: firstly a mouldering period, when the excreta exposed to oxygen decomposes; and secondly, a composting period, which pasteurizes pathogens and completes decomposition. Finally, a chemical treatment of the effluent takes place.

As the main treatment is a composting process the additional advantage is that the bulk of the household garbage is received and treated as well. The Biopot will thus yield very concentrated and rich manure. All the organic material can be used and instead of being a costly liability, becomes a valuable commodity. The system can be applied to existing neighbourhoods and the standard can vary according to the funds available.

The Biopot is basically a dry system. Although a limited amount of water may be used for flushing, there is no need for large quantities of water to by used to transport excreta. Little dilution of the raw sewage takes place and the volume which has to be treated is therefore low. The system should be safe and cheap in operation.

In the chamber currently in use as a latrine, ample oxygen is available, which ensures rapid breakdown of the excreta in the same way as organic material in the open decomposes and changes into soil. The wastes will be broken down by micro-organisms in an aerobic process. The availability of alkaline material is important to neutralize the urine acids, and for this reason, ashes should be thrown into the vault daily.

Paper and other household wastes will supply the cellulose which serves as a fuel in the decomposition process. When the vault is closed, a further decomposition will take place and complete the process. This involves micro-organisms and will be started by filling the pit with fresh green leaves. The temperature should now rise rapidly, destroying all pathogens, and the large organic molecules will break down into simple stable compounds, including nitrates and sulphates.

After six months, the process will be complete, the vault can be opened, and the dry manure can be removed so that a new cycle can start. The manure should be a completely inoffensive, odourless, dry, black soil, rich in nitrogen and potassium.

It is essential that fluids are available in the deposited mass throughout the process so that the chemical reaction can be sustained. But it is of equal importance that excess fluids are drained away and that there is no standing water. The filter is provided to ensure that excess fluids are disposed of. It consists of several layers of cheap material which can be partly removed with the compost at the end of the cycle, when a new filter is put into its place. The upper layer of this consists of leaves and coarse sand and traps the solid particles in the fluids. The next layer consists of coarse sand and charcoal, and will trap the remaining organisms and particles. Then finally, there is a layer of crushed limestone and ashes, which will neutralize the acids. The filter rests on a perforated stone slab which is a permanent part of the construction, (Figure 7.5).

Fluids leaving the Biopot and soaking away are thus treated so as to become completely harmless and without smell. In areas with a high water table, the fluids may be collected in a tank which is emptied periodically.

7.4 THE NEED FOR RESEARCH ON COMPOSTING LATRINES

Conference Working Groups[22]

Composting and mouldering processes

Because composting latrines seem to have considerable potential, while at the same time there is a relative lack of data on their performance, the major purpose of this working group was to review some of the questions which need to be answered in future research.

To begin with, the processes taking place in these latrines are not well understood, and not everybody accepts that there is a clear distinction between 'composting' and 'mouldering'. All types of composting latrine use a moderately dry process; sullage water cannot be dealt with and urine must either be separated from faeces (as in the Vietnamese system), or drained from the bottom of the vault (as in the Biopot and the Gopuri), or evaporated away (as in many Swedish types with ventilation). Which of these methods is used is significant because urine affects the carbon/nitrogen ratio in the compost; it can produce ammonia and thereby upset the bacterial action in the compost, and it can give rise to smells.

The different types of latrine can also be classified according to the inputs other than excreta which have to be provided. Most types require the addition of vegetable matter, kitchen wastes, and/or ashes, all of which contribute carbon and so affect the carbon/nitrogen ratio. The input of oxygen is enhanced in some systems by a design which encourages up-draughts, or by mechanical stirring, or by electric fans; but in other types, especially the Vietnamese double bin, the compost

Figure 7.5 A brick-built double septic bin in Vietnam; the picture indicates the importance attached to keeping these latrines clean (photo: Medical and Scientific Aid to Vietnam)

container is sealed during the period when the compost is forming. Heat is a required input in some of the smaller systems, especially in Scandinavian or Canadian climatic conditions, whereas most types generate sufficient process heat to keep themselves going. In general, tropical climates offer better operating conditions for composting latrines, but design must take the local climate fully into account — a latrine which worked well in Sweden behaved quite differently in Quebec because of the hotter summers there.

Priorities for research

The Working Group felt that the Vietnamese double septic bin is the most promising type; it is of simple, low-cost construction, and has been a proven success in one country. However, the Multrum type also seems to have potential; low-cost versions have been produced, including a $55 'Minimus' unit in Manila, Philippines. This installation has the latrine at first-floor level, while the compost is removed from a hatch at ground level (Figure 7.3).

Only the Vietnamese double bin has been extensively used. Many thousands have been built since around 1954, and the feeling of the Working Group was that these were the only composting latrines for which there is real experience of operation, though there is not yet much information deriving from this experience available in the West. Other composting latrines have only been tried on a small scale, and little information is available on their long-term performance by ordinary users, except, perhaps in Scandinavia. There have also been experiments in North America, and the trials previously mentioned in Tanzania, Mozambique, the Philippines and a few other countries.

Among the many questions still unanswered about the Vietnamese double septic bin, there are two particularly striking points. Firstly, the precise nature of the process is uncertain; the temperature said to be generated in the composting process is higher than expected, and rises within one or two days of sealing the bin. This may be associated with a short aerobic phase, and the succeeding process may be anaerobic, but none of this is clear. Secondly, the separation of urine from faeces is a striking feature: how efficiently is this carried out in practice, and how vital is it for the composting process?

The evident success of the Vietnamese system may be linked to the fact that night soil has been used as fertilizer for centuries in that region. The way the masses of the people have been mobilised since the 1950s is also certainly a factor. The acceptability of the system to other cultural groups is unknown; it seems certain that some degree of user education would be needed to ensure efficient and hygienic use of the double bin. The Working Group felt that the whole family of composting latrines should be studied with a view to defining the following data:

1. microbiological techniques necessary for study of microbe and parasite survival;
2. chemical and biochemical parameters of the process, such as carbon/nitrogen ratio of the material going in, temperature, acidity, oxygen need, degree of conversion, detention time, need to separate urine from faeces, etc;
3. production of heat, water and gases during the process and the effects of additives such as vegetation, lime, earth, and ashes;
4. the suitability of existing designs with respect to air flow, excess moisture, and product extraction;
5. characteristics and value of the fertilizer produced;
6. social acceptability in different cultures of the following aspects of operation and use:

     a) preferred method of defecation,

     b) personal cleansing materials which enter the system,

     c) ease of access to remove end-product,

     d) handling and use of end-product.

7. technical requirements, management skills, and institutional arrangements needed for operation and maintenance;

8. feasibility of the systems in relation to:

     a) population density,

     b) climate,

     c) water table location,

     d) carbon sources;

9. criteria for selection of a composting latrine system for a particular situation;

10. effects of overloading (surge loads, e.g. when a party in the owner's house results in a tremendous input to the system) and starvation (no material input).

Research into these topics need not cover all the complexities, but should aim to find out enough for the practical design and operation of composting latrines, and to secure the optimum use of the fertilizer produced. Such research should be pursued on an interdisciplinary basis, and should involve research workers from the countries where there is experience of operating composting latrines — Vietnam, Sweden, and some African countries.

NOTES AND REFERENCES

1. Working group members: A.M. Wright (chairman), R. F. Carroll (rapporteur), G. J. Ebrahim, Richard Feachem, J. M. Kalbermatten, Nomtuse Mbere, Joan K. McMichael, Krisno Nimpuno, C. Polprasert, Witold Rybczynski.

2. E. G. Wagner and J. N. Lanoix, *Excreta Disposal for Rural Areas and Small Communities*, WHO, Geneva, 1958, p. 118.

3. Information available from Overseas Division (R. F. Carroll), Building Research Establishment, Garston, Watford WD2 7JR, England.

4. *Technical Bulletin No. 1: Composting Privy*, IVS Package Program, Ambarkhana, Sylhet, Bangladesh, c.1977.

5. Joan K. McMichael is Joint Honorary Secretary, Medical and Scientific Aid for Vietnam, 36 Wellington Street, London WC2E 7BG, England. She has based this paper partly on a chapter of her book, *Health in the Third World: Studies from Vietnam*, Spokesman Books, Russell Press, Nottingham, 1976.

6. Nguyen Van Tin, *Vietnamese Studies*, no. 25 (1970), p. 28.

7. Hoang Thuy Nguyen, *Vietnamese Studies*, no. 34 (1972), pp. 101-2.

8. *Vietnamese Studies*, no. 34 (1972), p. 102.

9. *Ho xi hai ngan*, Hanoi, 1968, pp. 10-12; this 56-page booklet on the double septic bin was translated especially for use here by the Vietnamese Embassy, London.

10. *Vietnamese Studies*, no. 34 (1972), p. 102, and no. 6 (1965), p. 145.

11. *Ho xi hai ngan*, p. 15.

12. *Ibid*, pp. 16-17.

13. *Ibid*, pp. 18-20, 40.

14. *Ibid*, pp. 20-35.
15. Hoang Thuy Nguyen, *Vietnamese Studies*, no. 34 (1972).
16. *Ho xi hai ngan*, pp. 45-6.
17. *Ibid*, pp. 47-8.
18. Krisno Nimpuno's conference paper appears in two parts, of which this is the second; for part 1, see chapter 3, Section 3.2.
19. J. M. McKernan and D. S. Morgan, *Experience with Clivus Multrum and Mull-Toa Toilets in Manitoba*, Department of Northern Affairs, Province of Manitoba, Winnipeg, August 1976.
20. Witold Rybczynski, *Solar Age*, May 1976, pp. 8-11.
21. Krisno Nimpuno, *Appropriate Technology*, 3 (4), (February 1977), p. 28.
22. This is the second part of the report whose introduction appears as Section 7.1.

8

Bucket Latrines, Vaults and Night Soil Collection

8.1 CARTAGE AND CARRYING SYSTEMS FOR THE REMOVAL OF EXCRETA

Conference Working Group[1]

Applicability of cartage systems

The removal of night soil from individual houses in urban areas using trucks, carts, or manually carried buckets, is a system which was widely used in Europe until quite recently, and which is widely practised today in many Asian countries.

The system is most applicable in dense urban situations. Simple carrying systems, in which bucket latrines or very small conservancy vaults are emptied by 'sweepers' or collectors with very basic equipment are common in the urban slums of Asia. In areas with improved types of houses, built of permanent materials, large conservancy vaults become possible, with emptying and transport largely mechanized, as may be seen in Japan, Korea, and Taiwan.

Cartage systems are particularly suitable in places where the re-use of excreta is customary. Night soil collection covering large urban areas provides enough material for the operation of large and efficient composting or biogas plants. Advanced installations of this kind are to be found in Japan and Korea.

However, if a cartage system is to work well, there are a range of conditions which must be met by complementary inputs covering water supply, drainage of sullage water, refuse disposal, and the institutional arrangements needed to achieve the necessary organization. Efficient sullage and refuse disposal are needed to ensure that the excreta disposal system is not abused or overloaded. The importance of water supply arises from the use of water in personal hygiene; efficient excreta disposal makes hygiene possible only if water is available for washing also.

Many of the key problems in operating night soil removal systems have less to do with technology than with organization. The fundamental requirement is that night soil must be removed regularly. Questions of the design of containers for excreta and vehicles for transport are relatively minor compared with the crucial social and institutional problem of ensuring that latrines are emptied regularly with the maximum hygiene precautions.

In this chapter, the hardware aspects are discussed first, though, because they provide essential background information for the account of the social and management problems which follows.

Analysis of cartage and carrying systems

Any cartage or carrying system can be modelled in terms of four main elements, of which only the first three are considered here. These four elements, also illustrated in Table 8.1, are:

(a) The defecation area — the latrine and some receptacle to hold the excreta (marked 'd' and 'v' in Figures 8.1 and 8.3).
(b) The removal of excreta to some other container, or the replacement of a full container by an empty one (marked 'rl' in the Figures).
(c) The transportation system for moving excreta to a treatment or disposal area (marked 'tr').
(d) Treatment processes (if any) and disposal or re-use.

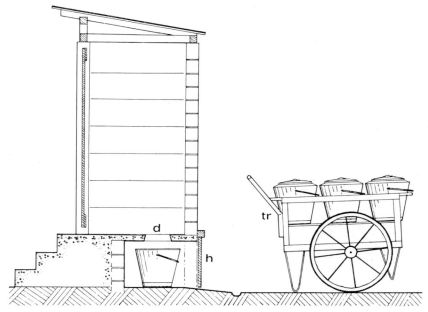

Figure 8.1 Bucket latrine with hand-cart for transport of buckets. The hand-carts and the lidded buckets are of an improved design typical of several produced in India (e.g. Ahmedabad, Department of Social Welfare; Nagpur, NEERI). The latrine, however, is not of improved design: the hatch (h) should be fly-proof and better drainage should be provided to cope with spillage

The *defecation area* consists of a latrine discharging into a bucket (Figure 8.1), or into a conservancy vault (Figures 8.2 and 8.3). In south-east Asia, latrines are usually separate from the house in a back-yard. However, indoor latrines can be linked to an external vault. In general, it is desirable for access to the vault for emptying to be from outside the householder's premises, so that night soil collectors do not have to enter the house.

The quantity of night soil to be dealt with varies significantly with diet. There

Figure 8.2 A sectional view of a latrine with a small vault, typical of many parts of East Asia. Removal of excreta is by means of a dipper with a long handle. Transport is primarily by buckets suspended from a yoke slung over the man's shoulder, but for transport from cities out to farms where the excreta are re-used, the buckets are emptied into a tank on an ox-cart or truck

are also certain variations in the quantities of other materials entering the latrine, depending on whether water or some other material is used for anal cleansing. In some places, sand or ashes are sprinkled through the squat hole to cover faeces after each defecation. However, with the Chiang Mai squatting plate used in Japan, there is a water seal between the privy and the vault, and the latrine is hand-flushed with a small volume (1 litre) of water after each use; this leads to a five-fold increase in the volume of material to be stored in the vault[2].

The size of the vault required depends on the total volume of all these materials, on whether manual or mechanical means of removal and transport are used, and on the frequency with which the vault is emptied. In Japan, vaults are cleared every two or three weeks. In rudimentary systems, a suitable frequency might be twice in every week, though extra capacity should be provided in the vault to allow for delays in service.

Removal of excreta from the bucket latrine or vault can be made by a large number of methods, including emptying buckets into other containers, exchanging buckets, using a dipper to ladle out the contents of a vault, or using a pump or vacuum truck to empty a vault. Figure 8.3 compares the use of a dipper with two mechanized techniques.

The *transportation system* for moving excreta to the treatment or disposal area may consist of men carrying buckets, men pushing hand-carts, animal-drawn or motor vehicles, vacuum trucks, or even railway vehicles which have been used in Lagos, Nigeria, and are suggested for a town in Bangladesh (Chapter 9). Hand-pushed vehicles or the carrying of buckets persists in some places because access by motor vehicles is impossible. Where large numbers of simple vehicles are used, maintenance is of key importance to ensure that leaks do not develop, leading to spillage and the possible spread of infection over a wide area. With modern vault systems, vacuum trucks are the norm. In the suburbs of Tokyo, small vacuum trucks of 1.8 m^3 capacity are used, because they can manoeuvre in congested streets more easily than large vehicles, and because they can use unstrengthened pavements for access. With vaults emptied every 2 weeks, one truck of this size can service 200 vaults.

Examples of cartage and carrying systems

In discussing some of the systems actually in use, it aids clarity to distinguish, firstly, bucket latrines and all other types which involve a portable container from, secondly, latrines with conservancy vaults. If the concept of cartage and carrying systems were stretched to the limit, it would also be necessary to consider aqua-privies and septic tanks (which require cartage after de-sludging), and cess-pools (which are effectively vaults with a very large capacity requiring infrequent emptying).

Bucket latrines can be very unhygienic because of the high probability of spillage during removal and transport. However, improved kinds do exist where there is a lid which can be firmly fitted and sealed before the bucket is moved, and there are some highly effective and advanced systems using the bucket latrine principle. Examples are:

(a) A man may carry buckets on a yoke slung over his shoulder, either replacing full buckets from the latrine by empty ones, or tipping the latrine bucket into separate carrying buckets. Where re-use is practised, as in Taiwan, there are usually separate buckets for faeces and urine. (In some places, water distribution is by vendors who carry buckets on a yoke in exactly the same way as these night-soil men.)

(b) In India, buckets with close-fitting lids have been designed, and special hand-carts which can carry six buckets at a time (Figure 8.1).

(c) The bucket latrine principle may be used with plastic bags, which may be sealed before being removed for disposal and replaced by clean ones.

(d) In Sydney, Australia, bucket latrines are used with tarred drums as containers. These are sealed for removal and transport, and replaced by clean drums.

(e) A container system operates in Sweden in the lake areas where people are prohibited from emptying sewage into lakes. The working group on communal latrines also studied the possible use of containers designed for easy removal by truck or rail.

Latrines with conservancy vaults are to be found with the following variant types:

(a) In Korea and elsewhere in east Asia, a dipper is used to empty small vaults by ladling their contents into buckets for carrying on a yoke (Figure 8.3A). This is unhygienic because of spillage, but provides much-needed employment in some cities.

(b) In the Indian sub-continent, systems similar to (a) widely exist, but vaults are less often excavated below ground level, and transport is often by bullock-drawn cart.

(c) Vaults like those in (a) may be emptied by hand-operated suction pumps fitted to tank-carrying hand-carts, animal-drawn vehicles, or small motor vehicles (Figure 8.3B).

(d) The emptying of vaults and the transport system may be completely mechanized using vacuum trucks, as is common practice in Japan, Korea, and Taiwan.

(e) Where water-seal latrines are used, a larger vault with mechanized emptying is required to deal with the larger volumes of fluid (Figure 8.3C).

Prospects for incremental improvement

It is evident from this analysis that cartage and carrying systems can be operated at various levels of sophistication, ranging from the collection of night soil on a daily basis by a man carrying buckets to the sophisticated vacuum truck systems in

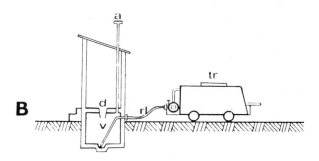

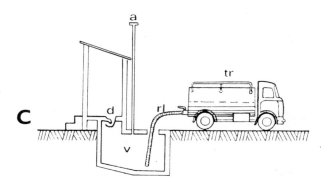

Figure 8.3 Incremental improvements made to latrines with vaults and to the cartage system serving them. The vaults are emptied (A) by a dipper, (B) by a hand-pump on a simple cart; and (C) by a vacuum truck. In each case, (d) is the defecation area, (v) the vault, (a) is the air vent, (rl) is the means of removal of excreta, and (tr) is the transport mode

Japan, some used with water-seal latrines. There is a whole host of intermediate stages, offering great scope for developing appropriate solutions applicable to specific, local situations, and equally, for introducing incremental improvements as conditions change.

A very simple bucket latrine in which the bucket must be emptied daily might first be replaced with a latrine discharging into a small vault with less frequent emptying. Then, when mechanized systems for handling the excreta can be introduced, the incremental steps represented in Figure 8.3 by changes from A to B and B to C become possible. These improvements achieve progressively better hygiene, and open up the possibility of larger vaults which need emptying less often.

Finally, to make full use of the capital investment which has been made in constructing the vault, it might be converted into an aqua-privy with a flush latrine and a low-cost, small-bore sewer pipe to carry away the effluent. There would still be a cartage element in the system, since a vacuum truck would be needed to desludge the aqua-privy, but this might need doing only once in 3-6 months.

The process of successive incremental improvements may take a very long time, and during that time there will be improvements in water supply also; this could necessitate the construction of drains or sewers to remove sullage, and these same drains might be used to take effluent from the aqua-privies, or as discharge points for night soil collection on a very local basis.

Table 8.1 is a model showing the possibilities for incremental improvement in a schematic way. Each of the arrows represents an investment, represents an improvement, and represents also its own particular set of constraints and time constants.

Starting with the simplest one, defecation, this can be behind a bush, or in a privy, or in a flush latrine. This in turn leads to the set shown in the rest of the table. Each of the processes shown can be short-circuited — the user of a privy can take his bucket and carry it directly to re-use on his own private garden. This is another factor that needs to be considered in trying to model an effective transportation system.

Cultural factors and Western influence[3]

It was objected in discussion that incremental improvement, as typified by Table 8.1, implies a linear model of development with the European and American type of excreta disposal as the ultimate goal. On this view, cartage is an intermediate solution eventually leading to full water-borne excreta removal. In fact, the prospects for incremental improvement do not inevitably lead in this direction — they could, for example, lead to the development of a progressively more efficient system for composting excreta. This could be based on a municipal composting plant, or alternatively, latrines with vaults could be converted into composting latrines so that the cartage system would transport compost rather than excreta, leading to fewer health hazards.

Table 8.1 Principal elements in cartage and carrying systems for excreta removal

---

ELEMENTS

---

1. Defecation area (and on-site storage)

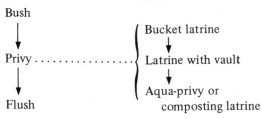

Bush
↓
Privy . . . . {
↓
Flush

Bucket latrine
↓
Latrine with vault
↓
Aqua-privy or
composting latrine

2. Removal of excreta

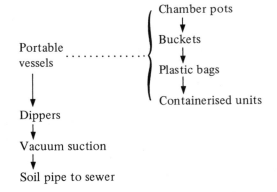

Portable . . . . {
vessels
↓
Dippers
↓
Vacuum suction
↓
Soil pipe to sewer

Chamber pots
↓
Buckets
↓
Plastic bags
↓
Containerised units

CONSTRAINTS
affecting all elements:

(a) Cultural/social
(b) Environment/climate
(c) Other services
{ water supply

refuse disposal

sullage disposal

(d) Institutions

3. Transport of excreta

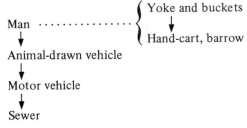

Man · · · · · · · · · · · · · · {
↓
Animal-drawn vehicle
↓
Motor vehicle
↓
Sewer

Yoke and buckets
↓
Hand-cart, barrow

4. Treatment/Disposal

Dumping
↓
Treatment
↓
Re-use

The advantage of many of the systems described here is that they can be developed in a flexible way. So long as the preference for following a Western pattern of development persists, they can be seen as stepping stones in that direction. But when perceptions change and people start wanting something different, a carrying or cartage system which has developed part of the way towards full sewerage will not have committed them. The chances are that the system will still be adaptable to the new objective, in the way that, for example, many cartage systems are adaptable to the use of composting as a method for night soil treatment.

It should be recognized that the influence of the Western model can work in two ways. Sometimes it can seem a very attractive pattern to follow, but sometimes also people may react against it and say, 'not for me', particularly if there is not much chance of getting there. There is also another ingredient in these attitudes, and that is vision. Surely, composting would be accepted in some communities if their leaders really went out and said, 'it is in our interest to use night soil to fertilize the land; the silly Europeans flush it down the drain, but we can take it and make crops grow'[4].

It is important in all this to distinguish between what people want (which is principally indoor plumbing), and what planners and administrators believe is required, for it is they who specify the objective as full sewerage. It is probably true that when Koreans and others opt for conventional sewerage, they are not necessarily saying they want underground pipes — what they want, essentially, is indoor plumbing. The average person may not know nor care how the effluent from this is transported away. So one important research need is to find ways of providing the private benefit of modern plumbing without the social costs and environmental damage associated with conventional sewerage systems.

Organization of night-soil collectors

The successful operation of a cartage or carrying system depends on a considerable social discipline among both users and collectors. Where this discipline exists, incremental improvements can be considered. Where there is no existing social discipline, or where it has broken down, the first step in any programme must be to establish a system of regular excreta collection. Once that is achieved, technical improvements can follow, and a community health programme can be introduced.

A checklist[5] of the factors which should be studied in any programme of improvement, is as follows:

(a) Examine the nature of the existing system, find out why the system exists and why alternative systems are not being used.
(b) If the improvement programme is necessary because the existing system has partly broken down, is the breakdown due to growth of population, changes in settlement patterns within the town, an inadequate number of night soil collectors, inadequate municipal organization, or other reasons?

(c) Determine who the night soil collectors are, what social group they come from, and whether they form a special interest group, e.g., will they be put out of work if a new system is introduced?

(d) Check any social customs which may affect the use of latrines; e.g. consider whether women in purdah are confined to the house and what effect this has.

(e) Consider whether methods can be devised to improve the status of night soil collectors, bearing in mind local attitudes regarding dirty jobs, ritually impure materials or actions, hygiene, night soil re-use, etc.

(f) Consider social discipline in the community, e.g. whether minor regulations are observed; also whether the municipal authorities behave consistently and observe the rules themselves, whether they stick to stated priorities, use money wisely, follow maintenance procedures correctly, etc.

(g) Consider whether the municipal authorities and the citizens are sufficiently interested to make a new system work; has there been wide consultation with users, operatives and other involved to check their willingness to co-operate?

(h) Study the relationship of the latrines to the houses, and the pattern of usage this reflects; study the access arrangements for collectors emptying the latrines.

(i) Consider whether the new system can be paid for and successfully administered in the long term.

(j) Study the scope for re-use of excreta and attitudes affecting it; e.g. in a Muslim culture, consider whether re-use would be possible at all.

One final point to stress is that unemployment is a major problem in many Asian cities. To carry night soil may not be much of a job, but at least it provides some income. Necessary improvements in hygiene should therefore not be made at the expense of throwing people out of work. Even with some mechanization, cartage and carrying systems are by nature labour-intensive. This is an important reason why they continue to be appropriate technologies in many of the places where they are still used.

8.2 THE SOCIAL ORGANIZATION OF NIGHT SOIL COLLECTION

Pieter H. Streefland[6]

The people employed

The existence of night soil collection systems such as those illustrated in Figures 8.1 and 8.2 immediately raises the question of who does this kind of work? What are their earnings? And, is collection 'organized privately or by the municipality? Enquiries reported from Taiwan and Korea suggested that there is no difficulty in recruiting night soil collectors in those countries, though their wages are well above the minimum. In Saidpur, Bangladesh, however, wages are pathetically low, and this leads to various abuses such as leaving night soil uncollected until householders offer a tip to supplement the collector's normal income.

Two years ago I studied a community of sweepers, cleaners, and night soil collectors in Karachi, Pakistan[7]. These people are Christian Punjabis, a minority group who are looked upon as second class citizens and treated accordingly by the Muslim majority. They live· an isolated, restricted life, but although they are regarded as the dregs of society, their economic position is quite strong and they cannot generally be classified as the poorest stratum. So far only a few groups in Pakistan have been willing to do the stigmatizing work of sweeping, whereas the services of the sweepers are indispensable. The result is a kind of monopoly situation that enables sweepers to earn incomes that are often quite high compared to those of other unskilled labourers.

My research, which took place in 1970-71, was concentrated on the Christian Punjabi sweepers living in the Slaughterhouse area of old Karachi. With almost 5000 inhabitants, this area is one of the larger sweeper quarters of the city. In the space of about two hectares, the Karachi Municipal Corporation has built blocks of flats for permanent employees and their families. Many houses have been built illegally between these blocks. In 1970, my census of the area showed that 80 per cent of the heads of Christian households in Slaughterhouse were engaged in one form of sweeping or another. Many other household members, both men and women, also worked as sweepers.

Sweepers who are employed by the municipality perform several kinds of duties. They include scavengers, coolies, motor coolies, *kundimen* (who maintain the sewerage system), and latrine cleaners. The work which implies contact with faeces and urine is characterized as 'wet'. The sweepers give it a much lower rating than 'dry' duties, because the sweepers' stigma derives from the wet duties.

The three categories of sweeper who have wet duties are the latrine cleaners, the motor coolies, and the *kundimen*. The former are in charge of cleaning public latrines which the Corporation has installed in several residential and market areas in Karachi. The duties of the motor coolies include taking away dirty water and urine in residential areas authorized by the municipality. The motor coolies work in teams consisting of two sweepers and a Muslim driver, and they operate a tractor/trailer combination. Finally, the *kundimen* work in areas with a conventional sewerage system, where they carry out repairs, sometimes having to enter the sewers.

Municipal sweeper-work is hierarchically organized. *Mukaddams*, often Christians or Hindus, supervise the squads and teams. Common sweepers are very dependent on their *mukaddam* as he plays an important role in the recruitment process, can make their work situation rather unpleasant, and can influence job security.

One of the tasks done by the *mukaddam* is to keep a list of absentees. Absence on a working day means loss of income for a sweeper, and dismissal if it happens frequently. However, most sweepers like to have the opportunity to be absent now and then, or to stay away from work for a couple of hours every day. The latter is more important for sweepers who want to make money via the more lucrative private sweeper-work, but who also want to keep their job with the Corporation. The *mukaddam* allows those sweepers to take some hours off before and/or after roll calls, and agrees to mark them as present for those hours. Of course, he can only do this because his superiors co-operate, and neither he nor his superiors offer this service free. At the end of each month, the sweepers have to pay for the help they have received in this way. The size of the gift they must part with varies with the help they have had, but there is a minimum charge which assures sweepers of a certain job security, and of future co-operation by the *mukaddam*.

Among the sweepers who work for the municipality, only the scavengers, by far the most numerous, use the exchange of gifts system to get time off for private work. Their working routine allows this because it is flexible. Motor coolies, latrine cleaners and *kundimen*, on the other hand, cannot neglect their work as the consequences would be an immediate nuisance in the areas affected. However, these sweepers who do 'wet' work often have other possibilities for earning extra income. Motor coolies, for example, can work overtime. Furthermore, people often tip the municipal sweepers who work in their street to make sure that the cleaning is done well and on time.

The most important work in the private sector is *khench-pot* emptying, which owes its name to the wooden boxes used in latrines in parts of Karachi. The sweeper pulls the box through a hole in the latrine wall and empties it into a basket he carries. The emptying of pits which contain fluid waste also forms part of the *khench-pot* job.

In Karachi, *khench-pot* work is organized in such a way that the customers of one sweeper are all located in the same street or streets. Among themselves, the sweepers speak of ownership of a street, based on rules that have validity within their community. The owner may do the work himself, but there are also other possibilities. It sometimes happens, for instance, that an owner employs labourers on a monthly wage, although in 1971, it was not easy to find labourers for this work as they prefer Corporation jobs, which at that time were easy to get.

Although the character of Karachi's growth is such that there is still plenty of private *khench-pot* work available, this may not continue to be so. The Corporation is taking over and improving excreta disposal in more and more areas. Another important factor in this connection is that in future the urban development of Karachi will probably be more and more planned, which may mean that sewerage facilities will be provided in new residential areas. Lastly, there is the possibility of a larger influx of migrants from among the Christians in Punjabi villages who at present work in agriculture as share-croppers and labourers. Such a development, especially if it is accompanied by rationalization of the urban sewage system, will cause increasing poverty among the Christian Punjabi sweepers.

Sweepers in Bulsar, India

From September 1971 till May 1972 my colleague Dr. L.Ch. Schenk-Sandbergen carried out research among sweepers in Bulsar, a small town in South Gujarat, India[8]. Her investigation focused on tribal people (Kuknas especially) and Untouchables (Bhangis). The tribal Kuknas try to make a living by doing part of the sweeper-work in Bulsar: sweeping the roads, scavenging, and cleaning open gutters. Night soil collection and latrine cleaning, however, is the work of the Bhangis, the lowest stratum among the Untouchables. In this way, both groups have their own sector of the cleaning work; the line between them is very strict.

If we take a closer look at the Bhangis we see that, in comparison to the Karachi sweepers discussed above, they are not only the dregs of society, but they also belong to the poorest section of society. Dr. Schenk-Sandbergen points out that the Bhangi night soil collectors in Bulsar cannot use their monopoly position as a means to improve their living conditions, because there are plenty of Bhangis, migrants from out of town, who are willing to replace them. Also, she stresses that the work available for Bhangis in Bulsar is restricted. The town is hardly expanding, and in this respect there is a big contrast with the situation in the city of Karachi, discussed above. Another important point is that the stigma of the Bhangis makes it impossible for them to find work outside their traditional domain.

In Bulsar, the work of the Bhangis is largely controlled by the municipality. Practically all toilets in the town are cleaned by municipal employees, and those Bhangis who are not working for the municipality are generally in the service of a hospital, or other public utility. The Bhangis who are employed by the municipality are 'class four' employees. There are official rules concerning their working conditions, and through the years several official committees have made recommendations for improvement of these conditions. There is, however, a big discrepancy between the rules and recommendations on the one side, and the very bad reality on the other. The Bhangis work too many hours a day, have too large a work-load, and do not receive the necessary working clothes.

Due to the manipulation of regional differences among the group by those in charge of the municipal sweeperwork, unity and solidarity among the Bhangis of Bulsar are not very strong. Also, education and the positive discrimination policy of the central government vis-a-vis the so-called Backward Classes do not form a way out for the stigmatized Bhangis.

There is a strong possibility that the situation of the night soil collectors of Bulsar will become worse in future. Already for a long time there have been plans to build an underground sewerage system in the town. The realization of these plans has met with severe difficulties: it was many years before permission was granted by the state government, sufficient financial means are lacking, and technically the work is not being done very well[9]. If the underground sewerage, or an important part of it, is completed, this will have disastrous consequences for the employment of Bhangis. In another town in South Gujarat, Surat, underground sewerage serving much of the town was completed in 1972. At first the sweepers welcomed the technological solution, because they saw it as a means of getting rid of their stigma as people who touch very impure things regularly. They quickly learned, however, that they kept their stigma, which made it almost impossible for them to find other work. For many of them it had become necessary to find alternative employment, because they lost their job after the coming of underground sewerage. The investigator observed that in Surat women often appeared to be victims of new technology because they were more often employed on a temporary basis than men, but male scavengers employed on a temporary basis were also dismissed. Young and middle-aged permanent class-four scavengers were trained to become street sweepers. The old scavengers were pensioned before their retiring age. They receive only a very small pension and besides had to leave the houses they lived in because these are reserved for permanent labourers in service of the municipality.

Night soil collection in China[10]

During a one month journey in 1974 Dr. Schenk-Sandbergen observed the ways in which various forms of waste are disposed of in Chinese cities. She was especially interested in the question of whether the position of sweepers had improved after the Revolution of 1949. On the basis of interviews and the study of the literature on China, she was able to reconstruct the situation before that time. In pre-revolutionary China, the condition of street sweepers and night soil collectors was comparable to the present situation of these groups in India[11]. In the big cities the collection of night soil was generally contracted out to private persons by the local police. These 'faecal despots', as they were often called in interviews, hired labourers to do the work, under the supervision of foremen. The night soil collectors lived in great poverty and were held in low esteem by the rest of the population.

After 1949, much was done to improve sanitary conditions in China. In Peking, for example, 'shortly after the liberation, 600 000 tons of refuse were transported from the city... Sewerage and drainage systems were constructed. Piped water became available to the majority of the inhabitants.'

In the Feng-Sheng and He Ping-Li neighbourhoods, it was possible to collect data at local level. In Feng-Sheng, the paving and the drainage for waste-water date from 1952; sewer construction started in 1972. Refuse is collected in litter boxes, each one of which is shared between about four households, and includes a separate box for waste paper. Water is obtained from pumps or taps, depending on the area, with typically one tap shared between a group of 4 to 8 families. In the new four-storey flats in He Ping-Li, there is one tap and one water closet for every two families. In alleys and side-streets there are public latrines to cater for households which are without access to a private latrine. In Peking, there are some 3600 public latrines. Many latrines are water flushed, but simpler types still exist and night soil collection is still practised.

The organization of sweepers in Peking demonstrates that sanitary work is considered a task for the whole population, not for any single group. There are three levels of organization. Firstly, there are the professional latrine cleaners and night soil collectors, numbering 5200 in Peking in 1974; 40 per cent of them are women. Secondly, there are members of street committees who do sanitary work on a part-time basis. They are mostly retired workers and housewives. Then thirdly, the whole population is mobilized in the Patriotic Health Movement. The mass of the people are actively engaged in sanitary and hygiene work. Well-known are the thorough campaigns to destroy the four pests: rats, lice, flies, and mosquitoes.[12]

NOTES AND REFERENCES

1. Members of the working group: D. C. Gunnerson (chairman), D. M. Farrar (rapporteur), James Fraser, Dong Min Kim, H. H. Leich, Duncan Mara, Ng Kin Seng, Pieter H. Streefland.
2. J. A. Hansen and Henning Therkelsen, *Alternative waste removal systems for urban areas in developing countries*, Technical University of Denmark, 1977.
3. This section is edited from points made in plenary discussion by Pieter H. Streefland, E. L. P. Hessing, DeAnne Julius, and D. C. Gunnerson.
4. Contributed by Donald Curtis.
5. Checklist drawn up by Pieter H. Streefland, with a contribution by Guy Stringer.
6. Pieter H. Streefland is from the Anthropological-Sociological Centre, South and South-east Asia Section, Keizersgracht 397, Amsterdam, Netherlands.
7. The research was made possible by a grant from the Netherlands Foundation for the Advancement of Tropical Research, The Hague, and has been published elsewhere as follows: P. H. Streefland, *The Christian Punjabi Sweepers*, Amsterdam, 1973 and Rawalpindi, 1974; and P. H. Streefland, 'The absorptive potential of the urban tertiary sector in Third World countries', *Development and Change*, 8 (3), 1977.
8. This research was also supported by the Netherlands Foundation for the Advancement of Tropical Research; see L. Ch. Schenk-Sandbergen, 'The people of Dhobi Talay', in *Modernization, Stagnation and Steady Decline*, ed. C. Baks and S. D. Pillai, Utrecht, 1976.
9. L. Ch. Schenk-Sandbergen, *Science and Technology: failing means to improve the lot of sweepers and scavengers in Bulsar*, unpublished paper, p. 16.
10. L. Ch. Schenk-Sandbergen, *Vuil Werk, Schone Teokomst?* (Clean work, dirty future?), Amsterdam, 1975. The study in China was supported by a grant from the University of Amsterdam.
11. L. Ch. Schenk-Sandbergen, *Sweepers and Night Soil Collectors in China*, unpublished paper.
12. *Ibid*, p. 6.

9

Technology to Serve the Urban Poor

9.1 SANITARY INNOVATION FOR A LOCAL SITUATION

James McL. Fraser[1] and James Howard[2]

The urgency of urban needs

The plight of the urban poor in the great cities of the developing world demands urgent and unconventional solutions in terms of housing, water supply, excreta disposal, and other services. One crucial aspect is how to provide sanitation for people who do not have proper houses to live in, and for whom a household latrine is therefore inconceivable.

Engineering design and research relevant to the problem have hardly begun, and this chapter therefore moves away from the accepted and widely used technologies discussed so far, to deal with novel and unorthodox techniques, some of which only exist as proposals in engineers' reports. These techniques fall into two groups. Some, already in use in Calcutta and in camps around Dacca in Bangladesh, use the aqua-privy or septic tank principle in very unusual forms. The others are based on the cartage principle, involving a railway in one case and special containerized units in another.

Our starting point for this discussion is Saidpur, a town of over 100 000 people in the north of Bangladesh. The only significant industry is railway engineering, and the local situation includes many features which are specific to a railway centre. The town has also borne its share of recent happenings in Bangladesh, which have included a war.

A survey which the authors carried out in January and May, 1977, highlighted the sanitary problems that exist. The town has no underground drainage system and has no likelihood of installing one. It has only the remnants of a night soil collection system by means of which less than 5 tons of excreta are satisfactorily dealt with each day. As the daily production of excreta has been estimated to be around 50 tons, the result is that over 40 tons of excreta per day are dumped in open ditches or drains or are consumed by pigs, dogs, and rats—or are just left to dry out and become the dust that is blown and trodden around the town.

Many individuals and families within the town have no proper houses, or are homeless people—'pavement dwellers'. Their sanitary needs must be met by public latrines. There are tens of thousands of such people in the larger cities of Asia, and there exists an urgent need for suitable public latrines to be designed, installed and maintained at a high standard in such situations: yet the essential need for information and knowledge on this subject has somehow been ignored. Is it possible that these needs are too basic to attract the attention they deserve from engineers, planners, and builders?

One positive element in the situation at Saidpur is that a supply of piped water is currently being installed. Another is that some sanitary needs are effectively dealt with by the Bangladesh Railway. The core of the town is built on land owned by the railway, and this area is served by 'railway drains' which are cleaned and maintained by railway personnel. The collection and disposal of refuse and excreta from the railway area is also efficiently dealt with.

Outline recommendations for Saidpur

Early in their study, the authors reached the conclusion that the immediate needs were so pressing in their urgency that short-term, practical relief was needed immediately, and it would be wrong to wait for sophisticated remedies, however excellent, if they could not be put into operation quickly. This is not to ignore the need for a long-term solution. But what is required is short-term relief measures that can be converted year by year, or area by area, into a more sophisticated system, as and when circumstances allow. Thus our proposals are basically as follows:

- (a) construct public lavatories at selected points throughout the town;
- (b) institute a proper system for the collection, removal, and disposal of excreta, covering the whole town;
- (c) continue to use the existing open drains for the conveyance of sullage;
- (d) institute a proper refuse disposal system;
- (e) improve the existing means by which storm water is conducted away from the built-up part of the town.

Many of the public latrines which the people use are in a ruinous and disgusting state. The fact that the latrines are actually used is indicative of the sense of propriety the people have for excreting in a place set aside for the purpose. The public lavatories whose construction is recommended would be places where people could attend to all their bodily needs in comfort, cleanliness and dignity. In the author's view, these people would not have to be persuaded to use the lavatories—they would welcome the opportunity to do so.

There are a large number of men at present employed on night soil collection under quite disgusting conditions. What is proposed is that these men—or others taking their place—be given a degree of authority and good remuneration. Measures would be taken to improve their morale and equip them to do a better job. They could, for example, be given a distinctive uniform, and efficient light-weight carts. with appropriate brushes and shovels. This would also apply to refuse collectors. Lavatory attendants would be treated in a similar way, and all manual employees would be given special instruction regarding their duties; they would have ready access to washing facilities where they could clean themselves before returning to their homes after the day's work.

Public lavatories would be conveniently situated in selected centres of population; there might be twenty or more. There would be separate facilities for men and women, each with a male or female attendant whose duty it would be to keep the lavatory clean, and to prevent any misuse. If there were thought to be a need for it, certain of the lavatories could provide facilities for the washing of clothes, and even for the washing of the person in privacy. Used water from the washing places would join the nearest sullage drain. The superstructure of the lavatories would be of brick, tiled or plastered on the inside, so that it could be washed down.

Every public latrine and almost every house in the town has been built to allow for removal of night soil by a cartage system. But this system has fallen into disrepute for a variety of reasons: obstructed access to cleaning doors, general dereliction of fittings, unsuitable receptacles, and clearance irregular or too infrequent. In the proposed relief measures, a 'regulation' receptacle would be introduced, repairs would be made to cleaning doors and vaults, and the cleaning arrangements would be re-organized to ensure regularity. With regard to sullage, the existing open drains would continue in use. Provided that excreta and other foreign matter are excluded, the drains will operate satisfactorily. The flow in them, when it is not obstructed, is sufficiently good; the drains are, for the most part, capable of being swept out, and if experience should show the need for the capacity of the drains to be increased, this could be effected by raising the banks. At certain seasons, flushes of clean water would be released into the heads of the principal drains to quicken the flow.

Some of the benefits that would accrue from removing the excreta and improving the drains would be lost if there were not a corresponding improvement in the service relating to refuse, which is composed, for the most part, of vegetable matter, but among it are plastics, rags, paper, broken pots, and the sweepings of road and market. An adequate system of refuse removal is therefore an integral part of the authors' proposals.

Conveyance of wastes to the place of disposal

The recommendations which have been made in relation to excreta and refuse assume that an effective means of conveyance can be devised. Provided the excreta and refuse are removed hygienically, each in its own vehicle or container, the specific type of conveyance is not important. It seems, however, that conveyance by rail has more advantages and fewer disadvantages than any other method, and it is on the use of rail transport that the proposals have been based.

The use of motorized road vehicles for this purpose cannot be considered at present, because all vehicles and spares must be imported and the town has no motor repair workshops or garage facilities. However, running through the centre of the town is a metre-gauge railway track which is not in use, and which connects with the site which is currently used for dumping excreta and refuse. If this track were rehabilitated and if a suitable locomotive and rolling stock were made available, there would exist a ready-made means of conveyance that would satisfy the needs of the scheme. There is probably no town in Bangladesh where railway technology is so well developed or where such excellent facilities for operation and maintenance exist as at Saidpur and neighbouring Parbatipur. However, it is worth pointing out that other towns with urgent sanitary problems, including Calcutta, are criss-crossed with railway tracks, and similar solutions could be adopted.

In Saidpur, at selected points along the railway, loop lines would be introduced which would serve as parking and loading places. The excreta and refuse would be brought to these loading points in proper sanitary wheelbarrows, buffalo carts, bullock carts, or whatever was appropriate having regard to the distance and the weight of material to be carried. At the loading points, the excreta would be transferred into railway tank cars and the refuse into open wagons.

Public latrines at first floor level could be discharged directly into tank cars alongside (Figure 9.1). The lower floor of such buildings could be used to provide laundry facilities, showers and wash-rooms.

Periodically, the train of tank cars and refuse wagons would be hauled to the disposal area and emptied. This might be done in either of two ways. The two discharge areas could be separate (as they are at present) or, if it were socially acceptable, the excreta could be mixed with the refuse and a compost produced for agricultural use. Whatever approach were adopted, however, waste disposal would have to be done in a more orderly way than at present. For example, the dumping could be into a bunded area with a capacity of about 30 days' production. This alone would be an improvement on the present practice of widespread, seemingly arbitrary dumping in several places at a time. Secondly, the pigs which at present wallow in the excreta, and which are responsible for spreading it around, would not be allowed to do so.

The institution of a proper night soil collection and removal system should be thought of as representing only the first step towards a more advanced system of community sanitation. The conversion could be carried out in stages, extending, if need be, over a number of years. One of the first advances that could be made might be the introduction of suction cleaning of the receptacles, whereby the collecting vehicle is equipped with a tank and a small suction pump. A hose from the pump is put into the receptacle, and by this means, the excreta are transferred to the tank (Figure 8.3B). Thus starting with a rescue operation on the existing night soil collection system, a steady but gradual improvement in conditions throughout the town could be effected.

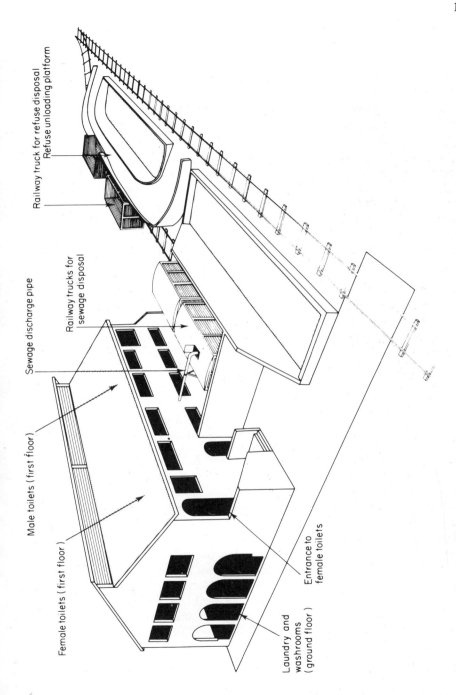

Railway truck for refuse disposal
Refuse unloading platform

Sewage discharge pipe

Railway trucks for sewage disposal

Male toilets (first floor)

Female toilets (first floor)

Entrance to female toilets

Laundry and washrooms (ground floor)

Figure 9.1 Proposed public latrine facility for Saidpur, Bangladesh. The latrines are on the upstairs floor, and sewage is removed by means of the metre-gauge railway. The ground floor houses laundry and ablution facilities

9.2 SANITATION FOR THE POOR IN CALCUTTA

M.S. Maitra[3]

Demography and administration

Calcutta has acquired an international reputation as a city of contradiction, confusion and chaos. But massive programmes, currently under way, are quickly altering the situation.

For years, civic improvement and development were hampered by lack of finance, and by division of responsibility between Calcutta City and some 35 separate municipalities, as well as smaller units on its fringes. However, in 1971, at the insistence of the Government of India, a large programme of development was agreed, finance was made available, and the Calcutta Metropolitan Development Authority (C.M.D.A.) was set up to administer it.

The C.M.D.A. was given a massive mandate to implement a wide range of linked developments, with budgets for a four-year period as follows:

(a)	Water Supply	..	285.7 million Rupees	
(b)	Sewerage & Drainage	..	289.6	..	..
(c)	Traffic & Transportation	..	438.6	..	..
(d)	Housing & New Area Development	..	100.0	..	..
(e)	Bustee Improvement	..	259.0	..	..
(f)	Garbage Disposal	..	26.0	..	..
(g)	Community Services including Primary Schools and Health Units	..	166.2	..	..

1565.1 million Rupees
(174 million U.S. dollars)

This represents a ten-fold increase in investment and effort. Organizing so greatly accelerated a programme was not easy. The C.M.D.A. gained the co-operation of various agencies of the Central and State Government and of numerous local oganizations, especially the Corporation of Calcutta and all the municipal bodies within the Metropolitan District. Many of these agencies played a part in implementing programmes while C.M.D.A. took on the role of overall management-formulating, co-ordinating and funding projects.

To understand the complexity of the sanitation and water supply works being undertaken, it is necessary to appreciate the Metropolitan Calcutta is a linear conurbation stretching for 80 km along the banks of the River Hooghly. This pattern was dictated partly by the importance of the river for transport during earlier stages in urban development. Of greater significance, though, is the fact that the best land for building is immediately alongside the river, where large quantities of alluvial silt form a natural levee of high land.

The slope of the land is, in fact, away from the river, and within about 3 km from either bank, the level falls considerably and ends up in low-lying marshes and swamps. This has limited the overall width of the conurbation.

The Calcutta Metropolitan District of today encompasses an area of 1425 km^2 with 8.3 million people recorded in the 1971 census. Of this, Calcutta city itself accounts for only 104 km^2 with a population of little over 3 millions; it is the most densely populated part of the Metropolitan District, but its population growth rate is less than 1 per cent per year. In contrast, the population of all the municipalities and smaller units taken together increased from 3.8 millions in 1961 to 5.2 millions in 1971, accounting for almost all the population growth experienced by Metropolitan Calcutta.

Existing sanitation

The topography of Calcutta has in a large way contributed to its problems for both sewerage and drainage. The highest point is only 10 metres above sea level; this limits the distance of gravity flow and involves substantial pumping of both sewage and storm water. The land slopes away from the River Hooghly on both banks and affords little scope for natural drainage. In fact, drainage depends on canals criss-crossing the landscape on both banks of the river—on the west bank three principal channels drain into the River Hooghly and on the East Bank drainage from the City of Calcutta and adjoining areas north of it is collected into three main canals discharging into the River Kulti. These systems, conceived and executed a century ago, were intended to serve a quarter of the present population, and apart from being grossly inadequate in capacity have suffered from heavy silting and large-scale squatting on the banks or even beds of the open channels.

Metropolitan Calcutta presents a dismal picture with regard to sanitation and public health. The drainage facilities are grossly inadequate, particularly in the City, where they are combined with the sewerage system. The result is that during the four-month monsoon period (July-October), the sewerage system often becomes overloaded with storm water, and sewage overflows into streets and buildings. Conditions outside the city are even worse—the contents of more than 200 000 open latrines float around openly in the streets, entering buildings and bathing places. The effect of this on the 20 000 shallow tubewells can well be imagined. There is a sharp rise in the incidence of cholera and other gastro-intestinal diseases during the monsoon months within a large section of the population. Besides the effects on sanitation and health, the flooding in Metropolitan Calcutta during the monsoon months also disrupts normal life, and caused the suspension of traffic movements in the affected areas.

The public water supply in Metropolitan Calcutta is characterized by its extremely uneven distribution. Over 2 million people are without any public supply of piped water, and have to rely on tubewells with hand-pumps, or ponds, tanks, and other questionable sources. For another 3 million people, the average level of supply of piped water is only 60 litres per capita daily.

Excreta disposal methods in Metropolitan Calcutta vary according to the district. In the rural fringes and non-municipal rural areas, one finds:

(a) absence of any facilities leading to use of open fields, water courses, etc.

(b) pit latrines; often simply a hole with an improvised platform on top; sometimes a lined pit with a proper squatting pan.

In the densely settled municipal and city areas, excreta disposal techniques comprise:

(a) service latrines, with earthenware containers supposedly emptied regularly on the bucket latrine principle.
(b) aqua-privies (and some septic tanks), all referred to simply as 'septic tanks'. Effluent from these discharges into surface drains.
(c) conventional sewerage exists within the city area and in four municipalities.

In terms of population, only 26 per cent of Calcutta Metropolitan District has conventional sewerage as compared with 68 per cent in Greater Bombay and 60 per cent in the Delhi conurbation.

Socio-economic background

These inadequate sanitation services need to be seen against the background of employment and urban poverty in Calcutta. In 1971, 2.6 million jobs were available, of which a large proportion were in the jute and engineering industries. Both industries have suffered a severe recession since then, and at the same time, the port of Calcutta has been dealing with less traffic than in the mid-1960s. Thus while population has been steadily rising, employment opportunities have been static, with the loss of industrial employment counter-balanced by some increase in 'informal' employment-petty manufacturing and street hawking.

There is little reliable data on incomes, but estimates indicate that average monthly earnings for two-thirds of the population were below Rs. 350/- or $40 per month in 1971, which represents the barest subsistence level for a family of five at the prices then obtaining. In the *bustees* or slums, average earnings for 97 per cent of families are below Rs. 300/- ($34) per month.

In the refugee settlements which have remained in Calcutta since the liberation of Bangladesh in 1971, earnings are higher than in the bustees, because of a significant number of factory and clerical workers. At the bottom of the income scale, however, are the pavement dwellers, who may number 100 000. A survey has shown that 22 per cent of these live by begging, and 63 per cent of the rest work as day labourers, hand-cart pullers, rickshaw-pullers or hawkers.

These, then, are the urban poor in Calcutta Metropolitan District who comprise 4 million people living in the following types of habitat:

(a) Bustees or slums where housing is within hut structures made of mud walls and tile roofs: 2.5 millions
(b) Refugees from erstwhile East Pakistan: 0.65 millions
(c) Settlements not classed as 'bustees' but consisting of congested, dilapidated buildings with shared facilities: 0.75 millions
(d) Pavement dwellers: 0.10 millions

It is evident that the 'bustees' constitute the largest group of urban poor. A 'bustee' is defined by law as 'an area of land occupied by ... any collection of huts', and in this context, a hut is 'any building no substantial part of which ... is constructed of masonry, reinforced concrete, steel, iron, or other metal'.

Bustees occupying a certain area of land are registered and have unique conditions of tenure and taxation, (though many smaller bustees are unregistered). One of the main characteristics of the registered bustee is its three-tiered system of land ownership, hut ownership, and tenancy. The landlords own only the land while the structure is owned by the middleman known as 'Thika tenant' who rents the dwelling unit to its occupants. The Thika tenant uses a part of the rent he collects to compensate the landlord. Most of the Thika tenants live in bustees—they do not form an affluent group. In fact, the rent they collect from one or more huts they own is, for a large percentage of Thika tenants, the main or only source of income. These Thika tenants form an interest group who oppose slum clearance schemes as these will deprive them of their steady income, but who may support environmental improvements within the existing bustees.

Programmes currently under way

Efforts to improve the situation in Calcutta have a long history, and include most notably an overall Basic Development Plan covering 20 years from 1966 and a 'Master Plan for Water Supply, Sewerage & Drainage' drawn up by WHO consultants and also dating from 1966. But until the formation of the C.M.D.A. in 1971, the institutional framework and financial resources needed to implement such plans were lacking. Now, however, programmes are under way in several of the main categories listed at the beginning of this paper, namely, water supply, sewerage, traffic and bustee improvement.

Action to rebuild or improve existing housing is outside the scope of the bustee improvement programme whose main emphasis, is on sanitary conditions. The programme aims to provide the following facilities:

(a) Conversion of existing service latrines to sanitary latrines working on the aqua-privy principle in unsewered areas, or connected to sewers where available, on the basis of one latrine for each hutment, or for every 25 persons.
(b) Water supply at 90 litres per capita daily through water taps—one for each hutment or every 100 persons
(c) Surface drainage facilities through underground conduits connected to the underground sewer system where available, or open surface drains.
(d) Paving of roads, streets and pathways and street lighting.
(e) Garbage vats, dustbins etc., at suitable locations.

The cost of providing these facilities was originally assumed as Rs.100/- ($11) per capita at pre-1970 prices. The programme was launched by C.M.D.A. in 1971 with an initial coverage of 1 million bustee dwellers at an anticipated cost of Rs.100 million. A physical survey of the bustees was carried out to prepare engineering plans and estimates for execution. The physical survey and schemes prepared on that basis revealed that the original assessment should be raised to Rs.120/- ($14) per capita. The first phase of the programme was completed by 1975 with a total coverage of 1.15 million bustee dwellers at a cost of about Rs.135 million. The second phase of the programme with a population coverage of about 650 000 bustee dwellers, now under way, is estimated to cost about Rs. 177/- ($20) per capita, reflecting inflation.

It is mainly due to the simplicity of the technology adopted for implementation of the programme that it was possible to achieve the targets, in spite of extremely difficult working conditions inside the bustees and their scattered nature. For instance, the latrines comprising the most important component of the improvement programme are simple structures, but location of each has had to be decided in consultation with the potential users living in the huts. Even a free space just big enough to locate the sanitary latrine is not available on most of the occasions, and the sanitary latrine has to be set up at the very spot where the service privy stood, involving removal of all the filth. Alternative location of group latrines at the fringes of the bustees would have simplified installation but this was not favoured, as it would have left the general upkeep and cleanliness of the latrines to a much larger group of families and thus make it uncertain. Sanitary latrines assigned to a small group of families living in one hutment or a quadrangle, have been kept reasonably clean and this shows the attitude of the users towards them.

In the bustees, the provision of sanitary privies is a wholly subsidized facility, mainly because of the users' inability to pay, but also partly because of the communal nature of the latrines. This free-of-cost arrangement, however, could not be extended to people outside the bustees, particularly those living in individual houses for whom an individual latrine is appropriate. As an incentive to these families, C.M.D.A. decided to grant a subsidy equivalent to 75 per cent of the total cost. Thus it is hoped to extend the use of sanitary latrines into all areas where existing facilities are leading to pollution of the environment.

Design of aqua-privy type of latrine

The design evolved by C.M.D.A. for sanitary latrines includes a septic tank in most instances where no connection can be made with a sewer, and is based on the use of prefabricated components. Such a latrine is an aqua-privy in the terminology of this book, though in India this term is sometimes used to denote a simpler type of latrine with a soakway pit, and the term 'septic tank' is preferred. In this instance, the tank is built up from eight standard reinforced concrete panels, 50 mm thick (Figure 9.2); it is roofed by three further panels of the same thickness, one of which has an opening to take the 450 mm long squatting pan. The superstructure is erected on top of that, using 38 mm thick concrete panels. A water seal is provided by means of a 100 mm diameter S-pipe.

All these components are manufactured at a production centre and transported to the respective sites to be put up by gangs of erectors. The erection involves minor on-site works like excavation of pits, preparation of beds, grouting of joints,

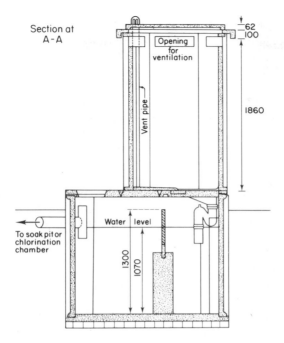

Section at
A-A

Opening
for
ventilation

Vent pipe

62
100

1860

Water level

To soak pit or
chlorination
chamber

1300
1070

Plan at floor level

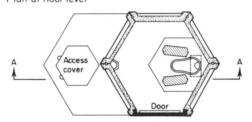

A

Access
cover

A

Door

Figure 9.2   Aqua-privy constructed from
prefabricated reinforced concrete panels. Over
30 000 of these have been installed in the
bustee areas of Calcutta (dimensions in
millimetres)

construction of the chlorination chamber, provision of a lead pipe up to the
discharge point, and so on. The erection time is usually three days, and the latrine is
commissioned within seven days, after testing the tank for leaks.

This design is preferred to the conventional one in masonry because of its
amenability to mass-production techniques, its low cost, and its quickness in
erection. There is also better control of the usage of materials, with much pilfering
and waste avoided. The current cost of this aqua-privy type of latrine with a
chlorination chamber is about Rs. 1900/- ($220) per unit, including the cost of
transport and erection. The C.M.D.A. now has more than a dozen production
centres for fabricating the components, which together have a capacity to make

about 10 000 complete latrines per year, most of which are used in the bustees. To date, about 30 000 latrines have been installed in the bustees.

An alternative aqua-privy design has also been evolved which has a tank consisting of a 1.225 m diameter reinforced concrete pipe, 2 m long, placed horizontally on the ground. This has the advantage of not needing grouting of joints on site, so it can be erected with less technical supervision. This design may not be suitable for the bustees because of the difficulty of manouvering the large-diameter pipe down lanes and alleys. It is more likely to suit those who pay 25 per cent of the cost for their own individual family latrine. It is marginally cheaper than the type built up from concrete panels. However, even with the 75 per cent subsidy, a householder must pay Rs. 450/- ($52) to get one of these latrines installed on his premises, and this is beyond the means of many people. It has therefore been suggested that the latrines might be provided without superstructures, leaving the householder to build this himself. Then the tank with squatting pan could probably be provided for a contribution from the householder as low as Rs. 240/- ($28).

These subsidized latrines are being made available to people living in the 630 refugee colonies in Metropolitan Calcutta, where other improvements include the provision of a piped water supply, with one tap for every ten households, the construction of open, masonry drains for surface water, and the filling in of insanitary ditches.

Evaluation of achievements

Providing sanitation for the urban poor is not an end in itself. It is a means to an end. Enrichment of human dignity, improvements in health, greater productivity, and changes in attitude should be the yardsticks by which the real usefulness of the programme can be judged. In the absence of a baseline survey, a correct assessment of the effectiveness of the programme is not possible. However, it can be mentioned that there has been a distinct decline in the incidence of cholera in those bustees benefiting from the environmental improvement programme. There is a growing awareness of hygiene among the inhabitants of the improved bustees, which is reflected in their efforts to secure the proper use and cleanliness of latrines, water points, and bathing platforms. The improvement in the environmental conditions can be noticed even during a casual visit, and the sense of relief among residents is very evident.

In terms of physical achievements, nearly 1.5 million people in the bustees of Metropolitan Calcutta have been covered so far by the environmental improvement programme, and under the refugee colonies' programme, works have been taken up only recently covering a first batch of about 7800 homestead plots or holdings. Schemes for the next batch will commence soon after authorization of funds is communicated by the Central Government. The enthusiasm among the refugee families over this scheme is clearly visible.

A very important question which still remains unresolved is the maintenance and upkeep of the improved facilities in the bustee and refugee colonies. While it is the function of the Corporation in Calcutta City, and of the Municipal and other local bodies outside the city, to look after these civic facilities, legal and financial questions have come in the way of involving these institutions in this task. The performance of the municipal authorities towards maintenance of public utilities has been on the decline for quite some time, mainly because of the very old fiscal-administrative structure. In fact, many of the development projects undertaken by the C.M.D.A. were necessitated by long accumulated maintenance deficits. While other steps are under consideration by the Government, the maintenance functions of improved bustees have devolved on the C.M.D.A.

There has been encouraging participation by the bustee dwellers in these programmes, and a good deal of interactions with them during the initial stages of surveys. The local youth clubs co-operated with C.M.D.A. officials on the location of the various facilities and in securing the co-operation and consent of the hutment dwellers and owners. The engineering staff were assisted by a small group of social workers recruited by C.M.D.A. to establish contact and interaction with local voluntary organizations in the bustees. The social workers also dealt with facilities like schools and health units covered by other sectors of the C.M.D.A. development programme. Contribution of physical labour as a measure of direct participation of the bustee dwellers, is not truly applicable. Most of the bustee people have to earn their living and have to depend on variety of jobs in the port, or factories, and many are self-employed. The type of work and the scale of operations in the bustees under the improvement programme were not conducive to an organized contribution of voluntary labour. A few of those who possessed skills as masons, carpenters, plumbers, or electricians, did participate in the programme, but as paid workers.

Conclusions

(a) For the given situation in Metropolitan Calcutta, the development perspective should envisage a number of goals: rescue and resuscitation in the first stage; consolidation in the second stage; and rehabilitation, revival and resurgence in the third stage.

(b) In Metropolitan Calcutta, with nearly two-thirds of the population below the subsistence level, and nearly 4 million people living in poorly serviced settlements, a 'sanitization objective' appears to be the most relevant for the first stage of development.

(c) In a development project addressed to a metropolitan situation like that of Calcutta a large welfare-oriented component is inescapable. Yet a purely welfare approach without active involvement of the community is likely to degenerate into a donor-receiver relationship which subdues community efforts and self-help, even in regard to upkeep and maintenance of simple installations.

(d) Contradictions are unavoidable in the employment of high-cost technology for basic infrastructure services—water-supply, sewerage, drainage and transportation, on a metropolitan scale. To serve the urban populace, the majority of whom are unable to pay for services, low-cost sanitation programmes and high-cost trunk facilities programme have to run concurrently.

(e) It has to be recognized that intermediate technology offering low-cost solutions may not be the end in itself but may serve as a 'holding action' during the period of transition.

(f) Improved and sanitized low-cost settlements are likely to attract migrants from adjoining States and Districts, thus tending to nullify the efforts and to proliferate the sub-marginal settlements. Calcutta is an 'oasis' in the desert of poverty extending over the entire eastern region, and this is unavoidable. But it can be contained within the desired level by matching efforts for development of rural areas in the adjoining districts.

(g) Benefits accruing through different programmes at the conclusion of each stage of development are to be evaluated against targets set in terms of inputs, population coverage and goals. Mere statement of outputs in statistical terms like lengths of water supply mains, or number of water treatment and sewage treatment plants built, is of little relevance so long as these facilities are not linked up with the households and the community.

(h) Operation, maintenance and management of installations and assets created under different programmes are generally overlooked, and tend to receive less attention in the zeal and enthusiasm associated with a massive multi-sectoral development efforts in a metropolitan area. These functions are crucial for maximization of benefits and should form an integral part of the programmes launched.

(i) Institution building to match and sustain such massive developmental efforts is a highly complex function. This is essentially a political process; it is time-consuming and may be subject to disabling compromises.

(j) Metropolitan development of the nature attempted for Calcutta does not simply amount to delivery of an assortment of public works; the 'hardware' content must be suitably supported by the 'software' component, including the delivery of social services, to make the programme really meaningful and viable. The timing, content, modality, mechanisms and institutionalities of delivery of 'software' components are of crucial importance—the complementary role of voluntary welfare organisations is of far-reaching significance.

9.3 TECHNOLOGY FOR COMMUNAL LATRINES

Conference Working Group[4]

A latrine to serve 1000 people

A perspective on the range of excreta disposal technologies needed by the urban poor in the major cities of developing countries can be obtained by viewing the material presented in the previous section from a somewhat different angle. Calcutta has unique problems associated with its great size, its location on low-lying, poorly drained land, and its unusual history, but the three main categories of people who comprise its urban poor are to be found in many other cities—they are the slum-dwellers, the pavement dwellers, and the refugees and squatters.

In Calcutta, slum dwellers are catered for by the mass produced aqua-privy already described (Figure 9.2), each one of which serves a group of 20-30 people living in a single 'hutment', that is, a group of shelters facing a small courtyard. These groups tend to function almost as an extended family, and take good care of any shared facility.

In slums where there is no convenient social unit such as this, and which are too congested for building large numbers of individual family latrines, there may be no choice but to provide a communal or public latrine. Experience in Bangladesh indicates that people living in these conditions are prepared to walk 100 m to use a latrine. Taking this as a maximum, and assuming a population density of 300 persons per hectare, it would be necessary for a communal latrine to serve 1000 people, and this can be taken as a design specification to aim at.

It is envisaged that a communal latrine of this type would often be the best solution for colonies of squatters or refugees as well as for old-established slums, and if pavement dwellers are to be adequately served, there is clearly no option but to provide public latrines.

There has been very little research or design work done on communal latrines serving the urban poor in unsewered areas. One existing system with the necessary capacity is described in the final part of this chapter (Section 9.4). It is a sanitation unit designed to provide facilities very rapidly after a refugee camp has been set up in an emergency; it is not suitable for longer term use than about two years' service, however.

A second approach discussed in this chapter is to provide public latrines at first floor level, with laundry and ablution facilities on the floor below. The upper floor latrines can then discharge directly into the vehicles used for transporting the sewage to a disposal area, in this instance, by railway (Figure 9.1).

A third approach was adopted in Ibadan, Nigeria, when consulting engineers for a sewerage master plan encountered a crowded area with no sanitation and no space for any of the conventional solutions. As described in Chapter 5, communal aqua-privies linked to showers and laundry facilities were provided, each unit serving a large compound of houses.

A fourth possibility, developed in the present study, is to revert to the idea of constructing latrines at first floor level, on a raised platform, which users would approach via steps. The receptacle for the excreta would then rest on the ground underneath the latrines, and not in an excavation. This was suggested with the high groundwater levels of Calcutta in mind, and also because the raised latrine offers the possibility of moving the excreta receptacle out at regular intervals; the receptacle could, indeed, be a standard ISO container, and the whole job of removing the excreta could be mechanized.

It was considered that a communal latrine of this kind should have 40 squatting plates, on the assumption that each one will be used 10 times per hour during the peak period of around two hours. With 1000 people using the latrine daily, each producing 2 litres of excrement, 2 tons of sewage would be produced each day. Assuming that the maximum load that can be carried by a container vehicle is 18 tons, this output of sewage would necessitate the replacement of full containers by empty ones at weekly intervals. Full containers would be moved to the municipal cleansing area and treatment works by a suitable adapted articulated truck, or by rail where facilities are available.

Where the local water table permits, the containers could be designed for the overflow of effluent water in such a way that they would function as mobile septic tanks. This would reduce the number of service visits required. A system of this kind would be most approriate in squatter settlements on the fringes of a city, where it would be possible to arrange good road access, though the penetration of railway tracks into crowded urban areas might extend its applicability if these were used.

Other options are, of course, possible where space is available and groundwater conditions allow. The latrine could simply discharge into a conventional septic tank. Alternatively, on-site treatment could be provided using oxidation ditches. However, the working group regard the concept of container technology as an important area for research. Several different kinds of container could be investigated, including:

(a) metal tanks,
(b) enclosed skips raised onto the vehicle by hydraulic gear,
(c) flexible tanks attached to the back of flat lorries,
(d) large tyre-like containers.

Costs and comparisons

The capital cost of the latrine suggested would be about $14 000. Spreading this cost over a 14-year operating period, and ignoring any interest payable, this sum is equivalent to $1.00 per person per year. The cost of maintenance, plus labour, and vehicles to transport the sewage out of the city was estimated at $3500 per year. Thus the total per capita cost will be $4.50 (or Rs. 41/-) per year. For the sake of comparison, the following calculations were made for other types of latrine:

(a) For a 1000-person unit attached to the main sewerage system—$0.91 (or Rs. 8/-) per person per year.
(b) For a 1000-person unit working on the septic tank principle requiring sludge removal only—$1.12 (or Rs. 10/-) per person per year.
(c) For an aqua-privy of the kind used in Calcutta, serving 30 people and desludged every six months, total costs calculated on the same basis as the above: $0.90 (or Rs. 8/-) per person per year.

Although the purpose of this report is mainly to emphasize the need for unconventional approaches to sanitation technology, it is recognized that none of the systems discussed can work without attention to a wide range of social factors. These include privacy for latrine users, separation of the sexes, orientation of the latrines (especially where used by Muslims), the social position and morale of lavatory attendants, and the danger of creating unemployment among the men who already clear night soil from the areas concerned. The organization of maintenance of mechanical equipment and latrines will be especially crucial.

Finally, the needs of particular categories of users merits some consideration. In communal latrines, a separate area could with advantage be allotted to children. Smaller squatting plates would be provided, and cubicles would be designed bearing in mind that privacy is less important but that parents should be encouraged to supervise their children. Latrines at first floor level might impose special problems for mothers with babies, old people and cripples, and the needs of these groups should be considered.

9.4 TESTS ON COMMUNAL LATRINES IN BANGLADESH

B.J. Lloyd and R.R. Daniel[5]

The Oxfam Sanitation Unit

As already observed, a significant component of the urban poor in many cities consists of squatters, refugees, and other categories of displaced or homeless people. In Bangladesh, a war and a series of natural disasters in the early 1970s left their quota of refugees, some of whose problems persist. These people, with squatters displaced from the capital city, are now accommodated in a series of camps located between seven and twenty miles from Dacca. An excreta disposal service for some 50 000 of these people is currently being provided by sanitation units developed by Oxfam.

The Oxfam Sanitation Unit was designed to meet immediate needs arising from a natural disaster, and is therefore constructed of components which can be easily transported and quickly erected. Thus the 'tanks' in which sewage is contained and digested take the form of butyl rubber bags, each with 18 000 litres capacity. The system has been adequately described elsewhere[6] and is illustrated in Figure 9.3. It works on the septic tank principle, with a communal latrine comprising 20 squatting plates feeding sewage into the butyl rubber tanks, two of which are normally connected in series. Effluent emerging from the second tank is passed through a percolating filter and a soakaway or discharged into a river which can provide a high degree of dilution.

Concern is expressed in many parts of this book that effluents emerging from septic tanks, aqua-privies, and other 'wet' systems can be highly dangerous in terms

Figure 9.3 A sanitation unit in operation. The squatting plates are inside the structure with the high roof. The sewage flows by gravity into the two pillow-shaped tanks seen under the lower roof, and the effluent then flows through the percolating filter on the left (photo: Jim Howard, Oxfam)

of their pathogenic potential. This is particularly worrying with systems designed for use in crowded conditions, such as the sanitation units and the Calcutta aqua-privies. This paper presents the results of bacteriological tests which allow this hazard to be evaluated, and which indicate that conditions might be very much worse if no sanitation were provided.

Location of units and pattern of use

The first sanitation unit in regular service was installed at Mirpur, a few miles north of Dacca, in 1975, as part of a small programme of improvement for several thousand people. A similar programme was undertaken at Bashantek. On Demra island, 25 units serve a population of up to 25 000, while at Tongi, the programme to provide sanitation for 17 000 people was completed in June 1977. At both Tongi and Demra, the sanitation work was combined with a housing programme, and the units are spaced at regular intervals throughout both camps and are served by tubewells and paths.

Detailed counts of the number of people using these latrines (Table 9.1) throw an interesting light on the discussion of communal latrines presented earlier in this chapter. Among the conclusions drawn were the following:

(a) about 1000 visits are made to every unit so far checked each day (± 20 per cent);
(b) there is little difference between male and female use;

Table 9.1 Specimen observations from a count of people using sanitation unit no. 2 at Mirpur, 23rd April 1977. (Young children are distinguished by height)

Time period commencing	Males (> 1 metre)	Females (>1 metre)	Children (<1 metre height < 6 years)
05.30	20	20	6
05.45	22	30	13
06.00	25	29	16
06.15	17	17	6
06.30	21	25	13
06.45	13	22	13
07.00	15	8	4
07.15	8	13	9
07.30	7	14	5
07.45	9	5	3
08.00	8	6	4
08.15	6	3	0
08.30	9	9	5
08.45	2	6	4
Sub-total	182	207	101

(c) early morning and evening are, as anticipated, the most intensive periods of use;

(d) children under about six years of age appear to use the facility less than the ratio of their age group to the total population would lead one to expect, although a more detailed analysis of the age structure of the community is needed. This is an important point, as it is this age group which is most seriously affected by diarrhoeal diseases.

Table 9.1 shows that the total number of individuals using the latrine during a peak period lasting 3.5 hours was 490. With 20 squatting plates available, each is theoretically used once every 8.5 minutes. In practice individuals spent from 3-7 minutes at the sanitation unit. Care was taken in collecting these data that the population was unaware that counting was going on.

Optimizing the efficiency of the containment tanks

The prototype tanks were originally tested at the Cholera Research Laboratories (CRL) Hospital in Dacca[7] by pumping 4600 litres of hospital sewage daily into the two tanks in series over a 6-week period. Physical, chemical, and microbiological monitoring was carried out on a daily basis. Several of the most relevant tests have been continued on the units installed in refugee camps from 1975 onwards. Table 9.2 shows some of the results, comparing data for raw sewage with observations made on the effluent from the second of the two tanks. Comparison between conditions at the CRL hospital and in the refugee camps can be made as follows:

(a) *CRL hospital effluent*

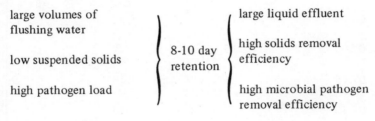

(b) *Present situation in refugee camps*

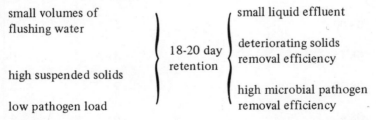

One factor in the situation at the camps is that the latrine attendants are probably pumping no more than 1000 litres of flushing water per day into the system. Add to this the ablution water and urine of the users, and the total fluid input becomes approximately 1000 litres/day; Given a total capacity for the two tanks of 36 000-40 000 litres and we have 18-20 day retention.

Not only was there over twice the volume of flush water passing through the CRL tanks, but also approximately half the numbers of people used the lavatories charging the tanks. The difference is compounded by the addition of sullage water to the effluent and explains the vast difference in strength of sewage indicated by the very high solids levels in the refugee camp sewage. Therefore although the

Table 9.2 Comparison of analyses* and removal efficiencies of prototype at CRL hospital effluent trials and units installed in refugee camps

Location	CRL	Mirpur 1	Demra 17
Suspended solids			
Raw sewage (mg/l)	1420	25 000	36 650
Tank 2 effluent (mg/l)	31	2200	375
Reduction (%)	98	91	99
Cholera vibrios			
Raw sewage (count/100ml)	5×10^6	Not detected	Not detected
Tank 2 effluent (count/100ml)	5×10^4	Not detected	Not detected
Reduction (%)	99		
Coliform count			
Raw sewage (count/100ml)	265×10^6	180×10^7	170×10^8
Tank 2 effluent (count/100ml)	8.3×10^6	2.3×10^7	4.9×10^8
Reduction (%)	96.5	99.7	97
Salmonella count			
Raw sewage (count/1 litre)	30 000		200
Tank 2 effluent (count/ 1 litre)	340		15
Reduction (%)	98.9		93.2

*All values are means of at least 10 sample analyses

percentage reduction of solids is comparable to that achieved at CRL, the actual levels remain high in the effluent.

The removal efficiency for parasitic ova by sedimentation will be impaired because their removal is dependent not only on retention time but also on the density of the sewage. In practice however, we can in part offset the increased number of parasites per unit volume escaping from the tanks by reducing the total volume of liquid effluent produced by each unit. Hence we must use as little water as is necessary to adequately flush excreta into the tanks, and where automatic flushing mechanisms have been installed it is proposed to experiment with these over the range 1000 to 2000 litres per day to assess the effect on effluent quality for a known number of users.

Evaluation of the percolating 'filters'

All of the sanitation units have included a percolating filter but unfortunately it is now clear that the mode of operation of the sanitation units renders the percolating 'filters' ineffective. The reasons for this are probably a combination of the following:

(a) The liquor from the effluent of tank 2 is excessively strong and prevents the establishment of the typical aerobic growth.

(b) The distribution arms and plastic corrugated perforated plates are not regularly checked by the attendants and hence ponding occurs and most of the substrate broken bricks are not wetted.

(c) The manual flushing is spasmodic and hence desiccation of the substrate medium occurs.

Although the recommended regime of flushing reduces the volume of effluent to a minimum, nonetheless every effort should be made to ensure the safe disposal of this liquid. Where the ground is porous a soakaway or ground drain may be satisfactory, but where clay predominates an alternative should be found. The only alternative may be open drains and in this case as long as length of shallow drain as possible should run inside the sanitation units enclosure. Model examples exist at Tongi where open drains run between the edge of the desludge area and the enclosing fence. Here the flow is so slow and the drains so shallow (2-3 cms depth) that further significant benefits can be expected to accrue by sedimentation and U.V. irradiation of the few remaining parasites and pathogens passing along these aerated ditches.

Desludging

Desludging of the tanks is a routine procedure which can be carried out by 2 or 3 persons in a little over an hour. When the desludge pipe is dropped into the desludge area the weaker supernatant liquid from Tank 1 comes out first and as emptying proceeds the solids concentration increases. To prevent siphoning of Tank 2 into Tank 1 the inspection cap on the interconnecting pipe is loosened or removed. Thus Tank 2 can be used in the later stage of the procedure, as a reservoir if required, to flush the remaining digested solids out of Tank 1 and into the desludge area for subsequent drying. The final stage in desludging is for two people to repeatedly shuffle across Tank 1 from the opposite end toward the desludge point.

Desludging is normally carried out every 10 weeks, though an effort is made to avoid the need for desludging during the monsoon rains. During sunny, dry weather, the sludge slurry in the drying bed evaporates rapidly, and a surface crust forms within 48 hours. The whole cake of dry sludge can usually be lifted and transferred to a stack for composting within ten days.

Desludging releases a partially digested sediment of heterogenous age. It includes the most recent excreta, less than 24 hours old, as well as fractions going back to the time when the unit was last desludged. The more recent fractions contain viable bacterial pathogens, and all fractions contain parasites. Therefore the temptation to use the material as fertilizer shortly after dewatering must be resisted. Preliminary tests on a number of sludge samples from the drying bed have revealed the presence of a minimum of 800 viable parasites per gram.

Simple stacking of the dry sludge seems to be adequate for composting to proceed. Examination of stored sludge samples invariably revealed thermophilic actinomycetes as a major component of the compost. No viable parasites were observed in repeated examinations of composted sludge which had been stacked for three months.

NOTES AND REFERENCES

1. James McL. Fraser is a consulting engineer of 95 Bothwell Street, Glasgow 2, U.K.
2. James Howard is Technical Officer, Oxfam, 274 Banbury Road, Oxford, OX2 7DZ, U.K.
3. M.S. Maitra is Director, Area Development and Bustee Improvement, C.M.D.A., 225C Lower Circular Road, Calcutta-700 017, India.
4. Working group members: B.K. Handa (chairman), B.J. Lloyd (rapporteur), Donald Curtis, Catherine Goyder, James Howard, M.S. Maitra, M.B. Pescod, P.H. Stern, R.J. Wall.
5. B.J. Lloyd and R.R. Daniel are from the Department of Microbiology, University of Surrey, Guildford, U.K.
6. James Howard and James McL. Fraser, *Aqua* (Pergamon Press), 1 (1), (1977), pp. 59-65.
7. James Howard, B.J. Lloyd and D. Webber, *The design and testing of a sanitation and sewage treatment unit for disasters and long-term use,* Oxfam Technical Paper, Oxford, 1975.

10

Putting Technology to Work:
The Social Factor

10.1 VOLUNTARY AND GOVERNMENT SANITATION PROGRAMMES

Catherine Goyder[1]

Public and private organisations

Discussions of technology are only of academic interest if people are unwilling or unable to put that technology to work. The implementation of the techniques discussed in previous chapters on a sufficiently large scale to meet current needs depends on people, organizations, and administrative capability to a crucial degree. It depends on whether there are institutions in the countries concerned capable of organizing the construction of latrines on a sufficiently wide scale. This not only means organizing supplies of materials and training skilled manpower—it also means conducting a dialogue with local communities and being sensitive to their needs, so that the latrines provided will be accepted and used.

Vietnam and Brazil are two countries which stand out in earlier chapters as having institutions effective in implementing their very different sanitation programmes, and alongside them we should consider the impressive programmes of Calcutta Metropolitan District. In Vietnam, the programme depended on the mass mobilization of the peasants to build latrines for themselves (Section 7.2); in Calcutta, progress depended on setting up an appropriate institution—the Metropolitan Development Authority—which in turn organized mass-production of latrine components and a system for consulting with local communities (Section 9.2); in Brazil, where there is less concern with local community involvement, State Companies are proving to be effective in planning and constructing water and sewerage systems (Section 4.2).

In each of these instances, the institutional arrangements strongly reflect the different social priorities of the countries concerned, and the choice of technology depends partly on social goals. In contrast to these successful examples, previous chapters have also mentioned technical innovations tried out in two African countries whose potential seems unlikely to be realized because of a lack of institutional back-up for servicing and maintaining latrines (Sections 3.5 and 4.3). Doubts expressed about the future of the technically very important Botswana project were especially striking (pages 64 and 65).

Because excreta removal is often undertaken by public bodies, either state-run or municipal, it is too readily assumed that the institutional development necessary for improved sanitation must always be in the public sector. It is easy to forget that there can be a large amount of private initiative in providing sanitation involving commercial institutions as well as informal community or village institutions. The influence of the latter on night soil re-use in India is discussed in Section 11.1, and village institutions must also have been actively involved in the Vietnames latrine construction programmes.

Private sector activity in sanitation includes night soil collection run as a private business (usually where the night soil can be profitably sold as manure); it also includes the provision by individual households of their own pit latrines, aqua-privies, or septic tanks (often by employing a private contractor, or buying from a builders' merchant). Perhaps one question that should be considered by those who wish to see wider provision of sanitation is whether additional help should be given to at least the poorer groups among those who wish to provide for themselves, both financially (perhaps through revolving loan funds), and through technical assistance.

Voluntary institutions

In a separate category from *private* enterprise, *village* institutions, and *public* institutions, there are, in many developing countries, *voluntary* institutions involved in the provision of sanitation. Typically they are hospitals or other agencies working in preventive medicine, but increasingly now there are village health workers supported by various kinds of health service, sometimes voluntary and sometimes state-run.

It is with voluntary bodies of these various kinds that Oxfam mainly works. Thus, although Oxfam's largest sanitation programme involves the specially designed communal latrine unit described in the previous chapter, some of Oxfam's smaller sanitation projects may be used to illustrate the problems and opportunities of voluntary institutions in this field.

Two hospitals in India, and another in a remote part of Malawi illustrate the most basic problem. This is that many health workers appreciate the importance of sanitation and tell people about it, but lack the resources or confidence to embark on practical work aimed at getting latrines built or improved. The Malawi hospital devoted half of its health education programme to discussing the value of pit latrines and methods of preventing schistosomiasis and hookworm, and one of the Indian hospitals organized educational mime shows to get over the same kind of message to village meetings. But the only practical measures that seem to have been actively advocated were the wearing of shoes when going to · the communal defecation ground, and the washing of hands with soap afterwards. The Second Indian hospital mentioned, in Maharashtra, was in the same situation until recently, carrying out health education in some twenty villages without much practical back-up. However, this work has now developed beyond education to support self-help projects in a number of villages where pit latrines are actually being built, drains are being laid, wells are being dug, and there is talk of biogas units. Health education has turned into practical extension work.

Public health in Zaire

In an attempt to stimulate more effective rural development, Oxfam has a team of specialists working in Zaire, who have helped to build up the public health work done by isolated rural hospitals and give it a practical bias. The country's Ministry of Health has been kept informed of all developments, and is gradually increasing its support for work of this kind. One recent response to the programme has been that the Ministry has asked for help in rewriting the nursing syllabus for Zaire to include a much larger public health component.

For a number of years, the leading work in this field was undertaken by the Vanga Baptist Hospital, and its methodology has now been adopted by many other projects in western Zaire. When work begins in any particular village, individuals from the village are first trained as health auxilliaries. Their subsequent work is encouraged by visits from a mobile team, who gradually get to know the village elders, and in due course hold public meetings to discuss the need for pit latrines and improved sanitation. This is followed by a massive latrine digging exercise, which aims to provide latrines for at least 90 per cent of the villagers in each place. After this is completed, the mobile teams continue to make visits to check whether latrines are being used and maintained. Once a village reaches a certain standard of sanitation, stool tests are carried out on the spot, and treatment is provided for all those with worms or other intestinal parasites.

This method depends for its effectiveness on rigorous and thorough fieldwork, but the result in a number of places has been a significant and measurable health benefit. A Peace Corps survey carried out in 1973 claims that the latrine programmes have reduced the prevalence of worms from 80 per cent of the population to 20 per cent.

To gain wider implementation of similar programmes in Zaire, Oxfam funded training courses for nursing auxiliaries from a number of hospitals, but discovered that if these people were to be encouraged to take up public health work, it was necessary to run seminars for senior staff as well. Once the backing of these senior staff had been obtained, the number of active public health programmes in the region expanded rapidly.

The long-term success of this work depends on it becoming less dependent on expatriate staff and external funding. Thus training is being offered to staff in rural dispensaries, village health workers, and similar people, and a need has been recognized for a simple handbook in local languages giving step-by-step instructions for digging pit latrines, and discussing related public health issues. Favouring the success of these developments is the evidence that in many villages, public health programmes have gained the respect and captured the imagination of local people. The visit of a mobile team to some villages is made into a great local event, with much singing and dancing, which brings the women in from the fields and encourages a good attendance at the public health talks.

Revolving loan funds

Where people want latrines but lack the financial resources to pay for them, the availability of loans can be very helpful, especially if money paid back by borrowers is continuously made available again in the same community as a revolving fund. This approach has been effective in Kerala (India) and in poor suburbs of Brazilian towns.

In a fishing community on the Kerala coast, the establishment of a revolving fund for latrines was one of several developments, the most important being projects to raise living standards by generating income. The basis of this was a successful fishing co-operative. At the same time, women attended adult literacy classes, took their children to a clinic, and were told about the health hazards associated with the open field system of defecation. They used a latrine at the clinic, and gradually the idea of having their own latrines took root. To obtain them, each family paid an initial deposit of Rs. 250/- ($26), the rest of the cost being covered by a loan, which was subsequently paid back in monthly instalments of Rs. 15/-. The total cost of each latrine was Rs. 750/- ($78). The latrines had brick superstructures and what are described as 'septic tanks'; these were not septic tanks in the usual sense but something much smaller — possibly just soakage pits.

Programmes of a similar kind have also been effective in Brazil, where the considerable progress made by conventional sewerage schemes still leaves many people in the poor suburbs of north-eastern towns without sanitation. In one instance, two Peace Corps volunteers launched a campaign in the small town of Cabrobo which effectively made 'privadas' the popular thing to have. The scheme received the support of the mayor and parish priest, and helped to stimulate other activities in the community. At public meetings, men got together to discuss the technical aspects of installation and maintenance, and women were told about disease prevention and the need for latrines. This was followed up by home visits, film shows on health, and the collection of small weekly amounts towards the latrine fund. Once a family had paid most of the required amount, a group of families dug a pit latrine and lined it with bricks. Prefabricated concrete squatting slabs were then provided at a subsidized rate, and installed by a mason. Building materials and transport were given by the mayor, and as a result, the scheme was able to help twice as many people as planned.

Once again, this is a project whose effectiveness is partly due to the way sanitation was introduced as part of an integrated development scheme involving a range of activities, with considerable community participation. But although many pit latrines were successfully constructed, there is some doubt as to whether they are being fully used.

Urban sanitation

In considering sanitation for crowded slum areas, one issue is the question of individual family latrines, as opposed to communal latrines. Family latrines often seem impracticable, but communal facilities are often neglected and misused.

In Korea, a local missionary hospital providing health care in an urban community persuaded the people to think about the need for better sanitation. Communal latrines were already available, but they were in a state of total disrepair. With a considerable self-help effort, twenty new communal latrines were built. Plenty of water taps were provided, somewhat reluctantly, by the local authority. The people seem pleased with the result, having built the latrines themselves and collected money sufficient to pay half the cost. Given this degree of commitment, the latrines seem unlikely to be misused.

One of Oxfam's major projects in urban areas has been to assist the Ahmedabad Study Action Group's project to relocate 2250 slum families from their flooded shacks on the banks of the Sabarmati River in Ahmedabad (India)[2]. The municipal authorities provided a new site, and undertook to lay sewers which were to be connected to the municipal system. What was interesting about this project was that it showed the extent to which poor people who have been living in conditions of the utmost privation care about proper sanitation and services once the opportunity is provided.

Building costs in the new housing colony were to be kept as low as possible, but the Action Group wanted to ensure that people had a say in the planning of their new settlement, and it became clear that people did not want communal latrines. Their willingness to accept shared facilities was only apparent once it was decided that each family should choose its latrine-sharing neighbours. Further, to keep costs down, no doors were fixed to the latrines, as it was assumed that people were used to a total lack of privacy. This proved to be unacceptable, so doors were ultimately provided, but people did agree to provide their own curtains to give some privacy in the washrooms. The municipal authorities were very slow in providing the piped water supply and sewer connections they had promised, and it took a tremendous amount of community effort to prevent a deterioration of environmental conditions while the completion of this part of the work was awaited.

In this review of projects supported by Oxfam and by the voluntary agencies in developing countries with which it works, a number of points have repeatedly cropped up. One is the need for health education to be backed up by practical efforts, both in the provision of latrines at clinics, and in active extension work, helping and advising people who want to provide latrines for themselves. A second point concerns the importance of community effort and the participation of people in programmes. Integrated programmes which mobilize people for a variety of development activities are undoubtedly the most effective way to bring about improvements in sanitation, hygiene, and other aspects of health in villages and slum areas.

10.2 OPERATION AND MAINTENANCE OF SANITATION SYSTEMS[3]

Five fixings

The question of how sanitation systems are to be operated and managed. has been mentioned in previous chapters as a matter of vital importance. Yet very little material is available on this subject, and there are few books to guide those who wish to improve the administration of excreta disposal or water supply. Significantly, though, Chinese literature on sanitation discusses management in parallel with technology. For example, in a document prepared by the Patriotic and Hygienic Campaign Committee, Province of Shantung[4], considerable stress is laid on the need for an effective and unified management covering night soil collection, animal wastes collection, and composting. Members of the local community appear to be recruited annually for a period of service with a 'professional composting team', which manages its affairs on the basis of 'five fixings'. These are five defined and agreed procedures to be used in carrying out the work, including the fixing of personnel, duties, quality, schedules, and hygiene. They can be roughly interpreted as follows:

(a) Fixing personnel—allocating duties to individuals, and forming small teams of 2-3 persons;
(b) Fixing duties—defining the tasks to be done, which include emptying household toilets, composting, keeping records and accounts, reporting any observed evidence of illness to health workers, and so on.
(c) Fixing quality—defining standards to be attained in each task, especially as they affect the quality of the compost produced;
(d) Fixing schedules—household toilets must be emptied at fixed time intervals, and there must be specific times for other tasks.
(e) Fixing hygiene—this seems to mean particularly, defining standards of personal hygiene to be observed by night soil collectors and similar workers to protect their own health.

These 'five fixings' could well be applied to almost any night soil collection service, and with suitable modifications, to the services needed for desludging aqua-privies or emptying composting toilets. One of the reasons why these tasks are so rarely carried out satisfactorily in other parts of Asia or Africa is that not enough is 'fixed' or defined about individual responsibilities, and time intervals between latrine emptyings.

Maintenance and servicing

One of the 'fixings' which is most frequently neglected when low-cost excreta disposal facilities are installed is the definition of what responsibilities devolve on the householder and what fall on the operating institution. When composting latrines are introduced into African countries, for example, it is necessary to decide whether the householder will want to clear the compost from the latrine and use it on his own land, or whether a community service for emptying latrines and selling or using compost must be organized.

With any latrine system, it is wise at the outset to enumerate a regular maintenance tasks and all repairs likely to be needed. Then it is possible to define which of these tasks may be left to the householder, and which must be carried out by the responsible institution.[5] When these tasks have been defined, it is possible,· on the one hand to give householders clear instructions, perhaps in a users' handbook, and on the other, to build up an institution with the necessary management capability, manpower and equipment.

For example, in a town with large numbers of aqua-privies of a specific, basic type, maintenance responsibilities might be subdivided by first defining the following tasks to be carried out by householders:

(a) cleaning squat-plate (daily);
(b) emptying two buckets of water into the tank to maintain the water level (daily);
(c) cleaning superstructure (weekly);
(d) repairing and painting superstructure (as necessary);
(e) reporting evidence of leaks from tank and other faults.,

Successful operation of the aqua-privies, and the achievement of the health benefits they can provide, clearly depends on householders being fully aware of these points and carrying out all these tasks. However, institutional responsibilities also need to be clearly defined, possibly as follows:

(a) desludging tank (every 12 months);
(b) discussing problems with householders (at desludging, with more frequent visits to problem latrines);
(c) record keeping to ensure that desludging is regular and latrines with persistent faults are identified;
(d) repairs to leaking tanks or blocked soakaways as necessary.

One reason why latrine projects frequently fail is that institutions capable of providing a sustained, long-term emptying (or desludging) and maintenance service are more difficult to organize than institution which can administer rapidly completed construction programmes. One difference between the Chinese way of doing things and methods used elsewhere is that night soil collectors in China are members of the community who take their turn at this particular task, and are not an underpriviledged minority group (Section 8.2). The point is made because the status, pay, and morale of sanitation workers is crucial if night soil is to be collected regularly, if aqua-privies are to be properly desludged, and if communal latrines are to be well run.

It is also worth noting that some technologies are especially dependent on regular servicing, and have a built-in crisis point, at which time, a labour dispute leading to a neglect of servicing would lead to large overflows of sewage. The night soil collectors in Bangladesh who allow household latrines to overflow if they do not receive an adequate tip from the householder are exploiting this crisis point on a small scale.

There are many other reasons why sanitation systems are so often badly administered, including the patronage which gets involved in systems. People have sometimes not only depended on a patron to get their job, but also have patrons who protect them if they fail to do the work properly. Responsibilities can also be evaded where large numbers of administrators are employed, with each duty divided among a considerable number of them.

Bad administration may also arise from employing too many operatives. But if you look to the politicians who try and run these things, some of what they say is reasonable, namely, that they have got to provide people with jobs, and jobs come before hygiene. If this means employing too many night soil collectors, and not being able to control them properly, that is the cost of giving people livelihoods.

But sociologists who build up models of inefficient administrations are apt to forget that one can do things to improve administrative procedures, like planning better, setting goals, defining targets, and thinking much more about project design. It would be well worthwhile getting into this very mundane area if we are to achieve anything in sanitation[6].

The user's point of view

A final but fundamental reason why many sanitation projects fail is that the users of the system belong to different, less educated, less westernized strata of society than the planners and administrators. Latrines which may look ideal to the planner seem inappropriate and unusable to those for whom they have been provided.

In towns, this is less of a problem, because people strongly dislike the squalor and lack of privacy that accompanies defecation in the open. So any latrine that is cleaner and more private than the existing arrangement will be actively used. In the countryside, however, bushes offer privacy, the wind disperses smells, and there is ample space to avoid the excreta of others. Defecation in the open is pleasanter than in the majority of low-cost latrines, which in any case demand considerable effort and perhaps expense for cleaning and maintenance.

In the countryside, also, when we do get people to use latrines and then are able to probe their motives in social surveys, we find that their reasons are mostly to do with privacy, convenience and status, with health coming a long way behind. This is understandable. The health benefits arising from a few individuals in a community using latrines are usually very small and quite intangible to the user. And in the countryside, a low-cost latrine will rarely seem healthier than the open air. Only when a whole community takes up the idea of sanitation, perhaps with the aim of cleaning up a squalid defecation ground, is a real impact made on the health situation. So only when there is a degree of community solidarity sufficient to get everybody building and using latrines can a noticeable impact be made on public cleanliness and health. The programme in Zaire mentioned earlier in this chapter is one of relatively few examples where this kind of community action seems to have worked. In a number of other instances where a high degree of latrine usage has been achieved, this has been partly because the latrines have been designed to provide a useful compost (as in Vietnam), or to produce biogas for cooking. These tangible benefits from using latrines provide a much greater incentive than improvements to health which may only gradually emerge.

One lesson to be drawn from experience of users' attitudes may be that it is often futile as well as arrogant to impose our own values and perceptions about health on other people. We should be thinking more of a dialogue with them in which there is an exchange of perceptions. And rather than *us* designing latrines for *them*, the intended users should be brought into the design process, perhaps in a way that is being attempted in Botswana (Section 3.5). The remainder of this chapter attempts to look at sanitation from the point of view of the users, so that a beginning can be made in understanding their side of the dialogue.

10.3 VALUES OF LATRINE USERS AND ADMINISTRATORS

Donald Curtis[7]

The 'social factor' in sanitation programmes

In planning and development, the 'social factor' is often invoked to explain the failures of technically competent, scientifically convincing, and financially sound projects. When the sociologist is called in to provide explanations, those who request his services usually expect him to provide an analysis of social or cultural 'obstacles'. They hope that he will find something in the values or institutions of the community in question which is different, strange, exotic and capable of accounting for aberrant behaviour. But sociologists are generally very reluctant to accept this interpretation of where the problem lies[8]. There are two sides to these social problems, and planners, administrators, or health officials bring their own complex values and procedures into programmes. These, as much as the values of the people, may be the source of the trouble.

The more we incorporate the elaborate analytic procedures and weighty words of science into our approach to hygiene, the more invulnerable we consider our programmes to be. So if we are right, then it must be them, the users of the system we provide, who are wrong when the programmes fail. Everything in our predisposition towards the non-elites of this world, the poor, the uneducated, the primitive, the lower classes, or however else we regard them, will tend to confirm our view.

.Thus sociologists are called in to explain social and cultural 'obstacles': the *exotic* factors arising from the particular culture of the system's users, which we assume should be educated away so the system can work. But there are also a range of *mundane* considerations arising from the differences in viewpoint between clients and planners, and in most cases, it will be these differences in viewpoint which explain resistance to particular items within health and sanitation programmes. Furthermore, mundane factors are much more predicatable, amenable to analysis, and remediable than are the exotic. A common example of a mundane factor is that little children avoid using pit latrines for fear of the cavernous hole that opens below them. This is an argument for altering the design of the latrine rather than for conducting a health education campaign.

In like manner, when exotic factors in a community's culture really do cause problems, it is usually less fruitful to try and re-educate people than to modify designs so that they suit the users' requirements better. For example, an exotic factor found among the Lubale of Zambia is that sons-in-law and mothers-in-law avoid using the same latrine. Here it is presumably better to design sanitation systems that give them easy access to different latrines than to try to persuade them to alter their ways.

People's concepts of health and hygiene do vary greatly from one culture to another in ways which are significant for health programmes. So although the *mundane* factors, recognizable by common sense, are the most frequent cause of difficulty, there are *exotic*, unexpected variations in hygiene concepts, and the next few pages will attempt to map out a way of thinking about them.

Concepts of hygiene: the exotic factor

Central to the question of perceptions of planners and users is a concept of hygiene. In the scientific culture, hygiene is a question of creating the physical conditions and personal practices which will prevent the spread of pathogens, but among ordinary people, hygiene is usually a much broader concept. Certainly, it is about those conditions which prevent disease. But disease is the consequence of disorder, and for most people, whether they subscribe to the scientific approach or not, disorder has much wider connotations for their lives than the invasion of a bodily system by submicrosopic organisms.

For many of us, part of the proper order of things is that defecation should be done in privacy. But there is no scientific reason why this should be. For some of us also, 'cleanliness is next to godliness' and, as in our various approaches to God, cleanliness procedures are highly ritualized. They are ritualized because they express an order of things and our relationship to that order and place in that order. Nevertheless, in the West, religion and hygiene are increasingly segregated into discrete conceptual spheres. In many cultures, however, relationships with the powers that be are not so segregated. The rituals of getting on well with the gods are part and parcel of getting on well with the physical environment and with the neighbours.

For all peoples, also, the unhygienic has a special status. We avoid polluting materials or practices verbally as well as physically, inventing euphemisms like 'night soil' for excreta and all sorts of funny names for lavatories like 'privy', 'smallest room', or 'loo'. The special status of these things lends itself to jokes, the humour arising from the fact that we trespass upon forbidden territory. These things are taboo, and this special status, in some cultures, may have significance for the design of sanitary systems.

One way of understanding taboo factors is to note that all people encounter problems in their attempts to conceptualize the universe, and have difficulty in fitting certain things into a safe, understandable pattern. Mary Douglas[9] illustrates this point from the biblical record of the ancient Israelites. For them, the universe was divided between earth, waters, and the firmament. Each of these areas had its proper kind of animals. Birds with wings and two legs fly in the air; fish with scales and fins swim in the sea; and on earth, four-legged animals, hop, jump, or walk. But various kinds of creatures do not fit this classification well. Eels seem to be neither fishes nor land animals. Insects both fly and walk. In this way, the book of Leviticus builds up a list of creatures that break the rules and must be avoided.

Bodily functions tend to be taboo for the same sort of reason. In most cultures, a fundamental distinction is made between man and animal. Man is a thinker, a tool user, a cultured being, and the higher rank we claim, the greater emphasis we lay upon these values. Animals are the obverse: instinctive and propelled by uncontrolled natural functions. Yet this elementary distinction is hard to maintain intact. We hunger, desire, bleed, and die with disconcerting similarity to animals. So bodily functions are difficult to handle culturally. Some we surround with ritual, others we hide away discreetly. In the European tradition, eating is surrounded by a paraphernalia of plates and cutlery; sex is sanctified and put between sheets; defecation is confined to the smallest room. Much of the early upbringing of our children consists of convincing them of the demerits of eating like animals, and we fill both themselves and ourselves with anxiety as we discipline them into use of the potty.

In discussing ritual cleanliness and pollution, one tends to look to India, where the traditional values of Hinduism produce a highly pollution-conscious society. Different occupational roles entail different hazards of pollution. These occupations are therefore ranked in a hierarchy of ritual cleanliness, and certain residual functions like handling dead bodies or removing 'night soil' are left to categories of people who, for historical reasons, fail to make the grade in the ritual cleanliness stakes altogether. Such a system makes people highly conscious of the boundaries between groups; caste groups become clearly demarcated.

Mary Douglas uses for her exposition a study by Srinivas of the Coorgs, a group who have the status of a caste, although they live as a relatively isolated community in the mountains. 'The ritual life of the Coorgs gives the impression of a people obsessed by the fear of dangerous impurities entering their system', says Douglas. 'For them the model of the exits and entrances of the human body is a doubly apt symbolic focus of fears for their minority standing in the larger society. Here I am suggesting that when rituals express anxiety about the body's orifices, the sociological counterpart of this anxiety is a care to protect the political and cultural community of a minority group.'[10] Body relics, especially excrement, must not be touched if the body is to be protected, and by implication, people who must handle such materials have to be regarded as untouchable if the integrity of the group is to be protected.

In various cultures, sensitive body relics not only include excrement but the remains of food, finger nails, hair, blood, and even foot prints.[11] Much of their significance, I suggest, arises because things like finger nail parings and spilt blood trespass on the boundary between life and death. What leaves the body and becomes dead is a threat to the body.

Menstruation particularly lends itself to difficulties of interpretation in terms of life and death. Clearly, menstrual blood is the stuff of life, yet it is destined not to be. In many societies it is regarded as particularly dangerous, and women are avoided when menstruating. Among the Tswana, menstruating women avoid crossing the paths of men and vice versa.[12]

What is the significance of all this for scientific sanitation programmes? Clearly the logic of ritual purity and danger does not coincide with the logic of epidemiology, although in some cases the practices themselves may be compatible. For example, the frequent bathing, careful cooking, and other dirt avoidance practices of high caste Hindu families probably correspond with good 'scientific' hygiene, and are often explained away in this fashion. Others are definitely not. By the curious process of inversion, common in many cultures, dirt may be used in ritual cleaning practices. Also there is no agreement between science and ritual on the subject of what is dangerous and polluting. Hair, nail parings, and foot prints do not interest public health workers, while in many cultures, faeces may not be regarded as particularly threatening at all.

How do these values influence defecation habits? Sometimes they emphasize the importance of avoiding contact with excreta, or with objects that have had contact with them — the untouchability aspect. Sometimes also they encourage secrecy and anonymity in defecation. This latter may be different from privacy in the Western sense, in that the object may be to avoid having a sorcerer trace one's faeces and use them against one. Hiding in the bush during defecation may be a more effective way of doing this than using a pit latrine, where one's wastes can be all too easily traced.

With the exception of Hinduism, these examples of taboos affecting defecation are mostly to be found in small, relatively isolated communities with a distinctive cultural identity and history. Increasingly, such communities are being drawn into a wider economy and society where their own beliefs must exist alongside others. Here they must explore intellectually all sorts of things anew as they are embraced within the communications and education process of mass society. In this situation, those who are upwardly mobile, who see opportunities to improve their standing in society, may well aspire to the standards of living and lifestyle of those who they see above them. If now, sanitation technologies are prestigious, they will adopt them even if this clashes with their customary beliefs and values.

On the other hand, in most parts of the world there are groups at the bottom end of society, without opportunities of advancement, for whom modernization is a threat rather than an aspiration, who may maintain a reactive identification with traditional values and beliefs. They will take much more convincing that new technologies have something to offer for them.

The mundane factors: cash, organization, and convenience

Mundane factors require less interpretation. They are the social facts which applied common sense should reveal. Costs, project organization, sound engineering and maintenance are basic to good sanitation programmes, but the mundane factors which are sometimes not considered are the user's problems, and the cost, convenience and organization necessary for him if he is to make routine use of the sanitation system.

Costs to the user may be quite considerable. In some rural areas, pit latrines may cost each household as much as the rest of their accommodation, and may compete as a priority with extra living space or other home improvements. In other words, there is for each household an opportunity cost. Some systems may require new routine payments for disinfectants or cleansing materials if they are to remain hygienic. Under these circumstances, the needs, objectively speaking, for all households may be the same, but responses may differ according to household income levels.

Convenience is perhaps a rather all-embracing concept, but one should look at such factors as how much time is saved, how the location of facilities influences their use, and whether facilities are equally convenient to all household members.

Organization only becomes critical when facilities like latrines or water supplies are to be used communally by people who are not otherwise co-operating in the use of resources. Put in a latrine for every household and the householders should manage them successfully because there is no room for dispute about ownership and responsibility (though servicing and emptying may still need to be publicly provided). But if facilities must be shared between households, then problems will arise unless somebody is specifically given control and adequately rewarded for doing so.

Evaluation of social factors

From the above, I draw two sets of conclusions about evaluating the 'social factor' in sanitation programmes. The first is that both the authorities' viewpoint and the users' or clients' viewpoint should be allowed to have some influence upon the design of the schemes[13], and the second is that mundane as well as exotic considerations are relevant on both sides.[14]

Table 10.1 expresses schematically the dimensions of the problem and provides a checklist of factors to be considered in each dimension. Below I apply the scheme to the latrines component of a housing project in India, but it could be used to check out any project component in the health and sanitation field where the co-operation of the public is essential.

Table 10.1 Evaluation of social factors in sanitation programmes

	Administration values and goals	User values, taboos and objectives
Exotic factors	— inherent values	— avoidance of dirt
	— assumptions about users	— avoidance of people (privacy)
		— own interpretations of hygiene and health
Mundane factors	— scientific objectives	
	— low cost to authority	— low cost to household
	— administrative convenience	— organization (if communal)
	— operational and maintenance procedures	— convenience of householders

The procedure may seem to be elaborate and its emphasis almost philosophical, but the objective is economy, and in two ways a careful appraisal of our own as well as our clients' values may be useful. By eliminating our own non-scientific predispositions from the project design, we can clear the ground for more careful consideration of how to achieve our scientific objective more cheaply. Also, by identifying more clearly our clients' perceptions and problems, we may make schemes more acceptable to them: and that in itself is an economy.

In one Indian city, squatters were recently moved into four-storey tenements in the course of a major rehousing programme. These apartments consisted of two rooms and an interior flush toilet. Housing managers complained about the misuse of these toilets. Some people damaged them by attempting to clear blockages with inappropriate tools. Others filled the pans up with sand and used the space for storage. Children continued to defecate in the open space surrounding the flats. In the fact of these malpractices, the authorities commissioned social workers to educate the tenants into new ways. For the officials, the poverty and social background of their clients was adequate explanation of the malpractices. The social workers soon came to a more sympathetic interpretation, and often found themselves representing the clients to the authorities. For instance, the social workers soon realized why the children fouled the pavements. In many households, both parents were obliged to work, so children were left to fend for themselves throughout the day and had no access to the toilets in the locked flats.

Such things were revealed through the mediating role of sympathetic social workers. No systematic study was conducted, but following the scheme outlined above, a number of questions could have been posed to both authorities and tenants to try to explain the emerging patterns of behaviour. I list them in Table 10.2. If this had been done at the beginning of the project, the relevant social factors could then have been used as design constraints[15] instead of being assigned the status of cultural blockages[16] that needed to be educated away.[17]

Table 10.2 Evaluation of toilet misuse: a checklist of questions

	Authorities	Tenants
Exotic factors	Are the authorities or architects predisposed to privacy as a value?	Is it offensive to have defecation activities within the margins of the household?
	What assumption do the authorities make about the sanitary habits of their clients?	What emphasis do households place on privacy in toilet use?
		What are the implications of people or dirt avoidance procedures for indoor toilet use? Or for outdoor public toilet use? Or for outdoor private toilet use?
Mundane factors	How much cheaper would private, outdoor toilets be at ground level?	Is there an opportunity cost involved in the use of interior living space for toilets?
	What servicing arrangements are in force?	Do interior toilets smell?
	Does the current design of toilet have adequate waste disposal capacity?	Would unattended children have better access to toilets if they were outside?
		How could communal facilities be managed in this setting?

10.4 CULTURE AND HYGIENE IN RURAL WEST BENGAL

Vijay Kochar[18]

Positive elements in folk hygiene

From the perspective of ecology, sanitation is a matter of 'regulations of man-environment relationships in the interest of health'[19] In the hands of technocrats, however, the word sanitation has become synonymous with a few technological interventions, such as latrines, water supply, and more recently, water pollution control. This has led to the neglect of a whole range of cultural and behavioural factors in man-environment relationships, all of which were originally signified by the term sanitation.

For example, among rural people in Bengal, notions of the pure and the sacred, and of the polluted and profane, are in many ways the rules for personal hygiene as well as for ritual. A popular text on daily rituals for orthodox Hindus includes procedures, prescriptions and even sacred chants to go with cleaning the mouth, applying oil, bathing, grooming, and so on.[20] Despite a way of life that makes it virtually impossible to emulate bookish, westernized notions of hygiene and cleanliness, the canons of 'folk hygiene' embody some very powerful notions of personal cleanliness. In fact, the concern of Bengali peasants for cleanliness of the person and of their dwellings results in an obsession for washing hands and possessions.[21]

In all human cultures, the agents and situations perceived to be connected with disease play an important part in influencing customs and habits. And constant changes and adaptions are made in health cultures as communities strive to achieve a balance in their relationships to perceived disease risks.

In the current situation, however, the folk health culture not only has to respond to environmental factors which may tend to be altering the pattern of disease; it also has to respond to influences arising from cosmopolitan medicine and planned sanitation programmes. The results may sometimes be negative, so that risks are enhanced (Figure 10.1), as when unsatisfactory latrines act as foci for the transmission of disease. But what is hoped for, of course, is a positive interaction between folk culture and cosmopolitan medicine, so that health is promoted. Figure 10.1 is adapted from Schaffer's model[22] of these interactions in order to highlight two basic contentions of the present author:

(a) *While some aspects of folk culture and hygiene are harmful, some are beneficial*, at least in a relative sense. The net impact of these beneficial practices could be enhanced by suitable interventions and reinforcements. And although complete elimination of harmful practices is improbable, there is ample scope for suitable modifications in these practices in order to reduce the risk involved, or to counterbalance the negative effects by suitable interventions at another level.

(b) *Sanitation and hygiene are integral parts of all lifestyles, including 'folk culture'*. Promotion of scientific knowledge, practices, norms and techniques does not occur in a vacuum, therefore. So the 'scientific' paraphernalia itself has a cultural significance associated with the cosmopolitan-urban social milieu and the group culture of public health professionals. Lack of fit between this *cultural load* associated with sanitary devices, and the *competing elements* of folk culture create strong conflicts. While the epidemiological, engineering, administrarive and economic components of the sanitation programmes are well advanced, much groundwork is needed before adequate socio-cultural accounting can also be built into these programmes. We even lack the basic data such as White *et al.*[23] have provided with

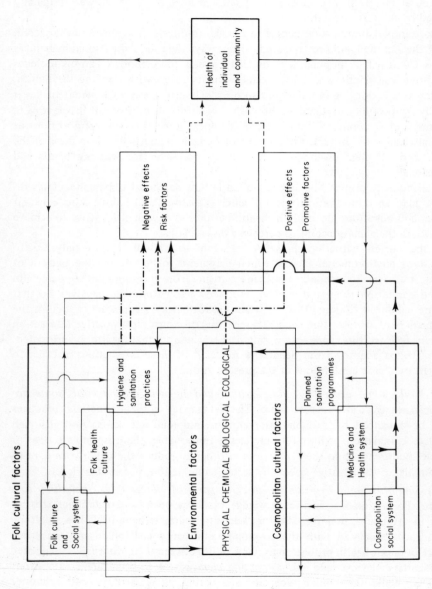

Figure 10.1 Schematic representation of the interaction of ideas about health within local 'folk' cultures with other human and environmental factors

regard to the use of water. The present paper describes the hygiene and sanitation practices of people living in rural West Bengal, and attempts to show how traditional practices have a beneficial influence on the transmission of hookworm, and how they might be reinforced in this respect.

Living conditions

A survey of twelve contiguous villages in West Bengal was conducted in 1968-70, during which a sample of 100 households was studied, with a more detailed investigation of a sub-sample of 50 households. The research was related to work on hookworm transmission already discussed in this book (Section 2.4), and full details have been published elsewhere by Kochar[24] and Schad *et al.*[25]

The survey explored the whole agricultural ecology and housing environment of the communities concerned because this was considered essential for understanding sanitary habits. For example, bamboo groves are an important source of firewood; they are used as places for defecation; and they are regarded in Bengali culture as a place of evil spirits. Bamboo groves are often used as a dumping ground for various kinds of refuse such as worn-out brooms (associated with witchcraft), and earthen pots used in mortuary rites. We therefore enquired into attitudes to the use of bamboos and studied firewood collection within the community in rder to understand the role of the groves as defecation grounds.

A census of cattle in the sub-sample households was also taken, and this revealed an average of 5.3 animals per household. Duties such as cleaning cattle-sheds and making cow-dung cakes for fuel are obviously relevant to sanitary conditions. A few people were found to be sleeping in rooms where fowls and goats were kept at night, enabling parasites and micro-organisms to pass freely from animals to man.

Most households have one or more ponds close to the dwelling. Drinking water is obtained from wells with hand-pumps, which are usually within three minutes walk of the home, but all other water usage takes place in or near the ponds, including washing clothes or pots, bathing, and watering cattle. Observation of a typical pond indicated that during the day, it was entered by one person or another sixteen times each hour. Women and children enter the pond more frequently than men. A quarter of the ponds dry up during the early summer, and the others become progressively more dirty.

A typical household occupies five or six huts with mud walls and gabled roofs thatched with paddy straw; the group of structures is usually enclosed by a mud wall, and includes a separate cattle shed (in 80 per cent of examples) and a separate kitchen or store room (69 per cent). There is usually a veranda outside the main room where people spend a lot of time. Hut floors are usually built up 0.5 to 1.5 m above ground level to avoid damp and flooding. Houses are very crowded, with about 3 m^2 of floor space per person, and an average of 2.8 people occupying each bed (sleeping platform or bedclothes unrolled on the floor).

Ash and miscellaneous items such as broken pots swept from the house are the most visible waste products around the houses. Wood, cans, and paper all get re-used. On average, about 6-7 trash heaps or dung-pits were observed around sub-sample households. Refuse from the cattleshed is generally thrown into the dung-pits, which have increased in numbers recently. The cow dung is largely used as fuel.

An attempt was made to assess fifteen common indicators of insanitary living so that different households could be compared. These indicators included the condition of the pond, excessive numbers of trash heaps, overcrowding, and so on. Among the upper social groups, whose members were not employed in agriculture, 74 per cent scored well on this basis, whereas among landless labourers, only 18 per cent passed the same datum of sanitary well-being. Farmers partly or wholly owning their own land came in between. The families who scored best seemed to enjoy slightly better health and had a lower level of hookworm infection. But since all families have many insanitary conditions in common, these differences in health were only small.

Hygiene practice

In the communities studied, people take a bath in a pond every day, sometimes just rubbing face and arms, but often applying oil or soap and carefully scrubbing the body with a cloth or gourd. Soap is used mainly by people who have relatives working in a town, though most people have some for washing their hair.

Ash or charcoal, or very occasionally, tooth paste is used for oral hygiene. Some men make a brush by chewing the end of a suitable twig. Vigorous cleaning of the mouth before and after every meal is a rule necessitated by notions of purification, and is invariably followed by the adults. The sequence of washing feet, hands, and mouth in that order is repeated many times each day. Washing clothes is a tedious and prolonged operation, carried out by the oldest women in each household, on average, once in twelve days (though more often with children's clothes). The bed clothes are washed less frequently. Laundry consists of first boiling the garments with washing soda, and then rinsing repeatedly in the pond.

About 95 per cent of people were observed to choose a place for defecation within three minutes walk of their homes. Men on average walked a little further than women. Most people go to recognized defecation grounds, and spend a minute or so walking round to find a suitable spot for squatting. They squat for about three minutes, on average, then immediately go to the pond for a wash. This ablution involves rubbing the peri-anal skin with water while crouching in the squatting posture. Then the hands are rubbed with soil as a purification act. Termination of defilement is symbolized by taking by hand a mouthful of water and then spitting it out. Many people also prefer to take a bath as a continuation of this ritual. In any case, clothing worn during defecation is changed. Most adults change from the normal 'clean' clothes before going for defecation. The left hand only is used during ablution. Rural Bengalis scrupulously avoid the use of the left hand for eating or handling any food materials (particularly cooked food) since it is defiled. These norms are followed with high conformity, and children are often reprimanded for not following the correct procedures. A visit to a faecally polluted bamboo grove for any purpose would normally require similar rituals.

Recognized defecation grounds are mostly in fields and bamboo groves. Monthly records were made during the survey which showed that only 0.8 per cent of stools were passed in latrines. The different villages in the survey varied somewhat, but on average, nearly 43 per cent of defecation occurred in fields, and over 22 per cent in bamboo groves (Table 10.3). Only 11 per cent of stools are passed near to the

Table 10.3 Age-sex differences in the choice of defecation habitat

| | PERCENTAGE OF TOTAL STOOLS PASSED IN EACH HABITAT | | | |
	Fields	Bamboo	Residential	Other
Adults – males	50.6	23.9	0.1	24.6
Adults – females	42.6	34.0	0.1	23.3
Children	34.8	12.5	28.9	24.0
All persons	42.6	22.4	10.7	24.3

houses, and then mostly by children and aged adults. Women tend to use shaded habitats more than men, who use the fields more, though this varies also with the season (Figure 10.2). In the wet season, especially July and August, most defecation takes place in the fields, whereas in the dry season, shaded defecation grounds are used more.

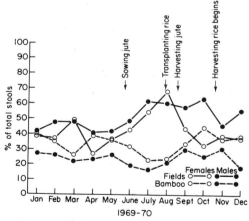

Figure 10.2 Use of defecation grounds in the rural West Bengal survey area, showing seasonal changes, and different preferences of the sexes. Peak use of the fields by the women corresponds with the season when rice is being transplanted. The men use the fields heavily throughout the growing season of the jute and rice crops

People do not like to defecate close to other stools. Their cultural norms of pollution and purity suggest they would carefully avoid stools in selecting a defecation spot. In the defecation grounds, as pollution increases in one corner, the people gradually shift to another suitable corner, and the intensity of faecal pollution in a given spot waxes and wanes. On the defecation grounds, about 45 per cent of the identifiable stools were within 2 m of other stools, and 55 per cent beyond that distance.

Only 9 per cent of households had some kind of latrine, and these were not much used. People tend to consider latrines as dirty, bothersome, difficult to service, unaesthetic, and uncomfortable[26]. Some simple latrine structures which were observed were simple pits with a platform and enclosure, or simply an enclosure on a natural slope (compare Figure 1.1).

About half the people possess some kind of footwear, but only use it on formal occasions. Only two persons said they used shoes when going to defecate, and observations confirmed that this was not the practice.

Sanitation and health

While sanitation is strongly related to culture, its relationship with health is more enigmatic. In Varanasi, the population of the university campus has modern water supplies, excreta disposal, and housing, but exhibits practically the same pattern of infection and disease as the villages nearby which lack these facilities.[27] In sanitation programmes generally, it seems that health gains are not achieved until the innovations have diffused throughout fairly large populations[28], and this only happens when many other changes in lifestyle are taking place simultaneously. The approach of linking the cost of sanitation programmes to definite gains in health as a key decision criterion, discussed by Feachem[29], is therefore not a sound administrative strategy. It overlooks the fact that sanitation in a rural mileu, particularly in its early phases, is more a matter of ethical, educational, aesthetic, and status values than a matter of epidemiological gains. People are more likely to perceive cultural values (and quality) associated with sanitary innovation than its health implications.

Sanitation and hygiene are, more than anything, parts of a way of life. The technology selected for rural sanitation must be so selected and adapted as to become part of the existing rural lifestyle. This can be achieved by incorporating epidemiologically useful components of the local culture into sanitation programmes. Professionals who are obsessed with absolute standards, high technology and cosmopolitan values are unlikely to be sensitive to this.

To illustrate the necessary approach, it is useful to consider hookworm infection in rural West Bengal. The high prevalence (90 per cent), yet at the same time, the low intensity of infection in this area has puzzled scientists for half a century (Section 2.4). It appears, however, that the traditional hygiene practice of rural Bengali society is at least partially effective in limiting the infection. In the present work, positive and negative consequences of various habits and practices were explored in quantitative terms with reference to their impact on the survival and dispersion of hookworm eggs and larvae (Table 10.4).

Table 10.4 List of protective (low risk) factors for hookworm in the villages studied

1. Simple latrines, natural latrines.
2. Strict avoidance of stools in selecting a squatting place leading to diffuse soil pollution, decreasing the larval population per unit area.
3. Restricted frequency and duration of activities in defecation areas.
4. Defecation in open habitats, decreasing the chances of survival of larval populations, particularly in the afternoon.
5. Universal avoidance of pollution of fields under crops.
6. Defecation away from maximum interaction zone of the settlement.
7. Many defecation grounds (large area per person and lesser aggregation of larvae).
8. Shift from shaded areas to open fields during the monsoon season.
9. Strict socialization of defecation habits.
10. Universal practice of ablution soon after defecation (or other activities in defecation grounds) and careful scrubbing of feet.
11. Recognition of the risk of infection, recognition of early symptons of high infection and early health action.
12. Better foot condition and care of lesions on feet during the monsoon season.
13. Short squatting time and lesser frequency of stools.
14. Higher intake of iron in the diet.
15. Non-agricultural family environment.
16. Non-agricultural occupations away from the villages.
17. Stable agricultural occupation (rather than agricultural labour)
18. Better socio-economic status.
19. Use of shoes and other footwear during defecation activity.
20. Use of latrines.
21. Provision of proper defecation areas around schools.
22. Recognition of risk from obliterated stool spots.

Thus rural Bengali society observes some habits which aid the hookworm—and these are *risk factors* from the human point of view—but people have other customs which restrict the hookworm population, which are *protective factors*. Some of the latter have developed as a direct response of human communities to percieved environmental risks.

Both risk factors and protective factors are simultaneously present in the culture. Yet epidemiology and public health have become concerned with the risk factors only. This has led to a negative view of indigenous cultures. But the knowledge of protective factors is of no less public health importance, and Table 10.4 lists a number of aspects of rural Bengali culture that have been identified in the present author's study as being protective These factors have nearly all played some part in the natural regulation of hookworm infection in the study population.

The benefits of these existing practices can be reinforced by incorporating indigenous protective factors into hookworm control programmes[30]. From Table 10.4 it can be seen that stricter avoidance of old stool spots, prompt ablution and washing of feet after defecation, and avoidance of defecation areas for other activities are among many factors which have a desirable effect on the hookworm situation. It was noticed that cultivation in banana groves which creates an undulating, furrowed surface seemed to provide a form of simple 'latrine'; people naturally walked and squatted on the higher ground, and defecated in the furrows. The possibility of furrowing important defecation grounds might be one simple measure which could significantly reduce contact of feet with hookworm larvae, without altering current hygiene practice.

The efficacy of the common folk medicines used for removal of 'worms' is highly suspect, but the possibility of some limited benefit from repeated doses of Ayurvedic and folk anthelminthics should be explored. Popularizing the use of these remedies during the season when hookworm infection is likely to be greatest should be easy, and people will benefit even if the medicine kills only a third of the worms. Some simple remedies for common foot complaints for use during the monsoon season might also be popularized.

While the goal of sanitary latrines and the use of shoes may have to wait for many, many years in the rural areas, behavioural control measures which are cheap, feasible, and acceptable offer a chance of some relief and benefit in the immediate future. The benefits from behavioural control of hookworm will be far from complete, and like other programmes, they will be difficult to pursue in the absence of any concurrent development[31]. However, once incorporated into the way of life, the behavioural and social changes will be self-sustaining. Could it be that the attainment of such changes are, in any case, the proper and ultimate goal of public health?

NOTES AND REFERENCES

1. Catherine Goyder is from the Joint Centre for Urban Design, (Department of Architecture and Town Planning), Oxford Polytechnic, Headington, Oxford OX3 OBP, England.
2. Ahmedabad Study Action Group, *The Repeat Potention,* prepared for Habitat, Vancouver, 1976
3. Edited from material contributed by John Briscoe, Donald Curtis, Michael G. McGarry, and Arnold Pacey.
4. *Compilation of Data on Experience and Sanitary Management of Excreta and Urine in the Village,* People's Hygiene Publisher, China, 1974, English translation by Thim Loy Lee, IDRC, Ottawa, 1977.
5. A comparable list of maintenance tasks is given by Arnold Pacey, *Hand-pump maintenance,* Intermediate Technology Publications, London, 1977.
6. Contributed by Donald Curtis.
7. Donald Curtis is from the Development Administration Group, Institute of Local Government Studies, University of Birmingham, Birmingham B15 2TT, England
8. J. Hamnett, *Journal of Development Studies,* 9 (4), pp. 493-507.

9. Mary Douglas *Purity and Danger*, Penguin, Harmondsworth, 1966, p.70.
10. *Ibid*, p. 148
11. R.F. Fortune, *Sorcerers of Dobu*, Routledge, London, 1932.
12. Isaac Schapera, *African Affairs*, 51 (1952), pp. 41-52.
13. Donald Curtis, 'Ideology and the impact of development agency activities', Ph.D. thesis, University of Kent at Canterbury, 1977.
14. I. Oxaal, T. Barnett, and D. Booth, *Beyond the Sociology of Development* Routledge, London, 1973.
15. D. Sears, and L. Joy *Development in a Divided World* Penguin, Harmondsworth, 1971.
16. M. Pflanz, in *Seminars in Community Medicine,* ed. R.M. Acheson and L. Aird, Oxford U.P., 1 (1976)
17. K.A. Pisharoti, *Guild to the Integration of Health Education in Environmental Health Programmes,* WHO Offset Publication No. 20, Geneva 1975.
18. Vijay Kochar is Senior Fellow, Indian Council of Social Science Research, Department of Preventive and Social Medicine, Banaras Hindu University, Varanasi 221005, India.
19. M. Schaffer, *Administration of Environmental Health Programmes: a Systems View,* WHO Public Health Papers 59, Geneva 1974.
20. T. Bhattacharya, *Nityakarm Paddhati,* Orient Library, Calcutta, n.d. (in Bengali).
21. L.C. Bhandari, *Transcultural Psychiatric Review,* 10 (1973), pp. 138-40.
22. Schaffer, *op. cit.,* note 19.
23. G.F. White, D.J. Bradley and A.U. White, *Drawers of Water: Domestic Water Use in East Africa,* Chicago U.P., 1972.
24. Vijay Kochar, 'Human factors in the ecology of hookworm infection in rural West Bengal', Doctoral Dissertation, Johns Hopkins University, Baltimore, 1975; also F.X. Grollip and H.B. Haley (eds.) *Medical Anthropology,* Mouton, Hagus, pp. 287-312.
25. G. Schad *et. al., Science,* 180 (1973), pp. 502-4.
26. K.A. Hasan, *The Cultural Frontier of Health in Village India,* Bombay 1967; also Planning, Research and Action Institute (PRAI) *Report,* Lucknow, 1969.
27. S.C. Seal. *Report of the resurvey of Singur Health Unit Area',* Calcutta, 1966.
28. Richard Feachem, Michael McGarry and Duncan Mara, *Water, Wastes and Health in Hot Climates,* John Wiley and Sons, London, 1976.
29. Richard Feachem in *op. cit.* note 28.
30. A.C. Chandler, *Indian Journal of Medical Research,* 14 (1926), p. 193, in twelve parts to 15 (1927), pp. 734-8
31. W.W. Cort, *American Journal of Tropical Medicine,* 2 (1922), pp. 449-62.

11

Night Soil as an Economic Resource

11.1 LABOUR AND ORGANIC RESOURCES IN THE INDIAN SUB-CONTINENT

John Briscoe[1]

Utilizing human excreta

Human excreta are seldom conserved in the Indian sub-continent, but cow dung *(gobar)*, crop residues, vegetable wastes, and water weeds are used for various purposes in the frugal village economies—for cooking food, fertilizing crops, feeding animals, and constructing buildings. Recognizing that traditional practices were often wasteful, scientists long ago devised methods for the efficient production of fertilizer and methane gas from these materials. By contrast, conventional economic planning has considered these issues to be unimportant, though the so-called 'energy crisis' is forcing some revision of this attitude.

Change is also taking place in the health ministries of poor countries. After decades of frustration with the disinterested response of villagers to latrine programmes, health planners are hoping that people who are given the means for producing fuel and fertilizer from their excreta may change their defecation habits.

The use of human excreta cannot be considered in isolation from the use of other organic materials. Human excreta will usually be digested with these materials, first because the quantity of excrement from one person is small and consequently the products are, on a per capita basis, small—and second, because human excreta is rich in nitrogen and can be mixed with carbon-rich matter to obtain carbon-to-nitrogen ratio suitable for efficient digestion.

So we know that resources are being used inefficiently, and that the technologies for improving these efficiencies are available; the problem is one of implementation. Some of the relevant technologies, particularly composting and the production of biogas, have attracted much interest as 'appropriate technologies', and in India, biogas is given official support with soft loans and subsidies for those investing in the equipment. But it is the farmers with most land, not the poor, who are benefiting, and there are many signs that the thrust for appropriate technology is coming from the top, and only helping those near the top. It is an imposed technology[2] when seen from the villager's viewpoint, and it is not always appropriate to the social and economic arrangements of the rural poor.

When I first went to India, I thought that appropriate technology was something new and very bright. I was brought down to earth in talking to Indians who had been around at the time of Gandhi and who had been thinking about the need for technology to be appropriate in the same terms thirty years ago.[3] In speaking with them about why they had failed, I found that there had been nothing wrong with their ideas, which often had high-level support in the government. The problem was that nothing was ever done to change the institutional arrangements that blocked the progress of these technologies. I think that the lesson we can draw from Vietnam and China is that, in these two countries, appropriate technologies are applied in parallel with the institutional changes that could make them work. To ignore these factors is to risk joining the 'stampede to quick solutions'[4], oblivious of the reaction of local people to new, apparently beneficial opportunities.

In fact, what we shall find is that the 'appropriate technology' of biogas production from waste is only appropriate to those farmers who have broken out of the traditional economy into the market economy. When looked at in that context, it emerges that biogas production and other improved waste recycling schemes may even act to impoverish the rural poor—the very people who the advocates of appropriate technology would most like to help.

One reason why these facts are not recognized is that our thinking is often influenced by the neo-classical economists' way of comparing different technologies, for example, in cost-benefit analysis. But the economists' approach is only appropriate to the market economy; it is not very useful for dealing with non-commercial resources[5] such as wastes, especially within the traditional economy.[6] Indeed, to understand the traditional economy, we need a different approach—and the key to that is to understand the way labour is organized. In this context, labour organization is 'only another word for the forms of life of the common people'[7].

This means that we need to understand certain social relationships in the community, and how they have developed historically, if we are to understand how that community uses the available resources.

'Customary' payment and resource use systems

The agricultural system which is referred to as 'customary' or 'traditional' in the Indian sub-continent is of relatively recent origin. Starting with the permanent settlement of Bengal in 1793, the British promulgated a series of radical land tenure ordinances. These succeeded in dissolving the ancient ties and usages of the villages, 'assessing and parceling out the lands which from time immemorial had belonged to the Village Community collectively.'[8].

Under the system that was created by these measures, social equilibrium depended on the surplus produce of peasant farmers being transferred to powerful local 'patrons'[9] in return for some minimal security.[10]. The revolutionary effect of the changes of land tenure was that now, 'patron-client relationships stemmed directly out of the possession of differential rights in land'[11]. All those working for a landowner, whether as tenants or servants, or as 'independent' artisans, tended to become his clients.

What are the benefits to patrons and clients of these relationships, which are still the norm in many parts of the sub-continent?

For the landowning patrons as a class this system provides a means for extracting the surplus value of labour while simultaneously ensuring social equilibrium. For individual landowners, too, there are benefits. Bigger landowners lease out land to tenants and sharecroppers in part to reduce their management problems and in part to assure a supply of labour during planting and harvesting when manpower shortages are common[12].

Poor villagers foster ties with powerful patrons as a way of reducing risk and improving stability. An ideal patron not only provides his clients with work and income, which is customarily paid in kind at the time of harvest, but also helps them in every way he can. 'He intercedes on the client's behalf with officials of local self-government bodies or co-operative societies, to secure for him a benefit or contract, introduces him to a lawyer or doctor, advances him a loan to meet an emergency, and tries to influence decisions in his favour in disputes.'[13] He also looks after 'the welfare of the client's children, particularly in the way of education and employment'[14]. A well-off person courts unpopularity if he does not maintain his side in these relationships, or if he neglects to sponsor village events and carry out community work.

Peasants have few options for meeting their needs for fuel, fertilizer, fodder and construction materials and their economies are consequently frugal in their use of organic materials.[15] The per capita availability of many of these resources is declining rapidly over large areas of the Third World.[16] In rural Bangladesh, the scarcity is manifest. Fuel collection has become a major task for women and children[17]; the number of *bichas* (village trials) arising from disputes over the ownership of trees, crops residues, and other fuel sources is large and increasing.[18]

The distribution of these scarce resources is governed by those mechanisms which control the distribution of food and other valuable commodities. A traditional landowner in Comilla District, for instance, may neither compost all of the available rice straw nor burn the straw on the field, where the ash is valued as fertilizer, but is expected to allow clients to clear a prescribed area of the harvest paddy field. Similar privileges may be extended for the collection of *gobar* from the cows of the rich. So a programme for the utilization of human excreta with the dung from a farmer's cows and the straw from his fields may not be attractive to the farmer, since the benefits may be insufficient to warrant the risk of damaging his customary relationships.

An awareness of these distributive mechanisms allows one to appreciate that when villagers are unenthusiastic about an innovation which urban or foreign 'experts' have thought up, 'it is because the latter are insensitive to the full implications of the innovation at the village level'[19]. The villagers live in complex, multistranded relationships with each other and with landowners[20]. To use straw or dung in a new way may threaten some part of that relationship. To use night soil, however, would not affect the relationship; the rich might object to it on grounds of ritual purity, but the poor would probably welcome it[21]. Innovation seems to work best when it involves something entirely new, and does not involve any attempt, 'to change the traditional methods and techniques of production'[22]. Thus there may be fewer barriers to introducing the use of human excreta than to altering the customary uses of rice straw and *gobar*.

Current changes in the resource use system

With the adoption of high-yielding crop varieties and mechanization of agriculture, the 'traditional' system has begun to disintegrate. In Purnea District of Bihar, as land values rose five-fold[23], payments in kind, sharecropping and the employment of permanent labourers gave way to money wages, owner cultivation and the hiring of daily labourers[24].

These processes are also under way in areas where there have not been dramatic increases in productivity, which is the situation in Bangladesh[25]. There, the decline of the traditional system and the rise of the market economy has led to a dramatic polarization in rural society. In the decade since 1966, about 15 per cent of households have increased their incomes, while the percentage of landless to total households has increased from 18 to 38 per cent[26]. Real agricultural wages have declined by nearly half, and nutritional standards have fallen drastically.

The causes of these changes

The customary system provided a channel through which rich and poor could reach their respective goals of power and security. A change now in the opportunities of patron and client alters the relative bargaining position of the two parties and consequently tilts the balance in the customary relationship: the terms of the relationship may change, or the ties may even be dissolved. In Bangladesh, several factors have contributed to the tilting of this balance against the poor, including:

(a) the impact of high-yielding crops,
(b) increased income from non-agricultural sources,
(c) decline in the availability of slack resources such as unused land, common pasture, and free fuel,
(d) changes in labour supply and demand.

It is probably the last of these which has had the biggest effect on Bangladesh.

With regard to high-yielding crops, if everyone has equal access to the new technology, modern agriculture offers the possibility of improving the lot of all. Since the demand for labour increases with the adoption of high-yielding crop varieties, even the landless could be better off. The hitch is, of course, that even in the better co-operatives in Bangladesh, the rich have access to new inputs which are denied to most of the small landowners and the landless[27]. Differential access to resources increases the squeeze on those who do not have access to the new technology—people are forced to sell land, sharecroppers' rents rise, and cultivators are evicted as landowners realize that it has become more profitable to work the land themselves.[28]. Market mechanisms are strengthened and traditional relationships decline.

In parts of Bihar, this process is associated with the introduction of new seeds and fertilizers, but in Bangladesh, where these innovations have played a much smaller part[29], similar changes are occurring for other reasons. One factor has been a low rate of growth in agricultural production[30]. At the same time, employment outside agriculture has barely increased, so in fact, the share of agriculture in total employment *increased* to over 80 per cent[31] in 1968. The result was that by the late 1960s, many more people in the agricultural sector were producing only slightly more than at the beginning of the decade. Real agricultural wages inevitably fell. And the widening gap between the supply of labour and a decreasing demand is probably the primary factor in changing the system of labour organization in agriculture.

In the 1970s, Bangladesh exhibits characteristics common to all societies which have been subsumed into the cultural system of the market economy—labour is sold, land is rented, and capital is freely invested[32]. In disposing of a man's labour power, 'the system is disposing of the physical, psychological and moral entity "man" attached to that tag', and it is clear that, 'robbed of the protective covering of cultural institutions, human beings are perishing'[33].

The consequences for the use of organic resources

There is little reliable data on the use of non-commercial resources, so it is difficult to assess how the rise of the market economy has affected this. But there are some indications. Thus some mention was made above of a village in the Comilla District where traditional landowners provided their clients with straw. In the same village, farmers who have acquired land through recent purchases, who farm their own land, and who pay money wages, burn the crop residues which they cannot use themselves. The disintegration of the traditional distribution system is endangering the stable combination of resources which had previously underwritten a minimal livelihood.

In India, 40 000 'gobar gas' plants have been installed under a government programme. The programme has been most successful where new seeds are widely used, particularly in 'progressive' areas of Gujarat and Haryana. Of their own accord, over 30 per cent of the biogas plant owners in Haryana have attached latrines to the digesters[34], suggesting that when customary norms have broken down, proscriptions against the use of human excreta may no longer be stringent.

Two surveys of gas-plant owners in Gujarat have been conducted. One showed that the individual families who own gas plants had, on average, 26 acres of land and 10 cattle. According to the other survey, most of the owners had 'an annual income of more than $1100 and a large number had an annual income over $2800 and their primary occupation was agriculture. They were literate and nearly 40 per cent of them had subsidiary occupations such as business, or service.'[35] The advantages of using biogas within this rather successful group have been at the expense of the poor, for whom the gobar excreted by the cattle of the rich was previously available as a basic fuel.

The findings of the differential adoption rate among big farmers, depending on whether they had subsidiary occupations, accords with the theory presented in this paper. Those whose traditional ties have been severed are able to mobilize their resources for their own purposes more easily than those whose relationships have a stronger traditional component.

Traditional ties are breaking down rapidly in many areas, with the result that the use of local resources is often 'rationalized' in a limited and capitalistic sense. Adoption of improved technologies for the use of these resources is hastening the deterioration of the resource base of the poor. The use of human excreta might shore up this base, but the Indian experience shows that unless programmes are explicitly tailored for the poor, they are likely to exacerbate an already inequitable distribution of resources.

11.2 BIOGAS SYSTEMS AND SANITATION

S.K. Subramanian[36]

The present status of biogas systems

Biogas systems have lately received considerable attention as a tool for decentralized approaches to development. They have been supported both as a means of fuel and fertilizer substitution, and as an aid to sanitary improvement.

However, the potential significance of biogas systems in meeting some of these needs is less then clear. On one hand, the installation of nearly 40 000 individual biogas plants in India and the use of biogas for fuel and lighting by over 17 million commune peasants in Szechuan[37], the most populous province in central China, together give an encouraging scenario. On the other hand, the Republic of Korea has decided to halt its programme after having earlier supported nearly 27 000 family-size biogas units[38], and this gives a more negative impression. This paper presents further contrasts and perspectives, based on a recent survey of biogas systems in Asia[39].

Most of the biogas plants in India, Korea, and other Asian countries operate either on cattle dung or pig waste. However, some units in India operate on the combined digestion of human night soil and cattle waste, and a small number, usually in large institutions, operate with night soil alone. Digestion of other wastes, including plant residues, algae, and other biological wastes, is being studied as a means of augmenting animal wastes, and spreading the benefits over a wider social spectrum.

The monthly production of biogas from one person's night soil would only be around 1.0 cubic metre, depending on dietary habits, whereas the monthly gas consumption for cooking would be around 4 to 5 cubic metres per person, assuming efficient burners. This explains why biogas plants using night soil are located in colleges or other places where they will collect the excreta of many people. It also explains why there is interest in using other wastes along with the night soil. In China, the feed to biogas plants includes weeds, leaves and crop residues after their preliminary decomposition for about ten days. The Office of Rural Development of the Republic of Korea has been engaged in the operation of a pilot village-level digester of 200 cubic metre capacity. Invariably all these units operate under mesophilic conditions (digestion temperature being at or below 35°C), whereas Japan has opted in favour of thermophilic treatment (around 55°C) for the treatment of urban wastes and other industrial effluents.

In India, the Gandhi Samarak Nidhi has been active in the installation of biogas units based on night soil and fifty-five such plants were in operation in 1976 in the state of Maharashtra alone. For example, a plant in a leprosy home near Poona was being operated with the night soil of its 187 inmates and the gas met part of the cooking needs. Another pilot unit at Nagpur Central Jail supported by nearly one thousand prisoners is presently run by the National Environmental Engineering Research Institute (NEERI) to demonstrate the total recycling of human waste. The gas meets part of the cooking needs in the jail. Among plants based on the popular design by the Khadhi and Village Industries Commission, but operating solely on the night soil, is an experimental plant in operation at a bus station in Maharashtra since 1975. This unit is connected to eight W.C. pans and the gas is used in the canteen.

Though a number of plants for rural and urban communities are being planned by welfare agencies and private firms, none is in operation yet. However, sufficient field data exist as regards small household plants and those owned by institutions. In the state of Haryana alone, over 30 per cent of the household plants are attached to toilets.

In the Philippines, a night soil digestion unit is in operation in a public school and the National Housing Authority is keen to introduce biogas technology for treating all wastes in new settlement areas. The Community Development Department had designed special toilet basins to avoid possible over-dilution of night soil fed into the digester and provisions were being incorporated in the design for diverting detergents and other harmful materials from entering the digester. In 1976, a hospital near Manila was exploring the feasibility of treating all hospital wastes and placenta. The most extensive application of biogas in the Asian region exists in Maya Farms, a piggery located at Angono, forty miles south of Manila.

Biodigestion of animal wastes helps to remove foul smell and to reduce breeding of houseflies, fruit flies and other disease carriers But the digestion of night soil warrants some additional precautions, as it contains many pathogens, worms and parasites. The most systematic work on the destruction of pathogens appears to have been done in China[40], and will be discussed in the next chapter.

So far, only a small number of designs for biogas plant have been built and tested, and there is considerable scope for technical improvement. The popular Indian design has the advantage of continuous run over a long period without the need for intermittent sludge removal. On the other hand, the Chinese model has to be opened up annually for maintenance and cleaning, but it has the unique distinction of dispensing with any moving part. Some farmers in Thailand as well as a few experimental units in the Philippines have successfully employed galvanised iron drums for the digestion of animal wastes, but corrosion problems may be more severe with night soil. The Japanese experience of thermophilic operation may be of interest at least for some large scale community plants, as the high temperature would ensure more efficient destruction of pathogens.

Social aspects

Resistance to the use of night soil in household digesters appears to be relatively less in China than elsewhere. In some areas, like West Java and Bangladesh, night soil is used as fish feed and it is not uncommon to see toilets constructed at the edge of fish ponds. On the other hand, in parts of Korea there are psychological barriers even to using animal wastes as manure.

In India, resistance to using night soil is not closely correlated with either education or religion. If anything, educated people voice the greatest objection. Religious sentiments sometimes discourage the use of gas generated from night soil for cooking, particularly the food offered during worship either at home or in the temple. Religious feelings could be the cause of objections found in parts of Uttar Pradesh, West Bengal and in the southern Indian states. But other, equally religious states like Gujarat and Maharashtra have shown a greater willingness to use biogas. For those who handle the slurry themselves, there are no problems. But those who have hired workers anticipate trouble due to labour unrest.

Where biogas generation is based totally on night soil, the hard fact that an individual depends on at least five others apart from himself to provide the gas for his cooking needs, could pose certain social problems. For example, a sugar factory in India constructed a biogas unit fed by toilets used by its watch and ward personnel, and presuming psychological barriers, it connected the gas supply only to the residence of the top officers. The operation subsequently failed, since the labourers decided not to contribute to the prerequisites offered to the senior staff.

Even in India, which has a sizeable number of biogas plants in operation, it is difficult to conclude that there has yet arisen a strong need-oriented demand for biogas. It has been the richer strata of rural society, who have installed biogas units. A host of factors have made it difficult, unattractive or impossible for relatively poor people to use biogas plants. The place of individually owned family units is a controversial issue, but countries like Korea and India are laying greater emphasis on large-scale village units.

The advantages of a community plant would be efficient, large-scale operation and opportunities for using gas for running refrigerators in health centres, generating electricity, pumping water, and so on. But all this would depend on people using community latrines and maintaining the cleanliness of the surroundings. To avoid excessive use of water, taps may have to be provided only outside the toilets and disinfectants cannot be used for cleaning. The equitable distribution of gas and manure could also pose a problem. The success of such schemes would be very much dictated by social attitudes and values of the community and also by its spatial patterns and arrangements. An understanding of the rural sociological practices would help in the identification of the sites for common facilities and in appreciating the operational problems to be tackled.

Biogas technology is certainly viable, but the economic performance of biogas systems[41] is dependent on a number of local factors like climatic conditions, local terrain, village setting, social practices, availability of water (and other inputs), and the ease of using the gas and the effluent effectively (taking into account the non-liquefaction of biogas at ambient temperatures). The economics is also very sensitive to fluctuations that occur outside the system. The high return on investments would have little significance when the necessary level of capital is not available to the villager. As said earlier, in order to produce sufficient biogas and to spread the benefits over a wide social spectrum, it may be necessary to think of community plants, and it would be essential to supplement the night soil feed with other materials like animal and agricultural wastes. This would not only help in improving the environment and controlling flies and other insects, but also in enhancing the manurial value of these wastes.

The way ahead

Biogas systems provide a means of hygienic disposal for night soil which could be more widely used if more attention were paid to the socio-economic factors necessary for success. Improvement in the technology is also needed, however, and one of the first steps should be the compilation of operating experiences from biogas plants in various countries.

Initial attempts with night soil digesters should preferably be confined to institutions like prisons, colleges, and schools, or public facilities like railway stations. This would help in standardizing the technology, and in alerting planners to possible technical and social problems. With that as a basis, one could then begin to identify places where community operations involving night soil digestion to make biogas have a good chance of success. These are likely to be places which already have large groups of people who co-operate in some productive process, which have few social restrictions on the use of night soil, and where a drive for betterment is already evident. Field experiences in these zones could be the starting point for spreading the activity to other areas, and for identifying extension workers who could help spread the technique at community level in new areas.

11.3 URBAN WASTE AS AN ECONOMIC GOOD

DeAnne S. Julius[42]

The theory of inferior goods

There is a small tentacle on the body of micro-economic theory which deals with the behaviour of what economists call 'inferior goods'. While this topic is rarely of any practical interest, I was delighted to discover a possible application in the field of low-cost waste disposal during the recent trip to East Asia. If the hypothesis is correct that urban wastes exhibit 'inferior goods' behaviour, then some interesting theoretical implications can be derived which may aid us in understanding and promoting the diffusion of low-cost technologies of waste disposal.

Three variables which affect the demand for all goods are the price of the goods, the price of other goods which may be substitutes or complements for the goods in question, and the preference of the consumer. A fourth determinant of demand is the income of the consumer. For most goods, as income increases so does the quantity demanded. When one diagrams this relationship between income and the quantity demanded the result is known as an Engel curve. For most goods the Engel curve is upward sloping when income is measured on the vertical axis and the quantity demand on the horizontal axis. For inferior goods, however, the Engel curve is downward sloping. That is, as the consumer's income increases he demands less of the good in question. One example of an inferior good which is often cited is the potato. Historical data in Ireland shows that during good years when consumers' incomes were high, fewer potatoes were demanded, while during bad years the consumption of potatoes increased. Of course, since potato sales formed a large part of many consumers' incomes, this demand behavior itself generated income cycles. Another example is beer. Consumption of beer by poorer families is much larger than the consumption of beer by richer families. Presumably this is due to the substitution of more expensive beverages as income rises.

Waste as an inferior good

In the spring of 1977, I spent three weeks in Japan, Korea and Taiwan in connection with a World Bank sponsored research project on low-cost waste disposal (described in Section 3.3). One of the particular questions with which I was concerned was the demand pattern for night soil. Japan, Korea, and Taiwan offered a unique group for comparison, because of the fairly similar cultural backgrounds of the three and the relatively large differences in income levels and general stage of economic development. Per capita income ranges from around $450 in Korea to $700 in Taiwan and $3600 in Japan[43].

Very little night soil is still used as fertilizer in Japan, the most affluent of the three countries—perhaps less than 2 per cent of all night soil collected. By contrast, in Taiwan, there is still considerable demand from farmers for night soil to put on the land, although this demand is decreasing. In Korea, however, the poorest of the three countries, night soil is still routinely used as fertilizer, often without treatment. These comparisons therefore illustrate the relationship between income levels and the demand for night soil predicted by the theory.

A second crude method of testing the hypothesis is to examine demand behaviour within a single country. In Japan, we talked to officials of the Kyoto night soil treatment plant about changes in the pattern of night soil use. Until about 1945, all the night soil was used by farmers, we were told. During the next 15 years the use of night soil as fertilizer declined steadily. Thus by 1960, almost no night soil was demanded or used by farmers.

The official with whom we spoke cited four main factors behind this change. These were the increased cost of farm labour, the increased use of mechanical equipment, the cleaner and easier application of chemical fertilizer, and higher farm incomes. In passing, one may note that during these decades, official Japanese policy focused on increasing farm income partly through subsidies on chemical fertilizer. Today, in the Kyoto area, some farmers still use their own night soil as fertilizer, and there have been instances of farmers obtaining city night soil to restore the humus content lost from their land through intensive use of chemical fertilizer.

At the same time that farmers' demand for night soil has decreased, the city dwellers' demand for modern plumbing has risen, so that the availability of night soil has also declined. In Kyoto, only about 40 per cent of city residents have access to underground sewerage, but septic tanks are becoming even more widely used.

Two cities in Taiwan provided relevant data. In Tainan, a city of about half a million people, only about 30 000 are now served by night soil collection. Since there is no underground sewer system, the rest of the city uses septic tanks and surface drainage. In 1961, when the population was around 100 000, nearly all used night soil collection. There has been a fairly rapid shift from night soil collection (which the city provides free) to private septic tanks (which cost about $80 to install plus another $80 for plumbing) as local prosperity has risen. The city's night soil is sold to people involved in fish farming, who use it to grow chlorella (algae) which is fed to the fish along with bean cakes. The farmers pay about $0.50 per tonne for the night soil, plus $0.50 per 2-tonne truck load per kilometre for transport. The entire operation is fairly profitable, even during years of poor weather.

We also visited a smaller city in Taiwan called Pingtung, located about 40 km southeast of Tainan. Out of a total population of 180 000, about 35 000 use septic tanks, 80 000 use the public night soil collection system, and the remaining 65 000 use their night soil as fertilizer or give it to farming neighbours. In addition, there are more than 200 household biogas plants in operation.

Public night soil collection is free, so the 65 000 people who do not use this service are demonstrating an awareness of the value of night soil as a fertilizer. Thirty years ago, night soil removal was organized privately throughout the city. Groups of 10-15 households each hired a man with a bullock cart to collect the night soil and sell it to the farmers. As chemical fertilizer became more widespread, and the demand for night soil decreased to the extent that farmers were no longer willing to pay for it, the city took over night soil collection. However, it was still able to give away all the night soil to farmers, and nowadays this practice continues, but the city treats the night soil before the farmers use it.

In Korea, we visited Chuncheon city and talked with the deputy mayor about his new night soil treatment plant. He stated that this plant was necessary because farmers were no longer willing to use aged night soil as fertilizer. In his opinion, this change was due mostly to rising farm income, and the country's self-sufficiency in chemical fertilizer.

Thus cities visited in all three countries have exhibited the same pattern of change over the last two or three decades: as incomes rise, the use of night soil as fertilizer falls. In addition, a rough cross-country comparison shows that less night soil is used today in the richest country, Japan, than in Taiwan and Korea. These two types of comparison lead me to suggest that considering urban wastes as an example of an inferior economic good may yield some useful policy implications.

Implications for policy

Among the four variables which influence the demand for a particular good, the first is the price of that good. Obviously, if one wishes to encourage the purchase of night soil, one should not set its price too high. We saw a case in Pingtung, Taiwan, where the price of night soil had dropped to zero at the time when the city first took over collection. As the quality of the night soil was improved for use as fertilizer, the price charged to farmers was again raised to a positive amount. Of course, the price of the night soil itself does not constitute the entire cost of using it. Since the application of such organic fertilizer is generally much more labour-intensive than the application of chemical fertilizer, the cost of labour is also an important determinant of the total cost of using night soil. In labour-scarce economies like Japan, the cost of farm labour may make night soil use uneconomical. In countries where minimum wage legislation distorts the price of unskilled labour, organic fertilizer may be rejected by farmers on financial grounds. Thus promoting its use may require politically difficult corrections in macro-economic policy, or some offsetting subsidy.

The second variable affecting demand is the price of other goods. The most important goods to consider are substitutes, for example, chemical fertilizers and bottled gas for cooking. In both Japan and Korea, when the government subsidized chemical fertilizers, the demand for night soil to use as fertilizer decreased. In Pingtung, the difference in price between liquid petroleum gas and methane from the biogas units was striking. One family we visited used the waste from four pigs plus night soil in its biogas unit and was able to produce enough methane to run a one-burner stove all the year round. This family had an additional stove which it used for large dinners on special occasions and which used liquid petroleum gas costing $6.25 per 20 kg cylinder. Before constructing the biogas unit, the family needed about one cylinder per month for cooking (thus costing about $75 per year). But with the biogas stove in use and the cylinder simply held in reserve for special occasions, it had lasted four years (costing $1.50 per year). However, the housewife told us that although she was very happy with the biogas stove, she might have to discontinue using it because the price of pig feed had risen so high that they were thinking of selling their animals.

The third determinant of demand is the preference function of the consumer. While it is difficult to collect actual data on preference in different situations, countries such as those visited in East Asia have a long history of using night soil as a fertilizer, and thus few ingrained prejudices against its employ. This situation might not obtain in other regions of the world. There, considerable education of

198

farmers might be necessary to induce them to use night soil even under optimal economic conditions. The example quoted in Kyoto of farmers returning to the use of night soil when they noticed a decline in soil productivity after intensive use of chemicals, is an illustration of a change in preferences growing out of education which affected night soil demand.

Income is the final demand determinant. If urban waste is indeed an inferior good, we can expect demand for it to decline as incomes increase. This implies that countries with relatively low per capita incomes are likely to be more susceptible to the spread of low-cost re-use technologies. There is nothing new or startling about this conclusion, of course; it is simply another example of the general principle that for a technology to be 'appropriate' in a given country, it must be relatively intensive in those factors of production which are relatively abundant in that country.

Another conclusion is possible. If the current burst of research activity leads to the development of re-use technologies which appear to have widespread application even in the labour-scarce (and increasingly energy-scarce) developed world, then the biggest obstacle to their diffusion may be the attitudinal block toward waste as an inferior good. In that case, rather than concentrating on making technology as low in cost as possible, an educational campaign stressing the environmental and ecological benefits of waste re-use may be the best marketing strategy. Through such an approach, it is even possible that innovative methods of waste disposal may become so fashionable as to need reclassification from inferior goods to what economists call Veblin goods—those status symbols for which demand actually increases as their price goes up.

NOTES AND REFERENCES

1. John Briscoe is Sanitary Engineer, Epidemiology Division, Cholera Research Laboratory, GPO Box 128, Dacca-2, Bangladesh.
2. Point made in conference discussions by M.G. McGarry.
3. Point made in conference discussions by John Briscoe. The modern idea of appropriate technology owes its origins at least partly to discussions of Gandhi's views. In one of his earlier papers on the subject, E.F. Schumacher quoted D.R. Gadgil, the Indian economist, writing about 'intermediate technology' in a book called *Appropriate Technologies for Indian Industry,* published by SIET Institute, Hyderabad, in 1964, before the idea of intermediate or appropriate technology had gained currency in the West. In fact, Gadgil was one of those who argued that the failure of Gandhi's approach 'lay essentially in not recognizing the need for. . . thoroughly demolishing the older institutional forms'. See Gunnar Myrdal, *Asian Drama,* Penguin edn., 1968, p. 886; also Schumacher's *Small is Beautiful,* Blond & Briggs, London, 1973, pp. 175-6.
4. Akhter Hameed Kahn, *History of the Food Problem,* Department of Economics, University of Karachi, undated; see also R. Cassen *Population and Development Review* 1 (1).
5. John Briscoe, 'Public health in rural India: The case of excreta disposal', Research paper no. 12, Harvard University Center for Population Studies, February 1976; and, Ramesh Bhatia, 'Bio-gas units in India's rural

development: A framework for social benefit cost analysis', presented at the Workshop on Bio-gas Systems, Management Development Institute, March 1977.

6. R.L. Heilbroner, *The Making of Economic Society*, Prentice Hall, Eaglewood Cliffs, N.J., 1962

7. Karl Polanyi, *The Great Transformation: The Political and Economic Origins of Our Time*, Beacon Press, Boston, 1957.

8. R. Palme Dutt, *India Today* (second edition), Modern India Press, Calcutta, 1947

9. Eric R. Wolf, *Peasant Wars of the Twentieth Century*, Harper and Row, N.Y., 1969

10. James C. Scott, *Journal of Asian Studies*, 2 (1), 1972

11. M.N. Srinivas. *The Remembered Village*, Oxford University Press, Delhi, 1976

12. Michael Lipton, in *The Crisis in Indian Planning: Economic Policy in the 1960s*, ed. M. Lipton and P. Streeton, Oxford University Press, N.Y. 1968.

13. Srinivas, *op. cit.*, note 11.

14. S.P.F. Senaratne, 'Micro studies, employment and the strategies for development', report for the World Employment Programme, International Labour Office, Geneva, 1975

15. Marvin Harris, *Cows, Witches and Wars: the Riddle of Culture*, Random House, N.Y. 1974

16. Erik P. Eckholm, *Losing Ground: Environmental Stress and World Food Prospects*, W.W. Norton, N.Y. 1976

17. A. Farouk and M. Ali, *The Hardworking Poor: a Survey of how People use their Time in Bangladesh*, Bureau of Economic Research, Dacca University, 1975.

18. Ahidur Reza Chowdhury, Chairman, Union Council, Fatepur East Union, Matlab Thana, Comila District, Bangladesh, personal communication.

19. Srinivas, *op. cit.*, note ll.

20. Ibid.

21. Prodipto Roy, 'Social aspects of biogas plants', Workshop on Biogas Systems, Management Development Institute, New Delhi, 5 pages, 1977.

22. Scarlett Epstein, *Themes in Economic Anthropology*, ed. Raymond Firth, Tavistock Publications, London, 1967.

23. Wolf Ladejinsky, *Foreign Affairs*, 48 (4), 1970

24. S.D. Biggs, 'Science and agricultural technology for Bangladesh: a framework for policy analysis', paper presented at Symposium on Science and Agricultural Technology, First Annual Bangladesh Science Conference, 38 pages, March 1976.

25. Edward J. Clay, *Bangladesh Development Studies*, 4 (4), October 1976; see also Mohiuddin Alamgir, *Bangladesh: a Case of Below Level Equilibrium Trap*, Bangladesh Institute of Development Studies, 1976.

26. A.R. Khan, 'Poverty and inequality in rural Bangladesh', working paper, World Employment Programme, International Labour Office, Geneva, 41 pages, 1976.

27. Akhter Hameed Khan, *Tour of Twenty Thanas: Impressions of Drainage, Roads, Irrigation and Co-operative Programmes*, Bangladesh Academy for Rural Development, Comila, 1971

28. Ladejinsky, *op. cit.*, note 23; also Douglas V. Smith, 'New seeds and income distribution in Bangladesh, *Journal of Development Studies*, 2 (2), January 1975

29. Clay, *op. cit.*, note 25

30. A.R. Khan, *op. cit.*, note 26

31. Ibid.
32. Edward J. Clay, 'Technical and institutional change and the agricultural labourer', Seminar at the Bangladesh Institute of Development Studies, January 15, 1977.
33. Polanyi, *op. cit.,* note 7
34. S.K. Subramanian, *Biogas systems in Asia,* mimeo, Management Development Institute, New Delhi, 1977.
35. Subramanian, *op. cit.,* note 34
36. S.K. Subramanian is Technical Consultant, Asian Productivity Organization, Minato-Ku, Tokyo, 107, Japan
37. 'Marsh Gas', Hsinhua News Agency, Peking, quoted in *Japan Times,* 30 May 1977
38. *Utilization Effects of Methane Gas as a Rural Fuel Source,* Office of Rural Development, Suwon, Republic of Korea, August 1976.
39. Subramanian, *op. cit.,* note 34.
40. *Experimental Research on Excreta Disposal by Biogas Plants, Preliminary Report,* Research Office for Parasitic Disease Prevention, Province of Szechuan, c. 1973
41. T.K. Moulik and U.K. Srivastava, *Biogas Plants at Village level. . . in Gujarat,* Indian Institute of Management, Ahmedabad, 1975; also, Indian Council of Agricultural Research, *The Economics of Cow Dung Gas Plants, 1976,*
42. DeAnne S. Julius is an economist in the Energy, Water and Telecommunications Department, The World Bank, Washington, D.C. 20433, U.S.A.,
43. Income levels for 1973, quoted from *World Tables, 1976,* International Bank for Reconstruction and Development, (The World Bank), Washington, D.C.

12

Treatment, Re-Use, and Health

12.1 RE-USE POLICIES AND RESEARCH NEEDS

Conference Working Group[1]

Policies on using excreta

The use of excreta and waste-water to provide fertilizer, nutrients for fish, or a gaseous fuel, can give a positive economic incentive for improving sanitation in developing countries. The economic benefits from using excreta in these ways are often more tangible than the benefits to public health, and may therefore provide stronger motivation for better sanitation.

However, we feel that re-use of excreta has been discredited needlessly or incorrectly by over-zealous and over-strict health authorities. They have rightly seen the dangers of the direct application of night soil to vegetables or to fish ponds, and they have correctly assessed the dissemination of pathogenic organisms which result. But in their reaction to this, they have set up such strict standards as to turn people away from re-use altogether, to the point where it is not considered socially acceptable by international agencies or local health departments. And under some circumstances, this restrictive attitude may actually slow down improvements in hygiene and sanitation, though it is supported in the name of better health.

A different analysis of the health aspect is possible, however, which needs to be formulated with some care: we felt that in a situation where there is no organized excreta disposal, and faeces are spread all over the place, and the population is exposed to large helminth loads, then the very act of channelling excreta onto a disposal site, and from there onto the fields, is a positive health gain.

Recognizing that all the health problems have not been solved, we feel that just by restricting the area of contamination and exposure, re-use can be beneficial in terms of health. Once the channelling of waste through an organized collection and re-use system has been accomplished, the introduction of a treatment process such as composting or oxidation ponds can follow as a second stage, and can lead to the reduction of health risks still further.

Agencies which have preached against night soil re-use, or have set up unreasonable standards such as total heat treatment or pasteurisation (which is not feasible from an economic point of view) have deprived many populations of a potentially valuable resource, that will become more valuable as time goes on because of world fertilizer and fuel price increases. In the long run—twenty to thirty years—excreta used to make biogas or fertilizer may play a key role in maintaining the energy balance or nutrient balance in areas where excreta comprise one of very few resources. Policies on fertilizer subsidies should be reviewed in the light of this. From this point of view, there is room for a new interest in night soil and organic waste re-use. There is room too, for public policies to be changed through policy-making organisations such as WHO, other international agencies, and the national health departments. These bodies should recognise not only the value of the resources to be gained in this way, but the incentives for better sanitation which may follow.

Another way in which re-use has been discredited is through people who over-sell it by talking about turning garbage into gold, and making other claims which cannot be substantiated. Municipal re-use programmes should *not* be seen as profit-making operations, but merely as ways of reducing costs, and as ways of motivating people to co-operate in sanitation schemes by demonstrating a tangible benefit.

Cultural and organization problems

There are several social and cultural problems associated with night soil re-use, aquaculture, and biogas production. Although in certain countries there may be local cultural constraints against the re-use of excreta, this rarely holds for the entire society. For every instance where a group of people object to re-use, there are other groups who do not object, and who see it as beneficial. In most societies, there are more than enough people already aware of the potential benefits for a start to be made on re-using wastes. With diffusion of new ideas, and with practical demonstrations of the benefits, even people who now oppose re-use may slowly change their minds. So this should not be seen as a closed situation. If there is opposition to a re-use plan in one place, its promoters should try it in another community where the people are in favour, and once it succeeds there, opinions in other places may change.

The organization of projects does not pose any special problems in rural areas, but will be of critical importance in urban conditions. Just to collect night soil hygienically and efficiently may require tens or hundreds of vehicles operating to a fixed schedule, which is itself a major organizational task. The operation of a sanitary night soil treatment system such as composting also requires a high level of organization, and there are problems of marketing and distributing the compost. The ability of a community to provide such management and organizational skills may be a major factor in determining the success or failure of a project. Management training should be included as part of any programme.

Re-use options

There is a surprisingly wide range of different ways of making use of either the nutrient content of excreta, or its energy value, or both. The main options, not all of them to be recommended, are as follows:

(a) Direct use of night soil on the land
(b) Compost making
(c) Use of waste-water for irrigation
(d) Aquaculture (i.e. fish production)
(e) Algae culture
(f) Use of excreta in feeding animals
(g) Biogas production

There are health hazards involved in most of these options, but measures can often be taken to reduce them. When it is wished to use night soil on the land, for example, health dangers can be greatly reduced by composting (which is discussed in Section 12.2) or by first storing the night soil in closed detention tanks, as is done in China.

Composting night soil can be operated safely and with great benefit to agriculture, and we suggest that governments should reconsider their subsidies on chemical fertilizers to include subsidies for night soil composting on a similar basis. This would not only encourage better soil fertility, but could lead to all night soil being treated before re-use, and hence to an improvement in human health.

Where urban areas have water-borne sewage facilities, the use of waste-water for irrigation can provide real benefits in increased soil fertility and productivity. Treatment of waste-water in a series of oxidation ponds with 15 to 20 day retention can provide a high degree of pathogen removal. Such treatment provides superior helminth removal to that obtained by conventional biological treatment methods. Restricting the crops grown to non-edible crops or to crops usually eaten when cooked can provide an additional degree of health protection.

Fish, pigs, and algae culture

Adding night soil in combination with other organic waste to fish ponds can increase fish production with important nutritional benefits. Prior treatment of the night soil in oxidation ponds can effectively reduce the risk of infection, as can placement of fish in post-treatment ponds for at least two weeks before being marketed and eaten.

Although the growth of algae in oxidation ponds may provide a potential future resource for growing low-cost food for animals such as cattle and pigs, it is felt that this subject requires further study before it can be applied and be of benefit in developing countries. Another approach to the production of animal feed is research which has been undertaken to find ways of separating nutrients from sewage. It should also be noted that in places without adequate sanitation, pigs are often observed to eat any human excreta they can find. This is hardly a recommended form of re-use, but the health hazards involved in consuming the meat of such pigs needs investigation.

Biogas

In China, there are said to be 80 000 biogas units (see Section 12.5) in Korea 27 000, and in India, where it is called 'Gobar gas' meaning cow-dung gas, there are 40 000 (Section 11.2). Biogas is an extremely attractive, all-encompassing re-use strategy, because one can use the gas as a fuel and still have a fertilizer, in the form of sludge from the plant.

There is a minimum critical size for a biogas plant, which depends on details of design and insulation. The size influences the temperature of the slurry and the process of digestion. Size is also relevant to economic performance, because a considerable capital investment is needed to build the plant, and there are economies of scale. Only at a certain scale does the process become feasible from a biological point of view, and only at a certain scale does it make sense from an economic point of view.

The economic factor should become less of a constraint as fuel prices rise, but it is unclear whether the units currently in use give an economic return. It is especially difficult to be clear about this where biogas programmes benefit from strong government support through loans, grants, and subsidies. In India, biogas has apparently been particularly attractive to moderately prosperous farmers with access to loans, and with a sufficient number of cows to keep the biogas units supplied with raw material—for example, farmers with two flush latrines and between 5 and 15 cows. But efforts should be made to develop a communal or co-operative biogas system serving a number of families, who would then locate their cooking facilities near the gas source.

The problem here is that the minimum critical size of a biogas unit is such that it does not fit the individual family unit. In India, only 12 per cent of the population have sufficient cows to support an individual unit of their own. If we try to reach people who do not possess these sorts of resources, it is inevitable that communal facilities will be required, and this point has been completely neglected (but see Section 11.2). We strongly felt that studies should be made to discover whether organizational structures can be arranged around family groups, extended families, or groups living in houses facing a common courtyard or hutment area—groups which would be large enough to feed a biogas plant, and at the same time capable of sharing the cooking facilities.

Research needs

This question of access to biogas by the poorest members of society was picked out as one of several areas where more research on re-use strategies seems to be needed. No attempt was made to establish an order of priorities, but it was agreed that research is also needed on:

(a) the use of currently unused vegetable resources (e.g. water hyacinth) in biogas or fertilizer plants along with excreta;

(b) The transfer of re-use technologies from developed to developing countries (and vice versa);

(c) the institutional framework for optimum implementation of re-use strategies, including integrated institutions for dealing with health, energy, and agricultural aspects;

(d) the agricultural value of night soil and compost as compared with chemical fertilizer;

(e) the health protection obtained by composting night soil in well-run municipal systems;

(f) the value of night soil in fish ponds and ways of maximizing fish yields;

(g) the rate at which pathogens die away when night soil is applied to fields and crops.

(h) the effects of feeding excreta directly to pigs, chickens and other animals, including the controls needed or the excreta processing required to develop a reasonably safe system.

12.2 COMPOSTING AS A TREATMENT PROCESS[2]

Choice of treatment technologies

It is obvious that if methods of recycling human wastes are to become more acceptable, waste treatment processes must be brought in which are suited to the type of re-use proposed, and are capable of reducing the health risks to a minimum.

Where conventional sewerage is in use, excreta will arrive at the treatment plant as sewage or waste-water, and will be most suited to re-use in fish ponds or for irrigation. The simplest and most appropriate treatment system in most hot countries will then be a series of *waste stabilization ponds* (often also called oxidation ponds), whose effectiveness is discussed in Section 12.3 and 12.4 below. These can reduce health risks considerably, but rarely eliminate them altogether. Further precautions are therefore needed during re-use, such as the use of irrigation techniques which avoid contact between the water and the edible parts of the crop. Drip irrigation is one technique which does this and the possibility of contact between water and the above-ground parts of the crop can be still further reduced by applying the water underneath a mulch of polythene sheeting. In contrast, an unsuitable method to use with waste-water is sprinkler irrigation, which can distribute pathogens very widely; salmonella from one spray unit in Israel were detected 100 m away as a result of water droplets being blown by the wind.

A different kind of re-use is involved where latrines make use of 'dry' systems, so that the excreta are not turned into a liquid sewage. Here the principal treatment process involved is *composting*. Two systems may be distinguished. In one, the excreta is removed from individual latrines as night soil and taken to a municipal plant for composting. The alternative is the use of composting toilets (Chapter 7) whereby the composting process takes place within individual latrines which are emptied at fairly long intervals. This section is mainly concerned with municipal composting practice.

Where 'wet' systems are in use, the sludge from aqua-privies, septic tanks and sewage treatment works can be dried out and made safe for re-use by composting. An instance where sludge is first dried in the sun and then made into compost for use in agriculture was described in Section 9.4.

Composting principles

Composting has been practised in many parts of the world from time immemorial, but efforts to understand the principles involved and devise systematic procedures for compost-making seem to have begun only in this century. Pioneering work in India by Howard[3] (1933) based on a study of the traditional methods of peasant farmers, led to the development of the 'Indore' composting process. Alternative layers of organic refuse and animal manure with night soil were piled in heaps on open ground, and were turned over at intervals of a few days.

Night soil can contain the full spectrum of pathogenic organisms including helminths and the bacterial, protozoan, and viral pathogens. Composting will greatly reduce the number of these pathogens (but not necessarily to zero) largely as a result of the heat generated by the process. There is a lot of evidence that a high level of health protection is given by composting, even though this does not give full pasteurization. Reports of compost heaps reaching 70°C are not realistic because such temperatures would destroy all the microflora. Very often, the centre of a heap goes up to 70°C while most of it reaches only 55°C, but even at this temperature, there will be a significant reduction of pathogens in three days. Composting also improves the quality of the material for soil fertilization, and the compost is further improved when other organic wastes are included, though the presence of plastic and glass refuse in the household wastes of some communities is a severe disadvantage.

The composting of night soil with other organic wastes is a particularly attractive option for municipalities, since it provides a relatively low-cost means of treatment with some economic return. It is said that 22 composting plants are operating in Indian cities. One example is Madurai, where the plant has worked successfully for about thirty years.

The Indore composting process was introduced into Nigeria in 1951, with the opening of a plant at Kano. This city then had a population of 130 000 and its composting depots were treating the night soil from 3 000 bucket latrines, together with most of the city's refuse and litter.[4] The compost was made by placing a carefully mixed batch of night soil and refuse in a pile between concrete walls about a metre high. In any one depot, these walls divided the plant into sixteen cells, each one capable of dealing with a two-day accumulation of wastes. The compost in each cell was turned after five days and fifteen days, and the cell was emptied after thirty days ready to begin a new cycle. The compost was then stacked at the depot to mature and to await collection by farmers from the surrounding groundnut-growing area. The Kano plants are still operating, though they have suffered through being designed entirely for manual handling.

The methods used in China for composting night soil include significant improvements over practices seen elsewhere in Asia (Section 12.5). One is that the compost pile is covered with a 5 cm layer of mud and straw mix which helps retain the heat developed inside the heap.

Much more data is needed on successful composting operations, and upgraded plant for urban areas needs to be demonstrated to make the feasibility of this approach more widely known. A satisfactory composting plant may either postpone or obviate the need for water-borne excreta removal which most developing countries can ill afford.

Although some composting schemes have met with success, a number of failures in developing countries have also been reported. Poor marketing of the compost may be an important factor in these failures, as well as the poor quality of the final product. It is recommended that in any proposed night soil composting project, a market survey should be carried out in advance and that project funds for the marketing side of the programme be provided to assure the proper movement of the final product to the agricultural consumer.

European researches on composting[5]

Traditional composting requires considerable manual labour for turning the material in order to sustain a satisfactory level of oxygen in the composting pile. This direct handling of the undigested material is not without risks to health. The results of technical developments in Holland and Denmark have been to avoid all handling by a reliable but very capital-intensive process, and there are now a great number of composting reactors, composting towers, and composting digesters on the market which have all been designed to replace the conventional water-based excreta treatment methods. The Scandinavian countries have pursued this in their search for more environmentally acceptable excreta disposal methods, and the State Environmental Protection Agency of Sweden has conducted a series of tests located in the town of Laxa. In most of these tests, sludge from sewage plants is mixed with shredded household refuse and treated with oxygen and by agitation in various types of reactor. It was found that all kinds of cellulose material could be used in such composting plant, including wood wastes and bark as well as household refuse.

Most of the modern composting installations have a rather complicated system aimed at imitating the traditional method of turning over the compost. Usually the material is stirred or mixed by mechanical means. The latest developments in this field, however, have indicated that no such complicated installations are necessary. The right balance between aeration, temperature and humidity can be achieved without a complicated installation. The Swedish Environmental Protection Agency found that mixtures of shredded household wastes and sewage sludge or human excreta can react very effectively if humidity is maintained by spraying water, and if air is forced through the pile through a system of ducts. This leaves the pile in a sufficiently porous state for full aeration. The present series of tests in Laxa has been very encouraging. A pile 2.0 m high and 200 m^2 in extent is treated by blowing air from ducts below it. A temperature of 70°C has been easily reached.

12.3 A WASTE-WATER TREATMENT AND RE-USE DEMONSTRATION

B.B. Sundaresan,[6] *S. Muthuswamy*[7],
and V.S. Govindan[8]

The need for low-cost treatment

Waste-water treatment and disposal systems are being given a low priority in developing countries because of their high cost, and water supplies are frequently constructed without any provision for disposing of the waste-water arising from them. Pools of water around community taps and near houses lead to profuse mosquito breeding and other health hazards. Thus low-cost methods for collecting and treating waste-water have become a necessity to combat environmental pollution.

Waste stabilization ponds (oxidation ponds) are now recognized as effective and economical units for treatment of domestic sewage as well as biodegradable industrial wastes. Low costs make it possible to bring this kind of sewage treatment within the scope of smaller communities and help reduce environmental pollution. The algae present in these ponds are a good source of food for edible varieties of fish. Effluent from the fish pond still contains nutrients, and is well suited for irrigating vegetables.

Principles of waste stabilization ponds

The driving force in a waste stabilization pond is solar energy utilized by photosynthesis. The action of sunlight on algae in the pond enables them to grow and consume the nutrients contained in the sewage. Also essential to the process are the large numbers of aerobic bacteria in the pond, which break down organic solids in the sewage, making their nutrient content available to the algae. The carbon dioxide released as the bacteria work on the organic solids is also utilized by the algae in their growth.

The algae and the bacteria are inter-dependent ('symbiotic'). While the algae use the nutrients and carbon dioxide released by bacterial decomposition, the bacteria make use of and need the oxygen liberated by the algae during photosynthesis.

The nutrients contained in sewage include nitrogenous compounds, phosphates, and potassium. In stabilization ponds, through the activities of algae, these nutrients are removed from solution and concentrated in the algal cells. Since the effluent from the ponds carries with it a considerable quantity of algae, the harvesting of algae from the pond effluent is a means of recovering nutrients from the waste-water. Results of earlier investigations have indicated the value of the algae as poultry feed and as a source of industrial raw material. Further, algal harvesting prevents the pollution of receiving waters due to the depletion of oxygen in the water by the endogenous respiration of the algae.

Waste stabilization ponds have been constructed and used in several places in

India and other developing countries. Performance of such ponds in places with sufficient sunlight is generally good. However, the effluent from the ponds has rarely been used effectively. Neither the direct harvesting of algae nor fish farming has been much developed, and where the water has been used to irrigate farm land, there has rarely been adequate evaluation of the results either from a production or a health point of view. Detailed observations are required with respect to physical, chemical, bacteriological, and biological quality of waste-water at different stages.

Experimental studies

A well developed sewage treatment demonstration plant with a stabilization pond, treating about 270 000 litres per day, forms part of the Public Health Engineering Department, at the College of Engineering, Guindy, Madras. It has a capacity of 2 160 000 litres at 1.0 m depth with a detention time of 8 days. Effluent from this pond is fed into a fish pond of 650 m^2 area with a depth of 1.0 m, which provides a detention time of over two days. The inner slope of the embankment is pitched with plain cement slabs to a height of 2.0 m to check erosion by wave action, prevent growth of weeds, and discourage mosquito breeding at the water's edge.

In the first studies, 500 fingerlings of *Cyprinus carpio* were introduced in the pond and their growth was observed. This was done by netting about 25 fish at random to measure length and weight. On a few occasions, well-grown fish have been dissected so that the algae in the gut could be studied.

The continuous flow of the final effluent from the fish pond is stored in a sump and pumped to irrigate about 150 coconut palms through a series of open channels. Coconut kernels growing at the tops of the trees are all that is consumed by people, and hence no health hazard is involved. This crop was also selected because it does not involve frequent agricultural operations such as ploughing and weeding. The palms start yielding after 5-7 years, and the coconuts offer a good source of revenue. A tubewell close to the plantation has been sunk so that any groundwater contamination can be monitored.

Over a long period, samples of raw sewage, stabilization pond effluent, and fish pond effluent have been collected periodically and analysed for various chemical, bacteriological, and biological parameters.[9] In view of increasing concern about the occurrence and survival of bacteria in the waste-water environment, it was appropriate to assess the performance of waste stabilization ponds for bacterial removal. Samples were analysed periodically for the presence of *Escherichia coli* and *Streptococcus faecalis.* In addition, an attempt was made to isolate and identify *Salmonella spp.* and study how far the low-cost waste treatment system brings about their removal. It was found that there is an appreciable reduction in faecal coliforms, faecal streptococci, and *Salmonella spp.* in the stabilization pond. However, it was felt wise to adopt only those species of fish which are well cooked before human consumption.

The potential importance of this type of waste-water treatment and re-use was stressed in discussion, and it was noted that research of this kind was gaining increasing attention. Similar studies have been in hand for some time in Israel, and the International Development Research Centre (IDRC) is now in touch with new projects beginning in Hong Kong, Kenya, Malaysia, Peru, and Thailand.

12.4 PARASITIC DISEASE AND WASTE-WATER IRRIGATION

Hillel I. Shuval[10]

Health hazards in utilizing waste-water

It has been said that in some tropical countries, more than half the food grown and consumed by the rural poor goes to feed the parasitic worms which infest their bodies.[11] Although parasitic disease is a particularly severe problem in the tropics, many parasites are widely distributed throughout the world[12]. The warmer parts of Europe and North America, as well as certain temperate areas, have fairly high infestation rates.

Many of these parasites, which are mainly protozoa and helminths, leave the human body and enter the environment in excreta. If, then, excreta are used as fertilizer, or if crops are irrigated with sewage, then other people may become infected when they eat the crops. In addition, because some parasites can penetrate the skin, farm workers may be at risk while working on land irrigated with waste-water.

It is therefore apparent that the efficiency of waste-water treatment processes in removing parasites is of paramount importance, as is some knowledge of the ability of these organisms to survive in soil and on crops. The parasites of most importance for this study are listed in Table 12.1, which stresses those aspects of their life cycles which are relevant to agriculture. All the helminths which appear in the table have previously been discussed in this book by Hawkins and Feachem, and are classified by these authors in Table 2.1 which also gives information about the prevalence of the parasitic diseases concerned. The same classification is used in Table 12.1, which is based on information given by Craig and Faust[13]. Data of interest here are the length of time which eggs or larvae can survive on crops, in soil, or on pasture, when they have been deposited there by irrigation water. The precise manner in which health hazards arise for humans is also noted in the table, and two helminths are included which become a danger when sewage is used for fish farming rather than in conventional agriculture.

The effective removal of these pathogens, or a very significant reduction in their concentration by appropriate treatment, is clearly of great importance wherever waste-water is to be used for irrigation or in fish ponds. It is necessary both to protect the health of the public at large, and to protect agricultural workers directly exposed.

In order to make a rough preliminary estimate of possible levels of helminth egg concentration in sewage, it can be assumed as an example that in a medium-level

Table 12.1 Important protozoan and helminthic parasites of man which may be transmitted by waste-water utilization

Parasite	Behaviour on soil, on crops, in fish ponds, etc.	Occasion of health hazard
PROTOZOA: People infected by a cyst ingested via the mouth		
Entamoeba histolytica	survives some days on soil/crops.	eating uncooked, contaminated crops.
Giardia lamblia	survives 12 days on soil/crops in moist conditions; dies in dry conditions.	
HELMINTHS: water-based (percutaneous)* type.		
Schistosoma spp.	eggs hatch in water, infect water snails, from which cercarial larvae emerge after several weeks.	irrigation workers with skin exposed to water.
HELMINTHS: water-based (raw food transmitted)*		
Clonorchis sinensis	parasite eggs in sewage infect first water snails, then fish.	eating raw or partly cooked fish.
Diphyllobothrium latum	eggs mature in warm water after 11-15 days and infect diatoms subsequently eaten by fish.	
HELMINTHS: soil-based (percutaneous)* — the hookworms		
Necator americanus	eggs deposited by waste-water hatch in warm, moist soil releasing larvae which may survive 6-12 weeks, but are killed by dessication of the soil.	farm workers with skin exposed to infected soil expecially when barefoot.
Ancylostoma duodenale		
Strongyloides stercoralis		
HELMINTHS: indirect faecal-oral* life cycles		
Ascaris lumbricoides	eggs in excreta need incubation in warm, moist soil for 20-40 days to become infective; in dry conditions, *Trichuris* eggs die but *Ascaris* eggs survive even in wind-blown dust.	eating crops grown in direct contact with soil; exposure to wind-blown dust.
Trichuris trichuria		
HELMINTHS: meat-based* life cycles — the tapeworms		
Taenia saginata	eggs in sewage used to irrigate pasture remain viable for 60 days and infect grazing cattle.	eating under-cooked beef.
Taenia solium	eggs in human excreta are consumed by pigs with access to night soil, or from sewage-irrigated pasture.	eating under-cooked pork.

* Terms introduced for the sake of comparison with Table 2.1.

endemic urban area, about 10 per cent of the population is infected at any given time with Ascariasis, Trichuriasis, and Ancylostomiasis. Let us also assume that in a conventional sewerage system, the water-borne sewage flow per person per day is 100 litres. Based on reported egg production rates[14], it can be calculated that one litre of fresh sewage should contain about 200 Ascaris eggs, 25 Ancyclostome eggs, and 6 Trichuris eggs.

Rowan[15] in Puerto Rico found Ascaris egg concentrations in raw sewage of 14-38 per litre, while Schistosome egg concentrations ranged from 0.7-1.2 per litre. Wang and Dunlop[16] found a mean of 30 Ascaris eggs per litre, and a mean of 52 *Endamoeba coli* cysts per litre in the raw sewage of Denver, Colorado.

Liebman[17] reports 62 helminth eggs per litre in the sewage of a Bavarian town of which a major portion resulted from slaughter-house wastes, while Kott and Kott[18] found a mean of 4 *Endamoeba hystolytica* cysts per litre of raw sewage in Haifa.

In raw municipal sewage in a highly endemic area of India, Lakshminarayana and Abdullappa[19] found about 200 hookworm eggs per litre and about 1000 Ascaris eggs per litre, while Trichuris eggs were found at about 1.0 per litre.

Based on the limited data available in the literature and theoretical calculations, it is reasonable to assume that pathogenic protozoa and helminths can often be found in raw sewage at concentrations ranging from 10 to 1000 per litre. It therefore may be concluded that for a sewage treatment process to be effective, it should be capable of removing or inactivating 99 per cent or more of such parasites. Let us examine the removal efficiency of various sewage treatment processes to determine whether this objective can be met.

Primary sedimentation and biological treatment

Conventional primary sedimentation of sewage used in community sewage treatment plants calls for a theoretical detention time of about 2—4 hours in rectangular or circular sedimentation tanks (having typical upward flow rates of 0.034 cm/sec). Septic tanks are commonly used for individual homes or small institutional waste disposal systems and provide theoretical detention periods from 12-24 hours. Conventional biological treatment reviewed here includes activated sludge and trickling filters.

Vassilkova[20] reported that treatment in an Imhoff tank removed 97 per cent of all helminth eggs present in the influent, while 87 per cent removal was achieved by a trickling filter. Roberts[21] reported on the *Cysticercus bovis* infection of 23 out of 45 cattle grazed on a sewage farm irrigated with primary effluent. Cram reports that after primary sedimentation, activated sludge and trickling filters effluent contained significant numbers of hookworm and Ascaris eggs which were completely removed only after chemical coagulation with alum and sand filtration.[22]

A study of five plants in Johannesburg showed that tapeworm eggs were found both in raw and settled sewage as well as in effluent of trickling filter and activated sludge plants.[23] Silverman and Griffith[24] also concluded that conventional primary sedimentation, even when followed by secondary treatment, could not be relied upon to remove tapeworm eggs from sewage effectively.

Kott and Kott[25] report a 50 per cent reduction in *E. histolytica* cysts after primary sedimentation and trickling filter treatment, but a 90 per cent reduction in the final effluent. Rowan[26] reports from a study on eight sewage treatment plants in Puerto Rico that primary treatment removed 35-74 per cent Ascaris and 83 per cent Schistosome eggs, while trickling filters and activated sludge treatment removed 95-99.7 per cent of the Ascaris and Schistosome eggs. However, in most cases, Schistosome eggs hatched during treatment, allowing large numbers of infective miracidia to escape into the stream with the effluent, serving as a potential source for dissemination of the disease. Post chlorination or other tertiary treatment was considered essential in preventing further Schistosome infections.

Bhaskaran *et al.*[27] reported only a 50 per cent removal of helminth ova in a number of Indian primary sedimentation plants and found that a septic tank removed about 70 per cent of Ascaris and hookworm eggs. Phadke *et al.*[28] reported considerable reductions of Ascaris and hookworm eggs in a septic tank effluent with 20 days detention, but positive helminth cultures were obtained for the majority of effluent samples tested.

Liebman[29] contends that while the larger helminths with a specific gravity over 1.1 should theoretically be removed effectively in primary sedimentation tanks, there are variations in detention times. The presence of detergents, among other factors, leads to non-uniform sedimentation conditions, and possibly to low efficiency in removal of pathogenic helminths. He recommends chemical coagulation for more effective helminth removal.

From the above, it can be concluded that primary sedimentation cannot be relied upon for effective removal of pathogenic protozoa and helminths from waste-water. Some additional removal may be obtained by conventional biological treatment but reported results are not uniform.

Oxidation ponds

Oxidation ponds usually provide detention periods of 5-30 days and should give better conditions for the sedimentation of protozoa and helminths than conventional primary sedimentation plants. However, there is relatively limited data on protozoa and helminth removal from oxidation ponds.

Wachs[30] found effective removal of cysts of *Entamoeba hystolytica* from sewage during treatment by stabilization ponds with about 20 days detention. Arceivala[31] reports that a municipal oxidation pond in India with a total detention period of seven days produced an effluent free of protozoan cysts and helminth eggs despite the heavy load of parasitic cysts and eggs in the influent ranging from 100 to 1000 per litre. He concluded that oxidation ponds could provide greater health protection when sewage is used in agriculture, with regard to both the protection of crops and the health of farm workers.

Lakshminarayana and Abdullappa[32] studied an oxidation pond having a total detention time of 6 days divided into three pond cells of about equal volume. They showed that a range of parasites, including Trichuris and Ascaris, were totally absent from the pond effluent despite high concentrations in the raw sewage influent. However, *Ancylostoma duodenale* (hookworm) rhabditiform larvae appeared in the effluent in significant numbers, while hookworm eggs rather than larvae were found in pond cells 1 and 2, and many of these eggs were deposited there. Thus there was more than a 90 per cent reduction in Ancylostoma.

These findings indicate that protozoa and helminth eggs do settle out effectively in about 3-6 days in an oxidation pond, but the free swimming larvae of hookworms or Schistosomes may hatch from the eggs during this period and some may appear in the effluent. Free swimming Schistosome miracidia larvae can swim at a velocity of 700 cm/hr, but cannot survive in the free swimming state for more than 10 hours.

Laboratory studies by the same authors indicate that anaerobic pond conditions can completely eliminate or destroy hookworm eggs. They suggest that the inclusion of primary anaerobic ponds prior to facultative and aerobic ponds would be effective in obtaining helminth-free effluent. Similar findings had been reported earlier by Kazuyoshi *et al.*[33]

These important recommendations have not been verified under controlled experimental conditions as yet and may be worthy of study since it appears that appropriate combinations of anaerobic and aerobic oxidation ponds may be the most effective treatment procedure for the elimination of health risks associated with protozoa and helminths. As an initial assumption, a minimum of 1-2 days of detention in anaerobic ponds followed by 4-6 days of facultative aerobic ponds would appear to be the minimum desirable treatment of sewage prior to agricultural utilization, in order to achieve effective control of helminths or protozoa which might cause infections among agricultural workers or infect crops, animals, or fish exposed to sewage.

Calculation of sedimentation rates for parasite eggs

From the foregoing review of the literature on the removal of pathogenic helminths and protozoa by waste-water treatment processes, it is apparent that there is a wide variation in efficiency in removing these various pathogens by sedimentation. In order to assist in the analysis of this phenomenon, a theoretical calculation of the rate at which parasite eggs should settle has been made using Stokes' Law[34] together with information on the size, shape, and specific gravity of the eggs given by Craig and Faust[35].

Although such theoretical calculations can give only broad, general guidance, and are not particularly accurate, they show a marked difference in sedimentation rates between the large Schistosome eggs and the much smaller protozoan cysts. Only the eggs of Schistosomes, which according to theory settle at 12.5 m/hr, and *Trichuris trichiura* which settle at 1.53 m/hr can be assumed to achieve a high degree of removal in conventional sedimentation tanks having upward flow rates of about 1.2 m/hr. Only partial removal of Ascaris, hookworm, and Taenia eggs could be anticipated with their respective settling velocities calculated as 0.65, 0.39 and 0.26 m/hr, while little, if any, removal of protozoa by sedimentation can be anticipated.

Other factors hamper ideal sedimentation conditions, such as short circuiting, non-uniform flow rates, detergents, and interfering floatables, which can lead to lower removal efficiency.

The hatching of certain helminth eggs and release of free swimming infectious larvae during the sedimentation stage may also lead to the passage of infective forms of the parasite to the effluent.

Oxidation ponds having several days of detention should provide ample opportunity for the sedimentation of most of the parasites not normally removed by 2-hour sedimentation tanks or even by conventional biological treatment. However, the smallest parasites, such as *Entamoeba hystolytica* may not completely settle out even under such favourable conditions.

In general, it can be concluded that conventional sedimentation or biological treatment cannot be relied upon for effective removal of protozoa and helminths, while 3-6 days detention in oxidation ponds should provide much more effective removal. In this, the theoretical calculations mentioned above confirm the limited field data available.

Few definitive studies have been made on the use of tertiary treatment methods to achieve an assured high level of protozoa and helminth removal following relatively less effective conventional primary and secondary treatment. There is evidence that chemical coagulation followed by sedimentation is effective. Sand filtration has also been considered as a possible polishing treatment for this purpose. Chlorination may be highly effective for some parasites but not for others, while microstraining has also been reported to be effective for some parasites but could hardly be expected to remove the smallest eggs and cysts. There is need for controlled quantitative evaluation of various sewage treatment processes specifically aimed at helminth and protozoa removal for waste-water utilization purposes.

12.5 EXCRETA TREATMENT AND RE-USE IN CHINA

Michael G. McGarry[36]

Sanitation and the health care system[37]

In China, the technologies and approaches used for environmental sanitation, and in particular, for excreta collection and re-use are integral parts of the overall health care system. This system provides continuing institutional support, information, and even motivation for the successful use of certain technologies in the rural areas. In contrast to the vast majority of other countries, health care and environmental sanitation are carried out by the villagers themselves and not by government agencies, although the latter act in a supportive capacity. Health care and environmental sanitation are intimately integrated into the political and administrative system.

Administratively, China is divided into some 70 000 communes which serve as the basic units, each comprising about 10 000 people. These are subdivided into 'production brigades' which are again divided into 'production teams'. The Ministry of Health operates largely in an administrative role at national and provincial levels. At the county level, the County Health Bureau maintains Epidemic Prevention Stations which are responsible for mass health campaigns, training of personnel, mobile health teams, and support for the health and medical care programmes. Health Centres are located within the communes to provide health and family planning services and to train barefoot doctors and health aides. Environmental sanitation activities are centred at the production brigade level and, along with other duties, are the responsibility of the barefoot doctors, who receive four months' basic training and and a month-long refresher and up-grading course each year. The barefoot doctor is supported by a sanitary worker at brigade and a health aide at team levels in his sanitation work.

Sanitation programmes are promoted through mass campaigns originating from the Epidemic Prevention Stations. The best-known national mass campaign was against the Four Pests (mosquitoes, flies, rats, and lice). The Epidemic Prevention Stations are also responsible for prevention of infectious diseases including the parasites, occupational diseases, and promotion of environmental health (through the county hospitals, commune health centres, and brigade health stations). The sanitation programmes depend heavily on the peoples' financial support and participation. Each activity is repeatedly described and discussed with the people and promoted through a variety of media including the radio, manuals, wall posters, group meetings, home and meeting-place visits, and personal contacts. The Ministry of Health does not enjoy any extraordinary enforcement powers.

Although this paper focuses on technologies used for excreta re-use, it should be recognized that the environemental health programmes in China do cover other activities such as waste-water disposal, pollution control, water supply, food and industrial hygiene, and solid wastes management. It is emphasized that success of the following technologies in practice has depended heavily upon active participation of the people and the administrative and promotional support described above.

As rural water supplies are fast becoming a focus of international health programmes elsewhere, some comment should be made on China's activities in water supply improvement. Compared to other activities in environmental sanitation, the provision of clean water has not been given high priority in China. There are no 'national targets' for improving water supplies. The most important source of water is still the protected open well in villages, sometimes provided with a cover slab and simple hand-pump. Where deep groundwater tables are encountered, wells are drilled and motor-driven pumps are used to supply piped water to village stand-pipes or house connections[38].

The Chinese biogas plant

It is reported that 80 000 biogas plants are operating in China, most of them located in Szechuan Province and operated at the brigade or production team level[39]. The Chinese biogas plant differs from the Indian and Korean designs in that it does not use a floating gas holder as a storage chamber for the gas, rising and falling as the gas is produced and drawn off for use in the household. Instead, a simpler, cheaper and more maintenance-free design is used which incorporates a fixed-tap gas holder.[40]. The plant comprises six parts, as follows (Figure 12.1):

(1) the inlet chamber which daily receives human excreta (10 per cent), animal faeces (30 per cent), crop stalks (10 per cent), and water (50 per cent);
(2) the rectangular or circular fermentation tank used to store the water during fermentation;
(3) the fixed-top gas storage tank, providing space for gas accummulation;
(4) the outlet chamber, receiving digested wastes from the fermentation tank at its mid-depth;
(5) the slurry displacement tank located on top of the fixed gas storage tank, which is used to store excess slurry as the gas accumulates; and
(6) the gas vent pipe and ancillary equipment.

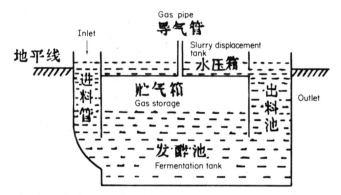

Figure 12.1 Schematic diagram of a Chinese biogas plant

As biogas is produced by digestion of the wastes, it accumulates under the inverted gas holder, forcing the liquid level in the fermentation tank downwards. The equivalent volume of slurry is displaced, moving through the outlet chamber and on top of the fixed gas storage tank where it is stored. As gas is used in the household, the displaced slurry returns to the outlet chamber. More detailed drawings of two versions of this plant are shown in Figure 12.2, and a household gas burner in Figure 12.3.

There are several disease-causing organisms which are transmitted through excreta and may pass unharmed through the biogas plant to reach the soil, crops, and eventually be ingested by man. Although some investigations have indicated that the biogas plant is capable of removing or destroying many parasites, it is by no means certain that the effluent from the plant is free from disease-causing organisms.

Research on transfer potential of biogas plants was carried out by the Research Institute for Parasitic Disease Prevention and the Revolution Committee of the

218

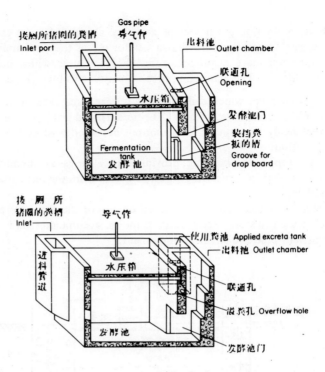

Figure 12.2   Two kinds of biogas plant used in China, both of them using the same principle as the one illustrated if Figure 12.1

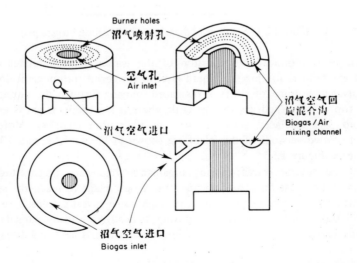

Figure 12.3 Earthenware biogas stove as used in China

Mien Chu County Communicable Disease Prevention Office, both of the Province of Szechuan[41]. The several plants under study were reported to be fed a mixture of swine and human excreta, with vegetable matter in the proportions noted above. The biogas plants normally had a capacity of about $10m^3$; Samples were drawn from the influent, the fermentation tank bottom, and the bottom and top of the outlet chamber. Total parasite eggs (including Schistosoma, Ascaris and hookworm) were counted; it was determined that there was a 94 per cent egg retention in the plant. It is emphasized, however, that the effluent still contained over 1500 parasite eggs per 100 millilitres; this was due to the fact that there were over 23 000 eggs/100 ml in the influent. The hookworm die-off was both rapid and effective. It is likely that the hookworm eggs settled to the bottom of the tank to digest with the sludge. Unfortunately, little could be said about the schistosomes, in that too few a number were observed. Later experiments did, however, indicate that even with improvements to the biogas plant's physical configuration, schistosome miracidia were found in the effluent liquid in four out of six examinations. Further, schistosomes were later observed to live up to 37 days in a simulated biogas plant experiment.

The hardiest egg of all is the Ascarid or roundworm ovum. The percentage of viable eggs in the influent was 68 per cent, whereas in the effluent it was 60 per cent; the total number of viable eggs in the effluent was 710 per 100 ml. Thus, the biogas plant had relatively little impact on the roundworms' viability. The reduction in levels of disease-causing organisms is due both to the physical separation of the organisms by their settling to the bottom of the tank and to their natural die-off in the tank under adverse growth conditions. Certainly, the major contributing factor to their reduction in the case of the hardier parasite eggs is that of physical separation. In one experiment, an improvement of the plant's effluent storage chamber and point of effluent removal from the tank clearly indicated an improvement in total parasite egg reduction from 80 to 98 per cent.

Although research has increased our knowledge of the relationship between man, parasites and their intermediate hosts, little information is available on the transfer of such organisms through excreta or manure reuse systems. This is also true of the bacterial and particularly the viral diseases. As described above, indications are that a healthy removal of some of the hardier and/or more prevalent organisms does take place in the biogas plant; but a significant level remain in the effluent, which is applied to land or aquaculture ponds.

The three-tank system

Much has been said but little published on the Chinese three-tank toilet system (also known as the three-vault septic tank and the two-partition, three-tank type toilet). The Epidemic Prevention Stations of Chiang and Chinkiang Counties of Kiangsu Province have provided us with full design, construction and operational details.[42]. The unit is made up of three tanks connected in series and constructed either separately or with common adjoining walls. Human excreta, as collected in buckets or flushed from a nearby toilet with a minimum use of water, are deposited directly through a vertical, aqua-privy type water-seal chute and let to settle in the first underground chamber. The liquid and some of the sludge pass through a horizontal connection in the lower portion of the tank to the second tank, where anaerobic decomposition of the wastes proceeds. The second tank discharges by means of an outlet at its surface which leads to the bottom of the third tank. This is used as a storage chamber from which digested liquid is removed by dipper bucket on a handle or rope for use in the fields or in aquaculture. The purposes of this design are basically twofold. Firstly, the digesting liquid moves very slowly through the system, being displaced only by incoming excreta and small amounts of flush water. Treatment is effected by anerobic digestion and settlement of the heavier solids (including parasite ova) on the bottom of all three tanks. Secondly, the overflow of liquid from second to third tanks allows for removal of excreta for use as a fertilizer only after the liquid has had the full retention period in the first and second tanks. Provided that the three-tank system is properly used, it effectively raises the barrier against using fresh excreta on crops. Based on a per capita output of 2 litres/person-day, the first two tanks are designed to provide ten days' retention each and the third one up to a maximum of thirty days.

Chinese composting methods

Composting as a method of night soil treatment and re-use has been practised for centuries in China[43]. However, two new methods have been developed since the 1950s which represent significant improvements over practices being used elsewhere in Asia[44]. They are (a) the surface aerobic continuous method; and (b) the large-pit, aerobic composting method.

The surface method is best for climates which do not reach freezing temperatures in winter. Human excreta, livestock manures, refuse, and soil are usually mixed in roughly equal portions by weight (although these vary considerably depending on location and availability of raw materials), and are first placed on the ground in a layer measuring 9 x 9 x ½ feet (3 x 3 x 0.15 m). Four three-inch (8 cm) bamboos are placed horizontally at three-foot intervals; four vertical poles are placed and supported where the horizontal poles cross. The rest of the compost material is added to reach a total depth of three feet. The pile is covered with a two-inch (5 cm) layer of pack mud, horse dung and straw mix, the poles are withdrawn, and the pile is left.

Aerobic, or at least micro-aerobic composting takes place over the following month, during which the temperature in the pile rises to 50-60°C over a period of 5-7 days. The average compost temperature was reported to be just over 40°C during tests in Hopei Province. Ascarid egg viability was reduced from 68.5 to 2 per cent in the final humus. Loss of total nitrogen was not reported, although ammonia-nitrogen rose from approximately 0.07 to 0.11 per cent.

The pit method uses a five-foot (1.75 m) deep pit or trench of 4 feet (1.4 m) width, with 3 x 3 inch (8 x 8 cm) air channels dug in its bottom which are covered with crop stalks. Vertical bamboos are placed and supported at channel intersections and later removed after the pit is filled with raw compost material and covered with a layer of mud. Although the pit technique requires more labour, it does permit composting in northern regions which reach sub-zero temperatures in the winter.

Excreta collection and re-use practices in China

The wooden bucket collection system is widely used in urban China. The buckets of about 10 litres in size are manually collected and tipped into sealed carts for delivery of night soil to holding tanks to await later sale and use as a fertilizer on the communes. Reduction (not total removal) of pathogens may be effected by tank storage, depending on the season and how urgently the excreta are needed. Public latrines are being favoured over individual ones. These use either a simple vault for storage or more preferably the three-tank system, which provides a further barrier to disease transmission. In the denser city centres, sewerage is being used as the only means of removing waste-water from high-rise areas. Conventional sewage treatement methods are employed and the sludge and treated effluent recovered for reuse on the communes wherever possible.

The bucket latrine is also employed in rural areas where concentrated excreta is reported as being valued higher than inorganic fertilizers. The shallow container latrines, which require frequent emptying and are open to insects and rodents, are being replaced by communal three-tank systems. With bucket and shallow-container latrines, the excreta is removed to a tank or sump from which it is distributed for use as a fertilizer. These tanks or sumps should be covered and the contents allowed to ferment anaerobically for 2–4 weeks, thereby destroying schistosome and hookworm ova.

In 1949, intestinal diseases were rampant throughout China, as were poverty, malnutrition and illiteracy. The government was faced with having to make do with a very poor resource base; thus, recovery of all reclaimable materials was mandatory. Despite a history of unhygienic practices in human excreta recycling as the primary cause of the spread of intestinal disease in the population, efforts were made not to eradicate the practice (as would have been the first reaction of Western governments) but to improve upon methods of collection and re-use to include treatment in as practical and inexpensive a way as possible.

Chao[45] has estimated the quantities of natural fertilizers used in China between 1952 and 1966, and has concluded that over this period, about one-third of the nutrients applied for plant growth was provided from human night soil.[46] During 1962, 70 per cent of human excreta was collected and used as fertilizer; this was pushed up to 90 per cent (298 million tons) in 1966, a truly remarkable achievement.

By 1953, the task of redistributing land was complete and the first five-year plan launched. Economies of scale were sought through collectivization and consolidation of land holdings. Land was reclaimed, and multi-cropping schedules were introduced to many areas. During 1954-5, there was a rapid acceleration of centralization and ambitious goals were set. Eager to raise agricultural productivity, an 'Accumulate Fertilizer' campaign was initiated and spread throughout China during the winter of 1955-6. Chao reports that 70 million rural youths participated in gathering 400 million tons of natural fertilizers.

The key to the successful reclamation of human waste in China has not been merely the innovation of appropriate technologies but their being developed and promoted through active participation of the people, backed by an effective information system and supported by motivated cadres at the village level. The technologies employed could be transferred to other countries in the region but care must be taken to ensure that they are not simply 'demonstrated and enforced' without the necessary administrative support and extension services.

Many questions can be thrown up as to the advisability of using excreta in the process of food production. In our ignorance of the mechanisms of pathogen die-off and transfer, it is tempting to take the path of least resistance and enforce unrealistic regulations which may prohibit such practices. It should be emphasized, however, that we are trying to improve an existing situation rather than force it to meet unrealistic standards. It is highly possible that the existing malpractices of excreta and manure disposal in other countries are far worse in terms of transmitting disease than what may result from the Chinese methods described here.

NOTES AND REFERENCES

1. Working group members: Hillel I. Shuval (chairman), Robert Mister (rapporteur), John Briscoe, Cole Dodge, Hemda Garelick, Peter Hawkins, DeAnne S. Julius, M.G. McGarry, Guy Stringer, A.V. Swamy.
2. Edited from material presented at the conference by Krisno Nimpuno, M.G. McGarry, and the working group mentioned in note 1.
3. A. Howard, *Journal of the Royal Society of Arts,* 84 (1933), p. 25.
4. C. Peel, in *Planning for Water and Waste in Hot Countries,* Loughborough University of Technology, U.K., 1976
5. This section was written by Krisno Nimpuno.
6. B.B. Sundaresan is Director, National Environmental Engineering Research Institute, Nagpur-20, India.
7. S. Muthuswamy is Assistant Professor of Public Health Engineering, College of Engineering, Guindy, Madras 600 025, India.
8. V.S. Govindam is from the Department of Public Health Engineering, College of Engineering, Guindy, Madras 600 025, India.
9. Results of these investigations are to be published separately.
10. Hillel I. Shuval is Director, Environmental Health Laboratory, Hebrew University, Jerusalem, Israel.
11. V.Z. Hyde, *American Journal of Public Health,* 41 (1951), p.1
12. M.R. Shephard, in *Water, Wastes and Health in Hot Climates,* ed. R. Feachem, M.G. McGarry and D. Mara, John Wiley & Sons, New York 1977.
13. N. Craig and E.C. Faust, in *Clinical Parasitology,* ed. E.C. Faust, P.F. Russel, and R.G. Lea and Febiger, Philadelphia, 1970.
14. *Ibid*
15. W.B. Rowan, *American Journal of Tropical Medicine and Hygiene,* 13 (1964), pp. 572-5.
16. W.L. Wang and S.G. Dunlop, *Sewage and Industrial Wastes,* 26 (1954), p. 1020
17. H. Liebman, in *Advances in Water Pollution Research,* ed. J.K. Baars, Pergamon Press, Oxford, 2 (1965), pp. 269-76

18. H. Kott and Y. Kott, *Water and Sewage Works*, **114** (1967), pp. 177-80.
19. J.S.S. Lakshminarayana·and M.K. Abdulappa, in *Low Cost Waste Treatment*, ed. C.A. Sastry, CHPERI, Nagpur, 1972, pp. 290-9
20. Z. Vassilkova, *Medical Parasitology and Parasitic Disease* (USSR), **5** (1936), p.657
21. F.C. Roberts Jr., *American Journal of Public Health*, **25** (1935), 122
22. E.B. Cram, *Sewage Works Journal*, **15** (1943), p. 1119
23. E.J. Hamlin, *The Surveyor* (U.K.), **105**, (1946), p. 919
24. P.H. Silverman and R.B. Griffith, *Annals of Tropical Medical Parasitology*, **49** (1955), pp. 436-50
25. Kott and Kott, *op. cit.*, note 18.
26. Rowan, *op. cit.*, note 15.
27. T.R. Bhaskaran,· M.A. Sampathkumaran, and T.C. Sur, *Indian Journal of Medical Research*, **44** (1956), pp. 163-80
28. N.S. Phadke, N.B. Thake, and S.V. Deshpande, in *Low Cost Waste Treatment*, ed. C.A. Sastry, CHPERI, Nagpur, 1972
29. Liebman, *op. cit.*, note 17
30. A. Wachs, *Study on Sewage Stabilization Ponds in Israel*, Sanitation Engineering Laboratories, Haifa Technion, 1961
31. S.J. Arceivala, *Waste Stabilization Ponds*, CHPERI, Nagpur, 1970, pp. 86-95
32. Lakshminarayana and Abdulappa, *op. cit.*, note 19
33. Kazuyoshi, Kawati, and C.W. Kruse, *American Journal of Tropical Medicine and Hygiene*, 1956, p. 101
34. W.J. Weber, Jr., *Physiochemical Processes for Water Quality Control*, 1972, pp. 112-17.
35. Craig and Faust, *op. cit.*, note 13
36. Michael G. McGarry is Associate Director, Health Sciences Division, International Development Research Centre (IDRC), P.O. Box 8500, Ottawa, Canada
37. This paper is based on a literature search and not on first-hand observation in China. Personal discussions with Somnuek Unakul assisted greatly in verifying the data, as did an IDRC-supported review of Chinese sanitation by W.L. Kilama, J.H. Lindsay, P.A. Oluwande, A.G. Onibokun, and U. Winblad in 1975. A special debt is owed to Lee Thim Loi for translating the document referred to in note 40
38. Somnuek Unakul, personal communication, 1976
39. 'Popularizing the use of marsh gas in rural areas', *Peking Review*, **30** (July 1975), quoting 1974 data; since then the number of biogas units has increased rapidly, perhaps to over a million, according to V. Smil, 'Intermediate energy technology in China', *Bulletin of the Atomic Scientists*, **33** (February 1977), p.27
40. M.G. McGarry and J. Stainforth (eds.), *Compost, Fertilizer, and Biogas Production from Human and Farm Wastes in the People's Republic of China*, trans. Lee Thim Loi, IDRC, Ottawa, 1978, pp. 53-6
41. *Ibid*, pp. 71-83
42. *Ibid*, p. 35
43. D.H. Perkins, *Agricultural Development in China, 1368-1968*, Edinburgh University Press, 1969
44. McGarry and Stainforth, *op. cit.* note 40, pp. 7-10
45. Kang Chao, *Agricultural Production in Communist China, 1949-1965*, University of Wisconsin Press, 1970
46. M.G. McGarry, *The Ecologist*, 6 (4), May 1976

13
Conclusion

13.1 TECHNOLOGY, HEALTH AND HUMAN BEHAVIOUR[1]

The social priority

Although this book has devoted more space to technology than to any other aspect of sanitation, it has also repeatedly emphasized that there are no wholly technical solutions to the appalling and urgent problems of sanitation in developing countries. The search for the 'perfect pit privy' may well characterize sanitary history, but 'no such devices really exist or can be devised' (Section 1.3). However well designed sanitation equipment may be, it will not work if people cannot be organized to service it regularly, and neither will it be effective if users do not clean it, maintain water levels, cover squat holes, or prevent blockages. Technology is not enough to solve the world's sanitation problems. 'Human behaviour dominates the scene' (Section 2.1).

There are two different levels at which human behaviour must be considered: the personal and the institutional. Hygiene, clearly, is a matter of personal behaviour, and so are defecation habits, although both involve interactions with other people which depend on local institutional structures. At several points in this book, but especially in Section 10.4, it has been pointed out that even in the absence of sanitation 'technology', even the crudest of techniques combined with appropriate behaviour patterns can safeguard health to a quite surprising extent. This is not to suggest that we should be content with the 'simple techniques' of Table 13.1; it is merely a salutary reminder that technology does not have all the answers.

The institutional aspects of human behaviour which have to do with the administration and organization of sanitation are crucially important if technology is to be effectively used. Very many excellently designed latrines, pumps, cisterns, and treatment works have failed because of inadequate institutional support. Such inadequacies include maladministration of maintenance and servicing, ineffective recruitment and manpower training, unenforced hygiene procedures in night soil collection systems, neglect of record-keeping, and difficulties in levying rates to pay for sanitation services. Other institutional problems have to do with health education and the organization of self-help construction programmes. The whole

224

question of the working conditions, health, morale and status of sanitation operatives is also crucial.

One often gains the impression, and it is strengthened by parts of Chapters 7, 8, 11 and 12, that it is the countries of East Asia which have a particular gift for operating intricately organized, labour-intensive sanitation services. In Japan, such services operate to perfection, but often using sophisticated technical equipment. In China, however, the efficiency of sanitary organization apparently compensates to some extent for the continuing use of relatively very crude equipment, so that considerable improvements in health and hygiene, and in waste recycling, have been achieved with very basic equipment.[2]

The Western habit, by contrast, is to simplify management problems by using technologies that reduce the number of people employed and operate for long periods without attention. Conventional sewerage achieves this objective very well, but since it is beyond the means of many countries, there seems little choice but to tackle the administrative difficulties which the more labour-intensive methods involve. So a strong recommendation emerging from Chapter 10 was that sanitarians who wish to achieve anything in their field should seriously tackle the theory of administration (Section 10.2).

The technological preoccupation

If this book gives less space to the foregoing issues than their importance would seem to demand, that is because it reflects the current state of thinking in the mid-1970s, which had just reached the point where public bodies as well as isolated individuals were prepared to challenge the widely held assumption that conventional sewerage is appropriate for all urban areas in developing countries. The resulting search for alternatives to the conventional technology has led to a series of technology reviews[3], the most important of which are those arising from the World Bank projects[4] described in Chapter 3.

Inevitably this book reflects this same approach. It devotes much space to reviewing technology, and illustrates no less than 29 different types of latrine. A key to the latter is provided by Table 13.1, and among this surprising variety of devices, the *composting latrines* (Chapter 7) stand out as having great potential, and there have been impressive improvements in *pit latrines* (Chapter 6). *Aqua-privies* (Chapters 4 and 5) have been attractive as an intermediate technology between the pit latrine and conventional flush latrines, but are currently under something of a cloud, partly because their servicing requirement seems to be beyond the capability of many of the institutions responsible.

Reasons for the disapproval with which conventional sewerage and cistern-flushed latrines are now often regarded include high costs, pollution, and implications for water resources. The pollution problem arises mainly because of the habit, promoted in the industrialized countries, of discharging sewage or treated effluents into rivers, lakes and the sea. In view of the wide range of opportunities now existing for reclaiming the nutrients, energy, and water that sewage contains, this habit of dumping wastes to the detriment of the environment seems not only mistaken, but also, in most instances, unnecessary. Chapter 12 demonstrated that suitable precautions can greatly reduce any health hazards which may arise from re-use of sewage effluents in agriculture or for fish farming.

With regard to water resources, conventional sewerage systems present a paradox. On the one hand, many dry, tropical countries have insufficient water to give everybody a conventional, cistern-flushed latrine. But on the other hand, countries that are short of water may ultimately need sewers as a means of collecting all available waste-water for reclamation and re-use. Sewers can be a positive water conservation measure, and Israel is one country where an acute shortage of water resources is mitigated by this means: 65 per cent of waste-water in rural areas is re-used, and 23 per cent from urban areas.

The demand for conventional sewerage in developing countries arises when standards of living improve and people install indoor plumbing and indoor latrines. Many of the excreta disposal systems mentioned in this book work well in a backyard, but there is still a need for techniques which will meet legitimate aspirations for indoor latrines. So work is still needed to devise ways of conserving water, meeting health requirements, and providing for people's wishes for indoor plumbing, but without incurring the high costs and damaging pollution which conventional Western practice seems so often to entail.

But to speak of the aspirations of people whose standards of living are rising seems almost an affront when there are many people in city slums (and in rural areas—Section 11.1) whose standards of living are falling, or have reached rock bottom. Their sanitary needs are amongst the most urgent anywhere, but yet have been neglected by researchers and by practical sanitarians alike. Chapter 9 recorded some very valuable achievements among the poor in Calcutta, and threw out many stimulating suggestions which the world's municipal engineers ought at least to take as a challenge. What can they produce, better suited to their own conditions, to provide for their urban poor? Some research on very elementary matters is needed—on the production of low-cost, easily cleaned squatting plates, and on the design of latrines suited to the needs of children.

With so little understood, and so much still to do, it is all too easy to be deluded by the promise of instant technical solutions. The installation of a conventional sewerage system may seem attractive, if it can be afforded, because of the hope that it will solve all these problems in one move. But a policy of gradual, step-by-step improvements, as suggested in Chapter 8, may be the most appropriate in many developing countries. It is a policy which allows benefits to be widely spread throughout the population, and it is a policy, too, where mistakes made in the choice of technology can be rectified before too great an investment is made, and the options are closed. Small improvements, made in steps, can also be kept within the administrative capability of the relevant institutions, and there is some hope that the strengthening and growth of these institutions may take place in parallel with the improvement of the technology.

It is this parallel development of institutions and technology, and these priorities concerning the problems of the urban poor which ought to be the keynotes of future work on sanitation in developing countries.

NOTES AND REFERENCES

1. This section is edited from *Sanitation in Developing Countries Today, Conference Bulletin No. 2,* October 1977, and from recordings of conference sessions.
2. A clear impression of the extremely basic design of many rural latrines in China in the 1970s is given by *Compilation of Data and Experience on Sanitary Management,* People's Hygiene Publisher, China, 1974; translated for IDRC by Lee Thim Loi, 1977.
3. E.g. 'Sewage disposal in developing countries: a survey of methods', by Krisno Nimpuno; extracts from this conference paper appear in chapters 3, 7 and 11 here.
4. Witold Rybczynski, Chongrak Polprasert, Michael McGarry, *Stop the Fecal Peril: a Technology Review,* IDRC Preliminary Report, Ottawa, July, 1977.

Table 13.1 (a) Key to excreta disposal methods described in this book involving *dry systems* with *on-site* treatment, and related types

TYPE OF LATRINE (also excreta removal and on-site storage methods where appropriate.)	ILLUSTRATION (figure no.)	TECHNICAL ASPECTS (page nos.)	INSTITUTIONAL ASPECTS (page nos.)	ASSOCIATED TREATMENT PROCESSES (with page nos.)
SIMPLE TECHNIQUES				
Open latrines	1.1	1, 2, 182	—	on-site dessication, composting, dung-beetle activity, 96–7
Burying	—	96, 104	—	
Trench latrines	—	97	—	
Defecation grounds	—	96, 164	180–1	
" " (furrowed)	—	183	—	
Overhung latrines	—	27, 28	—	dispersal and digestion in water.
PIT LATRINES (INCLUDING POUR-FLUSH LATRINES WITH SOAK PITS)				
Simple pit latrine	6.1	52–3, 89, 92–9	95, 97–8	on-site composting in dry pits, 108–9
Bored hole latrine	6.1	93, 98	—	
Vented pit latrine	3.6, 6.4	65, 101–4	—	
ROEC pit latrine	3.3	59, 60, 98	64	

Wet pit latrine with lined pit bottom	6.4	102–3	–	on-site anaerobic digestion in wet pits, 84
Pour-flush, water-seal pit	6.5	105–6	105–6	
Off-set soak pit	2.3	35–6, 89	37	
Watergate pit latrine	6.3	100–1	–	
COMPOSTING LATRINES				
Modified pit latrine	–	108–9	–	on-site composting, 108–9
Multrum toilet	3.1	53, 89, 109, 115	–	on-site aerobic 'mouldering', 110, 119
,, modified type	3.2	58–9, 63	–	
,, Philippines type	7.3	121	–	
ROEC derivative	3.4	60, 109	–	
Compact compost toilets	7.4	116–18	–	on-site aerobic composting, 110
Double vault composters	3.5	60, 108, 118–19	–	on-site anaerobic or micro-aerobic composting, 111–12, 119, 121
Vietnamese double bin	7.1, 7.2	53, 110–13	113–14	

Table 13.1 (b) Key to excreta disposal methods described in this book involving *wet systems*, and systems with *off-site* treatment

TYPE OF LATRINE (also excreta removal and on-site storage methods where appropriate.)	ILLUSTRATION (figure no.)	TECHNICAL ASPECTS (page nos.)	INSTITUTIONAL ASPECTS (page nos.)	ASSOCIATED TREATMENT PROCESSES (with page nos.)
BUCKETS, VAULTS & CARTAGE SYSTEMS				
Bucket latrines	8.1	125, 127–8	132–9, 202	off-site treatment, e.g. composting, 205–7, digestion for biogas, or waste stabilization ponds, 75–6, 208–10
Latrines discharging into containers or tankers	9.1	142–3, 153–4	–	
Conservancy vaults	8.2, 8.3	124, 128–9	–	
Chinese systems	–	221	137–8, 167	
Cess-pools	–	54, 85	–	
AQUA-PRIVIES AND RELATED LOW-COST WET SYSTEMS				
Basic aqua-privies	5.1, 5.3	83–91	168	on-site anaerobic digestion in water, 83–4, 158–60, 219–20
Calcutta aqua-privy	9.2	148–50	144, 147–8	

Name Index

(This index includes contributors and working group members only. Figures in *italics* indicate the page numbers on which contributors' addresses may be found)

233

Subject Index

activated sludge, 74, 212, 213
administration, 15-16, 162, 167, 224-5
  municipal, 132-6, 144, 147, 150, 175-6
  values of, 75, 132, 167, 170
agriculture, 51, 74, 179, 187-9, 202
  see also fertilizer, irrigation
algae, 77, 196, 203, 208-10
anaerobic digestion, 83-4, 217, 218-20
anal cleaning, 8, 70, 77, 91, 127
appropriate technology, 16, 48-9, 71,
  186-7, 198
aquaculture, 54, 74, 77, 203, 209
  see also fish
aqua-privies, 43, 46, 78-80, 83-9, 225
  in Botswana, 56-7, 60, 63, 64
  in Calcutta, 89, 148-50;
  maintenance, 88, 90, 91, 168
  surveys of, 7, 8, 57

bacteria, 19, 23, 47, 76, 208
Bangladesh, 49, 54, 109, 146, 155-61
  rural conditions, 1-2, 10, 33-4, 188-90,
  193
  urban sanitation, 1, 4, 127, 134,
  139-43
barefoot doctors, 12, 216
behavioural hygiene, 10, 22, 23, 177,
  182, 184, 224
bilharzia, *see* schistosomiasis
biogas, 84-5, 124, 186-7, 191-4, 196-7
  Szechuan system, 191, 192, 216-19
  use by the poor, 187, 189, 193, 204
BOD, 44, 45, 46, 76-7
Botswana, 42, 49, 56-65, 98, 108-9, 163
  aqua-privies, 56-7, 78, 83, 85
Brazil, 73-4, 162, 165

bucket latrines, 124-5, 127-8, 135
  surveys of, 7, 8, 69

Calcutta, 85, 87-8, 89, 142, 144-52, 162
Canada, 116-18, 120
cartage, *see* night soil collection
cess pits, 50, 54, 85, 127
Chad, 79, 83
children, 1, 32, 106, 157, 175
  latrines for, 99, 155, 226
China, 49, 54, 187, 215-22, 225
  biogas, 191, 192, 204, 216-19, 223n
  composting, 206-7, 220
  night soil collection, 137-8, 167-8,
  221-2
chlorination, 29, 37, 47, 213, 215
cholera, 5, 11, 20, 111, 145, 159
cleaning latrines, 14, 28, 94, 168
coliform bacteria, 76, 112, 159, 209
comfort stations, 86, 91
communal latrines, 137, 141, 143, 152-6,
  174
  attitudes to, 5-6, 9, 57, 98
  need for, 72, 91, 140, 153, 155-6
community development, 92, 95-6,
  113-114, 162-3
  see also participation, rural
  development
community health programme, 95, 97,
  105-6, 164-6, 170
composting processes, 54, 110, 119,
  205-7, 220
  parasites and, 28, 29-30, 112, 161,
  206
composting toilets, 46, 48, 58-63, 108-22,
  130

235

236